THE BEAUFORTS

THE BEAUFORTS

LINEAGE, AMBITION AND OBLIGATION
1373–1510

JOHN BRUNTON

AMBERLEY

First published 2022

Amberley Publishing
The Hill, Stroud
Gloucestershire, GL5 4EP

www.amberley-books.com

ISBN 978 1 3981 0382 5 (hardback)
ISBN 978 1 3981 0383 2 (ebook)

British Library Cataloguing in Publication Data.
A catalogue record for this book is available from the British Library.

1 2 3 4 5 6 7 8 9 10

Typesetting by SJmagic DESIGN SERVICES, India.
Printed in the UK.

CONTENTS

Introduction 7

1 A Brood of Royal Bastards 10

2 The King's Half-brothers 32

3 The King's Uncles 60

4 The Bishop and the Good Duke 86

5 The Cardinal's Crusade and the Coronation Campaign 112

6 War and Peace 129

7 The False Peace and the Loss of France 155

8 Faction and Fighting 179

9 Civil War 205

10 Somerset and Edward IV 227

11 The Last Beaufort Duke of Somerset 241

12 Margaret Beaufort 257

Conclusion 277

Appendix I: The Beaufort Estates 283

Appendix II: Genealogical Tables 289

Appendix III: Maps 296

Appendix IV: On Regalia and Liveries 298

Appendix V: Edmund Beaufort and Katherine de Valois 303

Appendix VI: Edmund Beaufort and the Siege of Calais, 1436 311

Notes 314

Bibliography 321

Index 325

INTRODUCTION

In every age the lives of men and women are circumscribed by different rules of status, opportunity and obligation. In the England of the fourteenth and fifteenth centuries parentage was the first decisive factor, and dictated not only what was possible but also what was expected of a life. This was the experience of the Beaufort family over three generations.

For most men born into the military class this meant a life engaged in warfare, usually in France, and service to king and overlord. As subdivisions within this class became increasingly defined roles were also pre-ordained. While an esquire, knight or baron would be expected to lead a smaller party of soldiers, an earl or duke would normally hold a senior command purely by virtue of his rank. A precise social standing also dictated the offices he could hold in the king's service. For women there were similar expectations and constraints; they would marry as their elders decided according to social status and produce a quota of children, ideally including at least one male heir. They were instruments in political alliances and transmitters of inheritances and titles.

For three sons and a daughter of John of Gaunt by his mistress Katherine Swynford, prospects were at first limited – illegitimacy was one of the worst social disadvantages. Once they were declared legitimate in retrospect, however, the four Beaufort children instantly gained respectability and senior rank. When their half-brother became king in 1399, the Beauforts – now two peers, a countess and a senior ecclesiastic – were propelled to the centre of royal affairs as servants of the Lancastrian monarchy. The Beauforts were earls and dukes, wives and mothers of all the greater nobles of England, and one even became Queen of Scotland. The most senior at any time was Earl (later Duke) of Somerset. They led armies into battle, defended towns and castles in the French wars, went on crusade, and remained loyal to three Lancastrian kings for better or worse.

Of this first generation Cardinal Henry Beaufort became a powerful, effective and often despised statesman of England, a prelate of international repute and a crusader, his influence of prime importance in England and France. His support bankrolled the English conquest of most of France, but his intransigence blackened the politics of his day during his lifelong feud with Humphrey, Duke of Gloucester.

A line of Beaufort earls and dukes of Somerset led royal armies, first against the French and then against Yorkist insurgents. It is often too easy to identify the Beauforts with the loss of the Hundred Years War and the misgovernment of the Lancastrian regime during the Wars of the Roses. Rather than the villains of either piece, they can in fact be seen as loyal associates of the House of Lancaster who laboured in its service only to face defeat due to factors beyond their powers to address.

Indeed, the story of the Beauforts is one of dependency and service to the House of Lancaster, from the protection of Henry IV through to following Henry V on his spectacular drive for conquest and maintaining the Lancastrian mission during Henry VI's minority and his later absences. Their commitment throughout cannot be faulted, despite their own vague and flawed claim to the succession. When the last Beaufort Duke of Somerset met his end on the executioner's block in 1471, the House of Lancaster soon followed and the Yorkist kings drew a line under both. The final surprise came when Margaret Beaufort's son Henry Tudor ascended the throne fourteen years later. In the female line the Beauforts were in part the origin of the Tudor monarchy, and their descendants have ruled this country ever since. This book in a sense seeks to rehabilitate the Beauforts from the negative image which the Yorkist perspective has informed.

Individually, Cardinal Beaufort has been the subject of several detailed studies, in particular that by G. L. Harriss (1988), for his crucial role in the affairs of the early fifteenth century as a political and ecclesiastical heavyweight, banker to the kings and also crusader. Similarly, much has been written on Margaret Beaufort and the part she played in her son founding the Tudor dynasty. The Beaufort earls and dukes of Somerset, meanwhile, played crucial roles in the military and political affairs of fifteenth-century England. Although they were not always successful, John, Edmund, Henry and the second Edmund were at the forefront of important affairs, as were the two Joans.

By virtue of their position, the Beauforts gained both opportunities and responsibilities. In a century in which the monarchy was subject to questions of legitimacy and challenge by force of arms, the Beauforts were among Lancaster's most enthusiastic champions – and it could be said that the last Lancastrian king failed them.

I

A BROOD OF ROYAL BASTARDS

For a large part of the fourteenth and fifteenth centuries England and France were intermittently engaged in a war of conquest. The Hundred Years War was not an accurate title: the conflict lasted longer, and the actual fighting was not constant. It began when Edward III of England used his dynastic claim to the throne of France as a propaganda statement in a vassalage dispute; as time went on, he and his successors began to take the claim more seriously.

In 1328, on the death of Charles IV, last in the male line of the Capetian kings, there was controversy over whether the French succession could include or be transmitted through Edward's mother, Isabella of France. Either through a distinct interpretation of the laws of succession or from a widespread dislike of Isabella's attitude, the decision went against her and a relative from the House of Valois was crowned Philip VI. Then fifteen, Edward was king of England but had no personal power; his mother ruled in his name with her lover Roger Mortimer, having forced the abdication of her husband Edward II in 1327 and had him murdered. It took Edward III three years to raise sufficient support to oust them, but once this was accomplished he enjoyed an eventful fifty-year reign. From the direct line of the Plantagenet kings who had ruled

England since 1154, Edward was one of its most successful and charismatic.

In 1337 a dispute with Philip of France concerning Edward harbouring a rebellious vassal escalated into a war over an attempted confiscation of Edward's lands in France. Edward had married Philippa of Hainault and begun to raise a family, and as his sons came of age they joined their father in waging the long war against France. The eldest, Edward, known as the Black Prince, was the most prominent and would lead the English into many a victory himself. Not as charismatic was the fourth son, John, who nonetheless led a full life in his own right.

For all those in England of the feudal military class, from petty gentry to the king himself, this state of continual war with France dominated everyday life. The higher their position in society, the greater the opportunities and responsibilities the ongoing war afforded them. The experience of John of Gaunt, Prince of the Blood and eventually Duke of Lancaster, was typical.

John was born in Ghent in 1340. Edward III, then campaigning in Flanders, had borrowed heavily from the burghers of the town and left his pregnant queen Isabella there as collateral; the son born to her was known ever after as John 'of Gaunt' from his birthplace. A product of the times, John grew up as a conventional prince, versed in the arts of warfare and chivalry; a man of action, not only a distinguished soldier but a lover of hunting, hawking and dice. He also gained his quota of book learning and, in an age of religious dissent, was conventional in his faith and outward piety.

In 1342, while less than two years old, John had been granted the earldom of Richmond with its estates and incomes. He later gained far more on his betrothal to Blanche of Lancaster, the most attractive heiress in the land. He and Blanche were third cousins, both descended from sons of Henry III, and were married at Reading Abbey in 1359. This marriage produced three children: daughters Philippa and Elizabeth, and son Henry, named 'Bolingbroke' after his birthplace. Of these three Philippa would in due course marry King João I of Portugal; her fourth son was Prince Henry the Navigator, who initiated the exploration of the world beyond Europe. Elizabeth married John Holland, Earl of Huntingdon. Following dramatic events at the end of the century, meanwhile, Henry Bolingbroke would become king of England.

Blanche was joint-heiress to Henry, later Duke of Lancaster, whose father Henry of Grosmont as Earl of Lancaster had been a valuable ally to Edward III in his struggle to wrest control from his mother in 1330. The younger Henry had inherited the earldom in 1345 and was created a duke in 1351; together with the Black Prince he was the first ever duke in England. The honour was not subject to automatic inheritance, and so the dukedom was first declared extinct when he died in 1361, but it was then granted to John of Gaunt a year later on the occasion of his father's fiftieth birthday. John of Gaunt inherited vast estates, with lands in almost every county in England forming an astronomical income between £8,000 and £10,000 a year. When Blanche's sister Maud, Countess of Leicester died in 1362 without issue, he gained the entirety of the inheritance.[1]

Over the next decade John would become known for his military escapades, although he did not produce the spectacular victories for which his eldest brother the Black Prince was credited. In 1367 he was commanding a force at the Battle of Najera and was also involved in the Black Prince's victory at Limoges in 1370; he was always in his brother's shadow. But the Black Prince was so much afflicted by an illness contracted in Spain that he was confined to a litter by the time he accepted the surrender at Limoges. The Black Prince returned to England in January 1371, leaving John as Lieutenant of Aquitaine.

On the death of his duchess, Blanche, on 12 September 1368, shortly after she gave birth to her last child, John of Gaunt was by all accounts visibly devastated. He first plunged himself into his role as a military commander while the war grew to absorb the kingdom of Castile. When he took a mistress, he set in motion far-reaching events.

When Edward III had married Philippa of Hainault in 1328, several from her home county in what is now Belgium came to England in her service. Some were prominent in Edward's court and armies, of whom the most well known were Sir Walter Mauny and the chronicler Jean Froissart. Another was Sir Paon de Roelt, a flamboyant knight who served the English royal family, as did his issue.

Sir Paon, whose real name was Gilles, was so named as a 'Peacock' for his colourful fashion, and his surname was spelled variously as Roet, Roët and Roulx among others. After a documented presence on the Crécy and Calais campaigns he was eventually created Guyenne King of Arms, a royal herald. Besides a son named Walter who inherited his estates, 'Paon' had three daughters, the younger two probably from a second marriage given the age difference with their siblings. The eldest of the three, Elizabeth, became a nun in a convent at Mons and the other two were taken into the queen's household as young ladies-in-waiting. Philippa married the royal official and poet Geoffrey Chaucer, but it was the younger daughter, Katherine, whose story would have such a profound effect.

Katherine Roelt was born in or shortly before 1350, probably near Mons. While in Queen Philippa's household, at about the age of thirteen she married Sir Hugh Swynford of Norfolk, a knight in John of Gaunt's service. Katherine was a member of the Duchess of Lancaster's household by the beginning of 1365, when the Bishop of Lincoln granted her certain privileges of private worship.[2] By all accounts she was said to have been very beautiful. Schooled in the ways of the royal court, she grew up cultured and well versed in court protocols, and was apparently well educated too. She was named after the saint whose symbol was the wheel, a whimsical allusion to her family name; her father's coat of arms displayed three Catherine wheels on a red field.

Katherine produced three children by her first husband. The eldest, Margaret, born about 1365, became a nun at Barking Abbey, together with her cousin Elizabeth Chaucer. Her only son of the marriage, Thomas, was later knighted and became a prominent royal servant. There was another daughter named Blanche. John of Gaunt gave his patronage to Margaret's taking of the veil and stood godfather to two of the other children. It was once suggested that a fourth child was Dorothy Swynford, who would marry Thomas Thimelby, also of Lincolnshire, but there is no clear evidence that she was issue of this marriage.

It is subject to debate as to when John of Gaunt and Katherine Swynford became lovers. Froissart laconically described him as a 'frequent visitor to the nursery' after his duchess's death, hinting that the affair began with him consoling himself on his loss in 1369. More recent assessments question this chronology as he was on continuous service in southern France when Sir Hugh was killed on campaign in Aquitaine in 1372, and Katherine was either appointed or continued as governess in Gaunt's household, charged with the keeping and education of his motherless three children. The affair might have begun after he returned to England in 1372. John had already shown his roving eye, conducting an affair with one Marie de St-Hilaire, another lady of his mother's Hainaulter entourage. Their daughter, also named Blanche, was born in 1369 and would marry Sir Thomas Morieux. This liaison also went on very soon after his duchess's death, if not before.

Froissart, fond of repeating gossip, insinuated that Gaunt and Katherine were first conducting their affair when both their partners still lived.[3] This is altogether possible and would explain the time discrepancies. There were even questions raised as to the paternity of Katherine's son Thomas.[4] It was only from about 1373 that she was known to bear children to Gaunt.

It was far from unusual for a man in public life to take a mistress. Questionable morality apart, many a noble might seek sexual gratification that the consort arranged for him failed to provide. Before deriding the culture of hypocrisy over sexual issues and double standards it must be remembered that aristocratic marriages were usually arranged by third parties, more for reasons of politics and inheritance than for personal compatibility. As a rule, the bride and groom went to the altar from a sense of duty to transmit claims to titles and inheritances, establish political alliances and produce a quota of children. Mutual attraction, let alone love, was a bonus in most cases. A man might wish to spend time with a mistress for relaxation and companionship. For a woman to do the same was officially frowned upon, but many did in secret, and a courtly culture made such dealings acceptable if conducted discreetly.

Even Edward III himself in his old age had taken the courtesan Alice Perrers as his own mistress. She made no secret of her position in the king's bed, dominating the court in his dotage, and by her intriguing she drew considerable resentment. Her brassy and high-handed manner gave royal mistresses a bad name and she was impeached and banished by the Good Parliament of 1376. She was soon reinstated by the king, only to be driven away again after he died in 1377. She remained with the king as he died and then immediately left, taking the rings from his fingers.

For all his affairs John of Gaunt was known to care about his wife, but he also showed his devotion to Katherine. She was his mistress for over a quarter of a century, although there were periods in which he did not see her, and she was more typical of a mistress; unlike the extreme example of Alice Perrers, she was as discreet as could be. She did lose some respectability as mistresses often did, for it was impossible to keep the affair a secret forever.

It caused some unease when Gaunt himself made public shows of affection for her; he would often hold her bridle when they rode together.

Katherine continued as governess as the affair progressed. At first she had all three of his legitimate children as her charges, and when the boy Henry of Monmouth reached eight and was assigned a tutor she continued to raise the two daughters – successfully, it seems, for they benefited from an education appropriate to young ladies. At times she might have also cared for his other children together with her own from Hugh Swynford.

Before departing on campaign in 1372, Gaunt gave orders concerning payment to Katherine of an annuity of 50 marks, to be paid 'without excuse' along with deliveries of venison and winter fuel. He also in 1375 made a payment to one Agnes Bonsergeant, a widow who was probably Katherine's wet nurse on the birth of John Beaufort.[5] He made many awards of money and household items to Katherine over their years together and apart.

Katherine almost certainly knew the score, and would likely have understood when Gaunt remarried, but not to her; to marry beneath him could be a serious political error. Given his ambition he was obliged to look for a consort who brought him advantage, and he soon met a candidate who offered him a kingdom by marriage. When Gaunt and the Black Prince allied with Pedro the Cruel, King of Castile, in the French wars in the 1360s, they fought off a rebellion led by Henry (or Henrique) of Trastamara, Pedro's illegitimate half-brother. Despite the spectacular victory at Najera in 1365, however, they could not stop Henry from eventually overthrowing and killing Pedro in 1369.

When the seventeen-year-old Infanta Constance (or Constanza), Pedro's heiress, sought refuge in Aquitaine Gaunt entered into a marriage with her on 21 September 1371. This was for John a means to a throne, while Constance simply wanted revenge on her uncle and to regain the kingdom. The marriage produced three children but John would later spend more time with Katherine than with Constance. He assumed the title of King of Castile and Leon in right of his new wife on 29 January 1372 and impaled his arms with those of the Castilian royal house. He then gathered about him a small court of dissident Castilians and required that English nobles address him as 'my Lord of Spain'.

In reality he was only a titular king and pretender, and his efforts to gain the kingdom itself made little headway over fifteen years. It was only in 1386, when King João of Portugal entered into an alliance with England, that he could actually campaign in Castile but his efforts that year and in the following expedition of 1387 saw little result. He then abandoned the project, renouncing his claim to Castile in return for the marriage of Katherine of Lancaster, his daughter by Constance, to the Trastamara heir. The one son of his second marriage had died in infancy.

Throughout the 1370s, Katherine Swynford bore John four children. Born out of wedlock, they could not inherit either estates or titles but Gaunt was determined that they would all be well provided for. He supplied them with the family name of Beaufort. This was possibly after Roger Beaufort, a French noble whose brother was the incumbent Pope Gregory XI and who was Gaunt's prisoner of war in 1377.[6] However, it is more likely that Gaunt took the Beaufort name from his own castle in France, as this was a link that he could either deny or acknowledge as it suited him.

John Beaufort, the eldest, was born in 1372 or 1373. John of Gaunt had only one legitimate son from his first marriage, whom he had named Henry after Blanche's father, and to name John after himself was a special acknowledgment despite his illegitimacy. In 1375 the second Beaufort, whom he also named Henry, was born and at further two-year intervals the third son, Thomas, and then a daughter, Joan, arrived. It is not certain where each was born; some would assume it was at Beaufort Castle, but it was more likely to be Kettlethorpe in Lincolnshire where Katherine resided.

They were all well educated as their father wished, although Henry was the most studious of the four and therefore destined for an ecclesiastical career.

In the same decade, Gaunt continued to campaign in France. Late in 1373 he attempted to regain more of Aquitaine with a landward raid from Calais. Other expeditions followed until in the summer of 1378 he sought in vain to capture St Malo. Gaunt found himself blamed for this failure, and others along the way.

As the long reign of Edward III drew to a close Gaunt was the most senior adult prince active in public life. The Black Prince had never recovered from the illness that ended his active career in 1371. As an added loss, his eldest son, Edward of Angoulême, who would have followed him in the succession, had died in 1371. This now left a small boy, his other son, who succeeded as Richard II aged ten. When Edward the Black Prince predeceased his father in 1376, an era of uncertainty began for the English monarchy. Since the death of King John in 1216, when his eldest son had taken his place as Henry III, there had been no need to question the succession as primogeniture had dictated the inheritance. But with Edward III's eldest son dying before him and his surviving son succeeding as a minor, the continuity was broken.

John of Gaunt was an able soldier and administrator, and some felt that he deserved a kingdom through his prowess. He might have made a suitable King of England, but his place as a younger son made this very unlikely. On Edward's death in June 1377, Gaunt had become the most powerful man in England next to the new boy king. His elder brothers – the Black Prince, William and Lionel – were all dead, as were six other siblings, and two younger brothers remained. Under his mother Joan of Kent's regency, Richard was somewhat accessible to John of Gaunt.

As he grew up, Richard proved a very difficult king. He lacked the martial virtues that characterised his father and grandfather, and his belief in his royal prerogative caused him to ignore procedures and concessions that many considered established; he made the fundamental mistake of not consulting his nobles and failed to address their various needs. Surrounded by favourites and flatterers, he acted in a somewhat abrupt and impulsive manner at times.

Like most in public life, Gaunt was controversial in his time. Although a popular figure, he made enemies both high and low. He was an advocate of ending the war with France, which he saw as unwinnable and an unnecessary drain on finances. This view enabled the Truce of Leulinghem in 1389, but it was unpopular with those who had long fought the French wars and had a vested interest in their continuation. He was also criticized for his campaigning in Castile, as it seemed that he was furthering his own ambitions in a foreign country rather than fighting for his king.

John never actively sought the throne of England himself, but he was much engaged in the political struggles during his nephew's minority and eccentric later rule. In fact, on the whole he proved a moderating influence. On his return from Castile in 1389 he was soon involved in easing one of the many crises between Richard and his nobles, engendering a compromise that maintained stability for some time. At times he quarreled with the king and for a while he gave protection to the Oxford preacher John Wycliffe, who spoke out for a revision of Church doctrine and wealth, but he dropped Wycliffe when his teachings became too extreme. He was disliked by many of the common people – during the Peasants' Revolt of 1381 insurgents ransacked his palace of the Savoy – and many believed that he wished to usurp the throne. But he always declared himself the king's loyal subject.

John of Gaunt did in fact have a strong claim in the succession. As the closest Prince of the Blood in Richard II's reign save for one small child, Gaunt was considered by many as an eventual candidate for the throne. There was growing concern when Richard's first queen, Anne of Bohemia, died childless in 1394, and

Richard, whose behaviour thereafter became increasingly erratic, entered into an ill-advised second marriage to the seven-year-old Isabella of Valois. Aside from the dubious match of a grown man with a child, the king was moving the possibility of an heir several years into the future. He was only thirty-one, true, but in an age of uncertain mortality, for someone of a markedly delicate constitution he was tempting fate. At best, if Richard lived to produce an heir the boy would have a long minority.

As the four Beauforts grew up in this troubled time, their father pulled every string he could to find each of them a place in the world. The stigma of illegitimacy was a serious impediment but all four had ability and drive to be reckoned with, and against the odds they would all become successful, prominent and influential. Both John and Thomas Beaufort were men of action, and as boys they were trained as knights, the traditional career for those of aristocratic backgrounds whether legitimate or not. Young John entered another household, probably that of the king, where with other boys he was raised as a page and then as a squire, learning the arts of horsemanship, fighting and chivalry, in which he would soon excel. John and his half-brother Thomas Swynford associated with his other half-brother Henry Bolingbroke, the three close in age. Thomas Beaufort apparently served in Gaunt's own household, where his education was much the same.

Appointed a king's knight in 1392 with an annuity of 100 marks, John Beaufort took well to his calling and gained opportunity for active service at about eighteen, and as a bonus lived the dream of every young knight: going on crusade. The Barbary Crusade of 1390 was in reality a poor imitation of those of previous centuries, effectively an attack on the Hafsid Caliphate of Tunis in response to the actions of the Barbary pirates. With some other young knights of the royal household John volunteered and joined a contingent led by Duke Louis of Bourbon. Though hampered by quarrels and a lack of siege engines, the crusade ended with the

Republic of Genoa extracting tribute and a substantial reduction in piracy from North Africa after a siege on Mahdia, a fortified city near Tunis. For John Beaufort it was the ideal knightly quest; to go east on crusade and fight the good fight against the enemies of Christ. He was lucky, as this was almost the last crusade that actually took place against the Saracens. He did not perform any conspicuous service, but at least gained experience and prestige.

In the early 1390s Gaunt purchased a number of manors from the Earl of Salisbury for John's material sustenance, mostly in Somerset and including Matlock, Bruton and Shepton Mallet. In themselves they were worth only about £300 a year in all, but were the beginnings of the estates the earls and dukes of Somerset would hold.[7]

In a time of little fighting in France, John Beaufort had opportunities for advancement in court but few for warfare. The lack of foreign wars in that time must have been frustrating, and the young man set off in 1394 to campaign with the Teutonic Knights in Lithuania in a party led by Henry Bolingbroke. Despite his illegitimacy, John gained a reputation as an able soldier. The third son Thomas was also earmarked for a military career but was then too young for any such action.

It was usual practice for a noble family to point at least one younger son towards the Church, normally whichever showed the greatest capacity for book learning. As senior churchmen were feudal landholders and sometimes powerful statesmen, there were plenty of opportunities. Henry, the second of the Beauforts, was clearly suited for such a calling. In 1388, in his mid-teens, he was sent to Peterhouse College, Cambridge and moved two years later to Queen's College, Oxford for further study. He also spent some time at Aachen studying canon law. By the time he was twenty, the future Cardinal Beaufort had already shown himself learned and mentally agile. He had a spectacular career as a churchman and politician ahead of him.

As the daughter of an aristocratic family, one of the only two careers open to Joan Beaufort was an advantageous marriage. She might, as was customary for one daughter in every generation of the Roelt family, have entered a convent but this clearly did not happen. She was a strong, pretty young woman and her greatest ability for the time was to produce many children, most of them healthy, and to take each pregnancy in her stride. This was remarkable in an age when a single childbirth might easily cripple or kill a woman; Joan gave birth to at least fourteen children and lived to a good age. She also had a flair for making the best of her opportunities. By arrangement she was married in 1394 to Lord Ferrers of Wem, whom she bore a daughter, and was widowed a short time afterwards. Like many widows in those days, she might have considered remarrying beneath her, but circumstances would soon make her eligible for a much better match.

About 1382, Gaunt declared his affair with Katherine Swynford at an end. He made a public atonement for his lecherous behaviour and took steps to have Katherine removed from his household. He still provided for her, but he declared that his life would be far more respectable from now on; he was in fact seeking to advance his claim to the Castilian crown at this time. He did not forget Katherine, though, and would call her back some years later.

Katherine and her Beaufort children now joined the household of Mary Bohun, wife of Gaunt's son Henry Bolingbroke. It is not known what exactly she did: she was probably not a governess, at least in the early years, for Mary's children were born later, but it is possible that from 1387 she supervised a nursery that included the future Henry V and his siblings.

From 1389 she was John of Gaunt's mistress once more. That year he returned from a long absence in France, Portugal and Castile, his Spanish ambitions now at an end, and from this time he and Constance lived apart. Several years later, in 1396, he made a decision that changed things for the Beauforts forever. Now in his late fifties, his deeds and aspirations behind him, he sought to put his affairs in order. Constance had died in 1394, and he was no longer in search of heiresses for his own advancement. Katherine had been his close companion for so long, understanding his absences and his need to marry for reasons of state, and it was a mark of his devotion to her when, after all the years that she had remained in the shadows, he finally made her his wife and duchess.

Froissart commented on this marriage by talking of the widespread shock it caused, and relating the comments of Eleanor de Bohun, Duchess of Gloucester, wife of Gaunt's younger brother Thomas of Woodstock. Not only had this gentlewoman been raised to the status of duchess, but her past as Gaunt's private whore was considered scandalous. Worst of all, Katherine was now the second most senior lady of the realm, yielding precedence only to Richard's child bride Queen Isabella. In his usual gossipy manner, Froissart wrote that the Duchess of Gloucester went on to say:

> We will leave her to do the honours all by herself. We will not go to any place where she might be. It would really demean us too much if that kind of duchess, who came from humble stock and was the Duke's concubine for a very long time, inside and outside his marriages were to take precedence over us. Our hearts would burst with vexation and rightly so.[8]

Of course the established nobility took umbrage at the new Duchess of Lancaster, as the status quo resents a parvenu. After her marriage she did become a friend to Queen Isabella, however, who though a child was in need of companionship. She also had little trouble being accepted by the wider court.[9]

There were problems obtaining the marriage itself; having been godfather to two of her children by her husband, canon law placed John of Gaunt within a prohibited decree, and Katherine had after all been his companion in adultery. Gaunt required a papal dispensation to overturn such objections, but this was not so difficult at that stage. The continuing Great Schism saw rival popes in Rome and Avignon, and the pontiffs could often be obliging if only for fear of losing the allegiance of their supporters.

This also provided an opportunity to revise the status of John and Katherine's children. Thus by dispensation of Pope Boniface IX in Rome not only would John and Katherine be able to marry, but their grown-up children would become the legitimate issue of this marriage. When on 9 February 1397 the marriage of John of Gaunt and Katherine finally took place, the four Beauforts instantly acquired legitimacy. Gaunt had their status confirmed by Act of Parliament.[10] The entry in the Parliament Rolls for January 1397 ratifies the papal dispensation and declares the Beauforts fully legitimate and free of any restrictions arising from their previous status. It specifies that all honours, dignities and titles were within their grasp.[11]

Modest pride of place was given to John Beaufort, knight; the text first names him. Richard II by then valued him as one in his personal service. Henry '*clericus*' is mentioned next, and Thomas and Joan are described respectively as '*domicellus*' and '*domicella*'. In Thomas's case it referred to his status as 'squire' or 'young man of a household'; '*domicella*' meanwhile could be translated at 'damsel' or 'young lady'. It had obviously passed notice that Joan was a widow.[12]

This raises questions of legality as opposed to common sense. The Act changed the Beauforts' legal status, but without reversing time it could hardly have made them legitimate by birth. The ease with which biological reality could be discounted through paperwork might seem unimportant in an age where the stigma of illegitimacy has faded to near-extinction, but in the fourteenth century, when the Church had the final word on morality, this was a deeply ingrained issue. Once the Beauforts had acquired their legal legitimacy, they found a world of possibilities opening for them.

But in reality the original stain was never completely removed. The question of their legitimacy dogged the Beauforts throughout three generations and prejudiced whatever claims they had to the royal succession. Such a matter was not foreseen at the time, but they would first encounter it in the next reign. Even in the final showdown of 1485, the culmination of the Wars of the Roses, Richard III's propaganda made much of Henry Tudor's two bastard descents, one of which was of his Beaufort forebears. Of course, such missives omitted Richard's own Beaufort origins.[13]

On the occasion of their legitimation there was no mention of whether the Beauforts could now expect a place in the succession. In 1397 there were no rigid rules and King Richard II was still confident of producing an heir. It would have been dangerous to openly consider alternative kings in those times, but the succession would become an intermittent controversy over the following century and the Beauforts were often in the discussion.

In 1397, soon after the legitimation was finalised, Sir John Beaufort was created Earl of Somerset. No longer illegitimate, he became a recognised Prince of the Blood and was granted a customary senior peerage. He also received a grant of precedence, between the Earl Marshal and the Earl of Warwick, and as a further honour became a Knight of the Garter. There had been no Earl of Somerset since the twelfth century, and this earldom did not automatically make him rich. Such titles were normally in the king's gift as extinct or forfeited peerages and usually came with a package of estates and incomes that would support the dignity. John received little more than the title to begin with, although various estates were cobbled together over the following years. He also married Margaret Holland, co-heiress to the Earl of Kent, at this time. On 29 September that year he was quickly promoted further, as Marquis of Dorset and Marquis of Somerset at the same time, although he was known then by the first of these titles. Richard was granting dukedoms and marquisates perhaps too freely, and some titles would be removed in the next reign, when John would revert to Earl of Somerset.

Henry Beaufort, the second son, was also swiftly promoted. Now in his early twenties, he was first granted the deanery of Wells, and it was understood that he could use the incomes and farm the position while he remained in Aachen at his studies in the hope of advancement in the Church. He was already allowed to farm the prebendary of Wedmore in the same diocese. That year, possibly as a result of his new status, he was elected chancellor of Oxford University, usually a two-year appointment.

On 27 February 1398, although still a deacon and not yet an ordained priest, Henry became a bishop. The king was persuaded to remove John Buckingham from the see of Lincoln and appoint Beaufort instead, which was an unusual action. Even though Bishop Buckingham was an old man and probably not much use in his role, he was translated against his wishes to the see of Coventry and Lichfield, recently vacated by the promotion of Richard Scrope as Archbishop of York. While elderly prelates were often secure in their sees despite being inactive, Buckingham's removal was abrupt. Unwilling to go quietly, in July he was still acting as bishop in Lincoln, and only when offered favourable terms for retirement did he agree to go. The king had exiled Thomas Arundel, Archbishop of Canterbury, by now and was making ecclesiastical appointments according to his own will.[14]

Young Henry Beaufort then gained his platform for wealth and power. Both Gaunt and Katherine had a long association with Lincoln Cathedral and were its regular benefactors, and Gaunt probably lobbied for his son's appointment. Henry would gain a more desirable bishopric a few years later, but Lincoln was a major promotion for a young man. He surrendered nearly all his minor benefices on his consecration.

Joan Beaufort was then a widow, but far more desirable than she had been as a bastard daughter. Also in 1398, obviously as arranged by her father, she married Ralph Neville, recently created Earl of Westmorland. As Warden of the West March towards Scotland, Westmorland shared with the Earl of Northumberland the responsibility for defending and policing the northern border region. Having gained his earldom, he was eager for association through marriage with the crown. Joan's new husband was at least thirty years her senior. With his deceased first wife, Margaret Stafford, he had a grown-up family of nine, mostly daughters. Joan would supply him with at least nine more children, and perhaps as many as twelve; this was the first generation of the Middleham Nevilles, as they were later called.

Thomas Beaufort was still a youth and did not receive the same sudden promotions, but he would come into his own later. He was married in 1397 while still a minor to Margaret, daughter of Sir Thomas Neville of Hornby, a knight of Yorkshire not closely related to Joan's husband. She was probably underaged too and lived in Katherine's household after her marriage. They had one son who died young. Thomas was granted Castle Rising, recently forfeited from the Duke of Norfolk.[15]

Now as legitimate royal issue the Beauforts were propelled from comparative obscurity into important roles in government. They had showed willing as servants of the crown, but soon the House of Lancaster with which they were decisively linked by parentage found itself in opposition to King Richard. Henry Bolingbroke, son of John of Gaunt and his first duchess, Blanche, became the focus of discontent over Richard's governance.

The main reason the Hundred Years War lasted so long was the failure to agree on terms for peace. After the battles of Crécy and Poitiers the English held the upper hand and could secure an agreement to keep what they had gained. In the Treaty of Brétigny of 1360 Edward renounced his claim to the French crown; at this stage it was mostly a propaganda tool, and he had gained what he wanted. But a violation of the terms by one of the French hostages invalidated it all, and peace eluded the two sides. The war thus dragged on for decades, often interrupted by truces but not resolved. The English lost some of what they had held, but they kept Calais and Guyenne.

By his early thirties, Gaunt's eldest son Henry Bolingbroke was a distinguished soldier. First Earl of Derby and then Duke of Hereford, he had some standing as a prince of the realm as heir to Lancaster; with Richard II still childless, he still had a vague claim to the throne. Richard was nearing a new crisis concerning his nobles. In 1398 the Duke of Norfolk and Bolingbroke fell into accusation and counter-accusation of treason, and the two prepared to settle the insult on the field of honour at Coventry. On 15 September the two dukes rode out in full armour preparing to fight to the death, but to their amazement Richard halted the duel at the last minute and banished both parties from the kingdom, Norfolk for life and Bolingbroke for ten years. Many thought the latter had been unfairly treated.

Richard II showed himself well disposed towards the Beauforts. He certainly approved of Henry Beaufort's consecration as bishop, and John had been a king's knight for some time before his legitimation. John was soon Constable of Wallingford for life, Admiral of the North and West, Constable of Dover Castle and Warden of the Cinque Ports. The banishment of Henry Bolingbroke was an unforseen blow, but if the Beauforts harboured resentment none of them were known to voice it.

On 3 February 1399, John of Gaunt died at Leicester Castle with Katherine by his side. Their marriage had lasted two years. In his will Gaunt had given her much in terms of plate, possessions and wealth. Her son Thomas by her first marriage was then Sheriff of Lincolnshire and her son Henry by her second was the bishop. She survived Gaunt by four years and on her death on 10 May 1403 was buried in Lincoln Cathedral.

Gaunt's death brought hopes that Bolingbroke would be recalled sooner than the king had initially ordered. Instead, Richard seized the entire estates of the Duchy of Lancaster. This caused outrage, as it was one thing that custom dictated kings simply could not do. In July 1399 Bolingbroke returned, the exiled Archbishop Arundel riding with him, and instantly gained support from many important nobles, including the earls of Northumberland and Westmorland.

There was little real fighting. Richard was then campaigning in Ireland and came back too late. He had left his troops behind, and lack of leadership in England prevented any organised resistance to Bolingbroke. One could wonder if Bolingbroke's personal popularity and the Richard's lack thereof decided the outcome of the revolt. Captured at Conwy on his return, the king was eventually forced to abdicate and Bolingbroke was declared King Henry IV. Richard was imprisoned at Pontefract Castle, Dorset's half-brother Sir Thomas Swynford charged with his keeping.

The Beauforts remained supporters of Richard's regime up to almost the last moment. Bishop Henry Beaufort had accompanied Richard to Ireland and was still in the royal party when the king returned via Milford Haven. It appears that Henry only defected when the king panicked and ran for Cheshire, leaving most of his entourage behind.

The behaviour of John Beaufort at this time is more difficult to ascertain. The Beauforts were as shocked as the other nobles when Richard appropriated their father's estates, but to rise against an anointed king was treason and not to be entered into lightly, especially for those who depended so much on royal favour. John Beaufort gave the impression of loyalty to Richard, but Bolingbroke was John's half-brother, and there was a conflict of loyalties.

John, still Marquis of Dorset, had recently been appointed Lieutenant of Aquitaine, a region of south-west France long held by the kings of England but by then reduced to the county of Guyenne. Given his father's recent death he was allowed to remain in England a short time before his departure, however, and when Bolingbroke landed both John Beaufort and his uncle Edmund, the elderly Duke of York and only surviving son of Edward III, raised armies to put down the rebellion, heading to intercept the insurgents at Berkeley.

Once they discovered that they were outnumbered, York and Dorset promptly surrendered. The outcome was straightforward for York, who was immediately pardoned by the rebels and afterwards supported the revolt. But John came very close to being executed when both the Earl of Northumberland and his son Hotspur called for it. It was Bolingbroke himself who spoke up to spare John, stating that they had been in correspondence in Bolingbroke's exile and that John was secretly loyal to the cause.

The truth of this assertion is uncertain. John was not only Bolingbroke's half-brother but had long been close to him, even on crusade. Westmorland, another leading supporter of the revolt, was John's brother-in-law; it was very much a family matter. At the same time, John was aware that he would commit treason by joining the rebellion against Richard. For one who had stayed loyal while many of the nobles plotted, it might have been distasteful to him. A true knight stood by his king, whether he thought him right or wrong in his judgment.

John was doubtless aware that if the rebellion failed after his defection he would face a shameful death by execution and the stain of treason would mark the family itself. It is likely that he hedged his bets throughout and only committed himself to Bolingbroke's revolt when it looked more than likely that it would be successful. It is equally possible that he deliberately made a poor effort to raise an army against him as a pretext to his early surrender; honour would then be satisfied. By doing so he succeeded in appearing loyal to the king until it was politic to change sides, but even then he played a dangerous game and narrowly escaped losing his head.

Perhaps also Bolingbroke saw John as more use to him alive than dead, even if he doubted his loyalty. While John did not contribute very much to the rising, it must be said that little actual fighting took place throughout the coup. Even with such a conflict of allegiances John was unlikely to fight his own brother, and he did show Henry clear loyalty afterwards. As a final consideration, Bolingbroke may not have wanted to see John killed no matter the part he played. Nor might he have wished for the mark of Cain. However minimal their contribution, both John and Henry Beaufort survived the coup and made themselves useful to the new king as soon as they could.

By virtue of their parentage the Beauforts could not fail to associate with the new ruling dynasty, despite their ambivalence during the coup of 1399. As their brother ascended the throne as King Henry IV, the Beauforts had their fortunes linked with the Lancastrian monarchy; they could do little else. The following two generations were just as closely associated with Lancaster.

Having grown up as a brood of royal bastards, the Beauforts had become a cadet and potential collateral branch of the ruling family. This brought them all manner of possibilities and responsibilities, shaping the progress of their dynasty. But they never completely lost the stigma of their origin, and this would complicate matters as events unfolded throughout the next century. Hurdling their illegitimacy was a major success for the four Beaufort children in their early adulthood, but regardless of papal and parliamentary pronouncements the mark of bastardy was never fully erased or forgotten. It was also their good fortune that the new king was their half-brother, much in need of trustworthy supporters to do his bidding.

2

THE KING'S HALF-BROTHERS

Henry Bolingbroke had made himself king in 1399 with a coup typical of more recent times. He mounted a military invasion and soon gained the surrender of those loyal to Richard II, and when Richard himself was captured Henry forced his abdication and proclaimed himself king. For better or worse, his route to power was little different from that taken by twentieth-century dictators and was therefore disquieting to most of his contemporaries. Rather than succeeding to the throne he *usurped* it, not only taking it by force of arms but displacing the anointed king in doing so. At the turn of the fifteenth century, revolt against one's king was the most terrible crime of all; to challenge the social hierarchy was tantamount to shaking a fist at God himself. Even given Richard's unacceptable behaviour, it was hotly debated whether or not Henry's course was justified.

The rules of succession lacked precise definition but there was a strong case for Edmund, Earl of March, only son of the third son of Edward III. Bolingbroke's father had been the fourth son. But March was eight years old and few wanted a repeat of the long regency that had fatally weakened Richard's reign. Bolingbroke had taken control by force of arms and none could challenge him at that point, but this left room for doubt that he was rightfully king.

When Edward II had been deposed in 1327 it had been accepted that, whatever the moralities of rebellion, his eldest son should succeed as Edward III. It was not as easy for Henry IV, and so he was left exposed to revolt and conspiracy. Moreover, the nature of his accession made it easier for others to countenance deposing kings; little wonder that four kings of England would be removed by force in the fifteenth century. Within a few months of Henry's coup a number of nobles loyal to Richard II tried to seize and possibly murder Henry. The pitiful attempt ended with most of the plotters executed, but it probably prompted Henry to have Richard murdered in his prison. It is not by any means certain that this actually happened – foul play is not established, nor whether Henry himself ordered it – but the accusation stuck to him thereafter. At the same time, rumours that Richard still lived plagued his reign and the next.

It was a sore point that so many of the greater nobles had actively sought to bring down the new king in 1400. A monarch needed the support of his magnates to run the country, both as royal office holders at court and as enforcers in the provinces, and it was obvious that many could not be trusted. He had the sure support of Thomas Arundel, Archbishop of Canterbury, who had spent time in exile with him, but this man expected positive action against the spread of heresy in payment. Thomas Langley, a priest who had risen by John of Gaunt's patronage, was another valuable counsellor and office holder who also attained episcopal rank. Without a long list of manors that most senior nobles held as sources of revenue, the Beauforts depended on various offices for incomes, and in return rendered loyal and trustworthy service.

The Beauforts were close to the centre of government from the start. John Beaufort, then Marquis of Dorset and previously a king's knight, took a military role as Captain of Calais and an administrative office as Chamberlain of England. Henry Beaufort, still Bishop of Lincoln, was an active counsellor and soon to be appointed chancellor. Thomas Beaufort was not long of age, but for some years was a knight in the royal household. He was knighted on or before 1400, the year he was admitted to the Order of the Garter, his distinguished career still before him.[1]

The presence of the Beauforts in the new regime was one of the reasons for the first division among the victorious faction, for some felt that they were too much favoured for doing so little in the 1399 coup. The Percy family, particularly its head the Earl of Northumberland and his heir and namesake Henry Percy, known as Hotspur, had given crucial support when Bolingbroke returned to England. The earl commanded the defence of the eastern half of the Scottish border region and held vast estates and important influence in the north. Hotspur had associated with John of Gaunt, particularly in his Spanish campaign, and was a popular hero. When the new king disappointed the Percys over the ransom of Scottish prisoners in 1402 and over lack of funding for the defence of the northern borders, however, relations began to cool.

Ralph Neville, Earl of Westmorland and brother-in-law to the Beauforts, was equally powerful in the northern region as Warden of the West March and also a strong supporter of the new regime. He was also a long-standing rival to the Percys and when the king appeared to prefer Westmorland over the former earl he was asking for trouble. But Henry already knew the dangers of displeasing the Percys and was obliged in this stage of his reign to placate them. To make Hotspur deputy to the Prince of Wales as Warden of the Welsh Marches was an unfortunate decision.

For half of Henry's reign, a tendency towards rebellion bubbled under the surface. There was a serious threat from Owain Glyndwr, a Welsh gentleman whose dispute with a Bolingbroke supporter led him to revolt. Styling himself through his lineage prince of a newly independent Wales, Glyndwr joined with Sir Edmund Mortimer, uncle of the Earl of March, and with Northumberland and Hotspur. By 1403 the House of Lancaster had a serious challenge when Mortimer, Glyndwr and Percy rose in revolt with the intent of dividing the realm between them.

Given their blood ties to the king and their evident acumen, the Beauforts came into demand. Henry had four sons who would in due course fill the military and viceregal roles required but at that point only the eldest, Prince Hal, the future Henry V, had reached an age where he could take on responsibilities of this nature, and even then only under supervision. The Beaufort men were all showered with offices and accompanying incomes, and despite their ambivalence in 1399 they did prove to the Lancastrian kings that they considered blood to be thicker than water.

John Beaufort was of a nature similar to his half-brother the king and their father, being an accomplished soldier, military governor and commander of men. He and the new king had crusaded together in Lithuania some years before. In the Scottish campaign of 1400 he was commissioned to lead a force of thirty-nine lances and 160 archers.[2] But early in the reign he lost his highest title. In 1400 the king stripped him of the Marquisate of Dorset and he automatically reverted to his previous dignity of Earl of Somerset. His was not the only degradation; several others who had been granted high peerage under Richard were divested of their inflated titles, including the dukes of Surrey and Exeter, demoted to their earldoms of Kent and Huntingdon, and the dukes of Warwick and Oxford also found themselves earls once more. Until Richard's time dukedoms had only been granted to members of the Plantagenet family and Henry was only reversing an ill-conceived policy of his predecessor.

On 6 March 1402, the Commons petitioned the king to restore John to his marquisate, protesting that he was a loyal subject and undeserving of the demotion. But before Henry made any pronouncement on this, John himself protested that he should not regain the title as it was 'estrange' to the realm of England; it was, after all, another of Richard's innovations.[3] The title, a French import ranking between that of duke and earl, returned to use later in the fifteenth century and remains today. The Dorset peerage would later be granted as an earldom to Thomas Beaufort, and three times more to Beauforts of later generations.

Despite the demotion, John had many other awards from the king. Partially as compensation, immediately after his degradation he was granted the office of Chamberlain of England, which gave him duties in the king's inner circle and an income from various designated sources. In 1400 he was given the lands forfeited by Lord Lumley after his rebellion. He also gained those of Lady Harrington, recently deceased, and the forfeited Welsh lands of Owain Glyndwr, although this last grant was purely notional for Glyndwr had declared Wales independent and was holding it against the English. Other, mostly modest incomes followed. His annuity of 100 marks from the Exchequer was confirmed and there was a further increase in revenues from various sources.[1]

There was some discussion on confirming John's lieutenancy of Guyenne, but it did not come about. Many other nobles treated their various positions as sinecures, delegating business to deputies; John Beaufort, however, did not. When he was created Captain of Calais in 1401, he took to the job personally. He was frustrated by chronic underfunding, sharing this grievance with Northumberland, who commanded the garrison at Berwick and suffered similarly. Shortfalls in revenue each year had resulted in the wages of the Calais garrison running into arrears over several years, making the soldiers there uncooperative and at times understandably mutinous. There was a growing concern over possible plans among the French, in particular the Duke of Burgundy, to lay siege to the town.

Henry IV did not usually attend his royal council, and as chamberlain John Beaufort was often his close advisor. John's standing is shown by his leadership of two important journeys in the early years. In 1403 he was in the bridal party for Henry IV's second consort, Joan of Navarre, Dowager Duchess of Brittany, bringing her to Winchester where Bishop Beaufort married her to the king in the cathedral on 7 February. The following year he headed the party that accompanied Blanche, the king's daughter, to Cologne for her marriage to Prince Louis of Bavaria.[5]

John's brother Bishop Henry also found opportunity in both Church and State. He appears from the beginning of Henry IV's reign as a witness to various charters and attended the king's council when he was in London, and on 20 February 1403 he was appointed Chancellor of England. As the keeper of the royal seal he was head of the medieval secretariat, where the will of the king was enacted. As this required both an education and some administrative ability, such a role usually fell to a senior churchman. It was not an immediate appointment; at first John Scarle, an archdeacon whom Richard had appointed, continued in the office, and in 1401 he was replaced by Bishop Stafford of Exeter. It was apparently considered a two-year appointment when Henry Beaufort took over. Still under thirty years of age, he had already risen further than most clerics could expect in a lifetime.

Like many outwardly celibate clerics Beaufort had an affair at this time, probably with Alice FitzAlan, widow of John Chilton of Powys. There was one illegitimate child, a Jane or Joan, born in 1402 and married in about 1423 to Sir Edmund Stradling, who served as Chamberlain of South Wales from 1423 to 1437. Beaufort did not acknowledge her but mentioned her and her husband in his will.[6]

Beaufort's main challenge was the handling of Parliament, which met twice in his two-year term. The king was obliged to summon Parliament in order to obtain money through taxation, and the Commons would often seek to bargain over grievances before granting the subsidy. As the need for funding over Wales, Ireland and Calais was acute, Parliament called for curbs on the expense of the royal household and pressed for reductions in customs duties. Beaufort as chancellor worked wonders navigating through these two difficult occasions. The government of Henry IV was faced throughout with an obvious need to balance the books without further discontent over taxation – a common problem that possible rebels could exploit.

It was customary for the chancellor to open each parliament with a sermon, and Bishop Beaufort had a particular flair for delivering sermons that set the mood to the kings' advantage. On 14 January 1403 he referred to the members as 'a multitude of wise men' that would give the king good counsel. He likened the nation to a body, a well-used image whose sides represented the Church and the laity, each of which required relied upon the other. He emphasised the many troubles of the realm and stressed the need for all to stand together and address the future. The sermon did much to swing the Commons to the king's needs.[7] Through his eventual three terms as chancellor, Beaufort would often use this strategy to put the Commons in a desired frame of mind, usually when the king needed money.

In May 1404 Beaufort himself made the first of many loans to the crown, of £1,333 *6s 8d*, to repay which revenues from Lincolnshire and clerical levies from the Lincoln diocese were earmarked.[8] Over the rest of his life Beaufort made periodic loans to the crown, which did much in all to ease its financial burdens.

One problem occurring on Henry Beaufort's watch as chancellor concerned the severance of trade agreements between England and the Hanseatic League. Beaufort set in motion attempts to restore normal relations, and an agreement with the Hanse in 1405 was formalised in a treaty of 1409.[9]

While still chancellor, Henry Beaufort gained a new ecclesiastical appointment. William of Wykeham, formidable Bishop of Winchester from 1366, himself chancellor at times under Edward III and Richard II and also a long-term enemy of John of Gaunt, died in September 1404. On 19 November, Henry Beaufort was translated to Winchester as his successor. This was technically not a promotion, for he was still only a bishop, but Winchester was the most prestigious of the bishoprics. It had been the capital of the late Saxon and Norman kings and its bishop ranked next in precedence after the two archbishoprics and before the sees of London and Durham, all of which were wealthy and powerful incumbencies.

The Beauforts and their parents had long associations with Lincoln Cathedral, and Beaufort had seen his mother laid to rest there the previous year, but this new see was the best possible move for a prelate with desire for wealth and power. There was after all nothing to keep him in Lincoln; he had not really made his mark on the bishopric in six years. Henry Beaufort might have had his sights set on Canterbury given the ambition he displayed throughout his life, but such a promotion would not materialise. Nonetheless, his position in Winchester worked to his advantage. In fact the resources of the see of St Swithin made him very wealthy indeed and able to extend his influence in the coming years. Beaufort resigned as chancellor on his translation to Winchester, handing the Great Seal to Thomas Langley.

It is interesting to note that Bishop Beaufort had performed the marriage ceremony between the king and his second consort at Winchester a year before it was his own see. There might have been issues of protocol with Wykeham, but perhaps his interest in Winchester began from that time. Winchester was basically a monastic foundation and Beaufort had few roles for patronage, although John Caterik, an associate from his time as chancellor of Oxford, knew his favour there as Archdeacon of Surrey.

Thomas Beaufort was also much at work as a knight of the king's entourage. As a king's knight he was granted an annuity and a number of estates in the king's hands by forfeiture. In 1402 he received his first command, the keeping of the castle at Ludlow at a time of Welsh raids. The following year he was commissioned to garrison the castles of Carmarthen, Newcastle Emlyn, Cardigan and others while the reconquest of Wales was underway.[10] Rising through personal prowess, Thomas impressed the king and gained such responsibilities on merit. Like John, he was confirmed in the annuity of 100 marks granted by the previous king and also incomes from forfeited lands and those of extinct tenancies in chief.[11]

Joan Beaufort had long before left for a life in the castles of Yorkshire, County Durham and Cumberland, where her husband performed his duties as a magnate of northern England. In 1400 she gave birth to her first son, Richard Neville, later Earl of Salisbury. For the next two decades she lived in continual pregnancy, producing some fourteen children of whom nine survived. It may have been in part due to Joan's influence that her husband Westmorland remained the loyal supporter of the House of Lancaster in this critical period. He was created Marshal of England in 1400.

Joan was determined to place her own issue at the forefront, even at the cost of Westmorland's heirs through his first marriage. The Middleham Nevilles, Westmorland's children by Joan, were a separate dynasty, all Beauforts on the distaff side. They and their Beaufort relations would become the most bitter of enemies in that rising generation and the next. From this second family would also come the House of York and the leaders of the Yorkist faction at court, including Salisbury and Warwick the Kingmaker, against which the second and third generations of Beauforts fought to the death.

In the early years too the Beaufort brothers set out on an endeavour that would remain intensely important to the English for more than a century to come. The town of Calais had been under English occupation for fifty years, and had already had its main military and economic functions established, but its maintenance needed attention. Led by Bishop Beaufort, the family successfully campaigned for this.

When Edward III gained Calais in 1347 after a year-long siege, he first expelled most of the French inhabitants and handed out properties there to English settlers. It was the closest French port to England and could always serve as a foothold by which armies could enter French territory, although in the course of the wars the kings seldom landed their forces there. Nor did they attempt a conquest of either Flanders or nearby Picardy; they only kept the town and a few square miles about it under occupation.

For some time the Wool Staple had been the principal economic concern of Calais. English wool was much in demand from Continental weavers, particularly those of the Low Countries, and the Staple made it mandatory to bring all exported wool to Calais for resale with few exemptions. Although it was sited in Bruges in its early days, since 1363 the Staple had been firmly set at Calais, where the wool supply could be controlled and taxed. But while it was not so difficult to bring wool and soldiers to Calais from England, communications from Calais to the Flemish towns and the greater part of France were poor.

As it was considered impolitic by some to reappoint him Lieutenant of Guyenne, John was made Captain of Calais instead. There was a separate command for the castle in the town and its garrison, which William de la Pole had held since the previous reign. As soon as he took up this appointment, John sought to correct the many abuses endangering the defence, with the support of his two brothers. One can often gauge the importance of an appointment at the time by the social status of the office holder, and this rule of thumb suggests that Captain of Calais had been a fairly low priority in recent times. Edward III had Lord Scrope as his overall governor in the latter part of his reign, but for the rest and throughout Richard's time the captain was of the gentry, usually a knight. The only other exception was the appointment of the Earl of Salisbury in 1379.[12]

From his appointment in 1400, John threw himself into the role. There is no direct evidence that it was he who alerted his brother the chancellor to the poor conditions prevailing there, but it is likely. To maintain such an overseas possession was expensive, and in an age when keeping a regular army was almost unknown the town had a permanent garrison. The French wars had not ended but there had been little fighting during Richard's time; there was a truce that ran from year to year and was continually renewed, but it was broken at times and would not last forever.

One chronic problem for royal finance at that time was a generally poor standard of accounting at the Exchequer and a tendency to leave less urgent bills unpaid. The resulting arrears of pay for the troops at Calais wrecked morale, and at times the soldiers reacted by seizing bales of wool from the merchants for sale. Other long-term problems included piracy in the Channel and the French occasionally attempting to blockade the town. Trade was often disrupted. At the parliament of 1402 John presented a petition insisting that arrears of pay to the garrison of the town should be met.[13] This was not immediately greeted with enthusiasm given the mood of the Commons, but Bishop Beaufort pressed for it successfully. The Beauforts had found a solution – for a time.

Sir Thomas Beaufort, now ready for a royal commission, was appointed Admiral of the North and he arranged a convoy system where merchant ships between the Tyne and the Thames sailed with the protection of warships. He and Lord Berkeley had the Channel patrolled, while Sir Thomas Swynford was appointed keeper of Calais Castle in 1405. John Beaufort, together with the Bishop of Rochester, Sir Thomas Swynford and others, was also commisioned to negotiate for the continuation of the truce with the French in 1403. The party was given a separate brief on keeping open dialogue with the main towns of Flanders. It is believed that John and Thomas Swynford were chosen for their affinity with Hainault through their common mother, which aided their dealings with the Low Countries.[14] A few years later their efforts counted to England's benefit. This would begin a long association of the Beauforts with Calais, although they were not always present themselves. From that time too the Captain of Calais was a senior peer, although most still had a knight as their deputy to perform the everyday duties.

It could be said that the politics of the reign of Henry IV had three definite phases. From the seizure of the throne in 1399 to the Percy–Mortimer–Glyndwr revolt in 1403 there was a time of striving for acceptance for the Lancastrian monarchy. Henry spent time placating the Percys and keeping Archbishop Arundel on side. By granting the *De Heretico Comburendo* statute in 1402 he created the mechanism for the English Church to burn the religious dissenters known as Lollards, but there was little room for manoeuvre and grievances multiplied. Poor administration and taxation of the clergy, even with Arundel's assent, were causing problems. Henry's unwillingness to offend Grey of Ruthin during a cross-border legal dispute had precipitated the revolt of his opponent, Owain Glyndwr.

It was obvious that by early 1403 many had lost confidence in the new regime. The Percys now had new grievances, complaining that the tallies issued from the Exchequer were not being honoured when presented for payment. Relations had turned very sour since the matter of the Scottish prisoners and Hotspur, then Deputy Warden of the Welsh Marches, had taken to intriguing with Glyndwr. Henry also committed the glaring error of not seeking to ransom Sir Edward Mortimer, then captured by the Welsh. Mortimer was uncle to the Earl of March, and could supply an alternative king when he joined with Glyndwr and Hotspur.

John was performing his duties at Calais when the rebellion of 1403 was threatening the Lancastrian monarchy, where the coalition of Glyndwr, Mortimer and Hotspur rose with the intention of dividing England and Wales between them and making the Earl of March king. The Battle of Shrewsbury on 20 July that year was hard-won for the new regime but Hotspur was killed in the fighting and Glyndwr and Mortimer routed, making it Henry IV's finest triumph. John was then called to subdue the region near Carmarthen soon after the king's troops invaded Wales. For a time he performed his duties there but he soon petitioned for the Duke of York to relieve him so that he could return to Calais, his principal concern.

Sir Thomas Beaufort was also needed to deal with the aftermath of the revolt. He was given the keeping of the castles of Hereford and Monmouth, and between 1404 and 1407 commanded the garrisons of four other castles as deputy to Prince Henry. By 1407 Glyndwr and his following were mostly confined to Snowdonia while Thomas and other English captains held the strongholds that Edward I had built in order to control the Welsh. Glyndwr would remain at large throughout Henry IV's reign and during the next, and it would take some years for the English to restore their hold over all of Wales.

Thus the Lancastrian monarchy had survived its most powerful challenge. The next phase in Henry IV's reign was characterized by further attacks from within and without. Northumberland's complicity in the 1403 revolt was not established, and he was soon plotting again.

In 1405 a second revolt did not go half as far, but it was nonetheless disturbing in its nature. That year, Richard Scrope, Archbishop of York threw off a lifetime of political neutrality and joined with Thomas Mowbray, Earl of Buckingham, son of the duke who had challenged Bolingbroke to the duel that led to their exile. Northumberland also caused trouble, but he was probably conducting a separate rebellion. The manifesto that Scrope issued bemoaned the taxing of the clergy and condemned Henry's usurpation. A time-server and lacklustre churchman up to this point, Scrope's motivation is a mystery. The revolt was halted before it really got underway with the rebels induced to disperse, the archbishop arrested and the other leaders in flight. Glyndwr was expected to join this rebellion but did not materialise and Northumberland, who had failed to meet with the main rebel force, fled to Scotland and was attainted in his absence, an act whereby Parliament rendered all his lands and titles forfeit.

The king was in a quandary when he came north to restore order. An archbishop was as much a feudal magnate and politician as an earl, but it was uncertain legal ground to execute one for treason: when Arundel had joined cause with Bolingbroke, Richard II had contented himself with banishing the churchman. On the other hand, Henry needed to make an example of Scrope, regardless of his place in the Church.

When on 3 June the king and his retinue entered the castle at Pontefract where Scrope was being held, the archbishop confronted him in a defiant manner clothed in his robes of office and bearing his crozier before him as if it entitled him to immunity. He seriously believed that Henry had no jurisdiction over him, and that the king would have difficulty finding anyone who would prosecute him. Sir Thomas Beaufort, who was riding with the king's party, immediately dismounted, wrested the crozier from Scrope's hands and took it to the king, breaking the spell that Scrope had hoped to present. Scrope became the only archbishop of the medieval period to be executed for treason. Mowbray also met his end on the block. Three years later, the former Earl of Northumberland returned to Yorkshire to lead a new revolt and was killed in an ambush on Bramham Moor.

Earlier in 1405 a different plot had been revealed when Lady Constance Despenser, sister to the Duke of York, attempted to abduct the young Earl of March and his younger brother and convey them to Wales. The fugitive party was soon overtaken, but when Constance was taken to the king she claimed that her brother had been the real author of the plot, and threw in other details of his plans to scale the walls of Eltham Palace and kill the king. The allegations were far from conclusive, but Edward, Duke of York since 1403 and previously the Earl of Rutland, who had survived the plot of 1400, was imprisoned. He was released and restored to favour a year later, after which he had the good sense to stay out of trouble. He served loyally throughout the rest of the reign and in the next, falling at Agincourt.

Also in 1405 John Beaufort saw his efforts at Calais vindicated when John the Fearless, Duke of Burgundy assembled an army at Saint-Omer in preparation for an attack. It is not known why the attack never took place. The campaign might have been countermanded by Burgundy's rival the Duke of Orleans, then in control of the government and able to issue a royal letter at the last minute. The plan itself may have been a mere show of force on Burgundy's part, again generated by the factional politics in France. Perhaps he simply thought better of it; Calais would not have been an easy conquest, as Edward III had learned. However, if the weak administration of Calais had not been addressed when the Beauforts raised the matter, a demoralised garrison might have given John the Fearless a better chance. Soon afterwards there really was a raid of the Calais march when the Count of Saint-Pol, another Burgundian, led an assault on the castle of Marcke near the town. John fought off the attackers, relieved that he had worked so hard to improve defences.

There were now serious concerns over France. Henry IV had never been assured of funds to renew the wars of conquest that his grandfather had waged, whatever his own intentions. But France could not be ignored, for no agreement had been reached over the remaining English possessions there, nor had the Plantagenets formally renounced.

The aborted Burgundian attack on Calais of 1406 was planned in conjunction with an onslaught on Bordeaux. There was also French aid for Glyndwr. The Beauforts were faced with a Commons that refused to vote funds for the victualling of Calais, so John and his brothers raised a loan from the Merchants of the Staple, for an enemy siege would have seen supplies seriously depleted. Again Burgundy decided against aggression, and in March 1407 the duchy entered into a formal truce with England. The Bordeaux campaign proceeded but melted away after failing to take a single castle. French activities in Wales and on the Isle of Wight also came to naught.

It was obviously on the Beauforts' urging that the council then made a serious attempt to address the disaster of Calais' financing. Together with some of the most recent subsidy granted by Parliament and a series of loans from various merchants totalling £8,000, they sought to reduce the arrears of pay to the garrison and make the situation a little more manageable.[15]

Events in France soon gave the English opportunity and beckoned a new campaign. It had long been obvious that the French king Charles VI was insane and unable to rule; he could not lead an army while he believed himself to be made of glass and could easily shatter. Court factions struggled for control, and by the mid-1400s John, Duke of Burgundy and his cousin Louis, Duke of Orleans were in open warfare with each other, as were many nobles of their separate factions. A brief period of cooperation between the dukes had produced the planned Calais–Bordeaux campaign, but neither really trusted the other and their quarrel would render France unstable for three decades. Burgundy had Orleans murdered in 1407, but the latter's brother-in-law the Count of Armagnac took over the leadership of his faction and Burgundy was soon driven from Paris.

From 1407 to the end of his reign, Henry IV could be described as more secure on the throne. There were no more serious rebellions after 1405, Glyndwr no longer controlled most of Wales and the capture of the future James I of Scotland in 1406 reduced the threat of Scottish invasion. In France the Burgundian and Armagnac factions continued their civil war and therefore could not easily threaten English possessions. Many even thought this state of affairs provided an ideal opportunity to resume the English wars of conquest, but the expense was an effective deterrent to any planned campaigns.

One cause for concern was the king himself; an illness he clearly developed soon after the northern campaign of 1405 showed no sign of a cure. Henry had always been in rude health, but now he suffered from a skin disease. Some believed he had leprosy – one source talks of a 'sekenese of lepre'[16] – but a more modern analysis suggests a skin condition that affected his immune system. There was also the possibility of a brain lesion, as he was given to momentary losses of consciousness from 1400.[17] Rumours circulated about the nature of the disease – leprosy had negative Biblical connotations – and whether it was divine retribution for the execution of Archbishop Scrope. Although Henry knew times of respite, he never fully recovered. The fact that the king neither died nor recovered for eight years was not conducive to stability in the realm.

By 1407, three of the king's sons had reached an age where they could participate in the business of government. Princes Henry, Thomas and John were now respectively lieutenants of Wales and Ireland and Warden of the East March towards Scotland. Each had a more experienced deputy and advisor and these three royal appointments had varied successes. The fourth, Humphrey, was not given office at this point, though he was only a year younger than John. There was much ill-feeling over the fact that Prince Thomas was designated to administer the king's rule in Ireland while he remained at the English court and showed no sign of embarking for a long time.

Bishop Thomas Langley, who had succeeded Henry Beaufort as chancellor, resigned the post in 1407 on his appointment as Bishop of Durham and was replaced by Archbishop Arundel. The three Beaufort men were as active as ever in the king's service, but now received what could only be an affront, with implications that affected the family for generations to come. In Parliament that year, the king issued a confirmation of their legitimation of 1398. Such a confirmation would have been welcome, since some of Richard II's actions had been challenged as contrary to custom, but there was a sting in the tail. In the statement it was repeated that the Beauforts had all the rights and opportunities legitimate issue could expect, but with one addition to the original test: '*excepta dignitate regali*', 'apart from the succession to the throne'. They may have been raised to the status of legitimate children of John of Gaunt, but according to this statement none of the Beaufort line was eligible to ever succeed as King of England.[18]

The original Act had not mentioned the succession and so had not specifically excluded the Beauforts from it, yet in 1407 it was unlikely that such an issue would ever be raised. Henry IV had four healthy sons approaching manhood, all unmarried but all expected to produce heirs in due course. The Beauforts must have questioned the justice of this new declaration; they might have reasoned that they had a place in the succession, if not a clear one given the various other lines of the Plantagenet family, but accepted without question that Henry's four sons and their issue would come before them. To be told that they would never succeed in any event was an unwelcome suggestion of their previous illegitimacy.

During the previous parliament in 1406 the line of royal succession had been defined and limited to the sons of the House of Lancaster. It affirmed that Prince Henry, the eldest son, would succeed and his own male issue would follow in order of seniority. Each of the three younger sons and their issue would follow in turn, but the succession halted there without any reference to the other descendants of Edward III, leaving the House of York, the Earl of March, the Hollands and the Beauforts without any defined order.[19] This would become a major problem when at a later stage the House of Lancaster proved less fertile than expected.

It may have been Archbishop Arundel who persuaded Henry to exclude the Beauforts. Perhaps he feared their ambition, or resented Bishop Beaufort's sudden rise to such a senior rank in the Church. Arundel was conscious of his own seniority in both Church and State and this young Beaufort was in his eyes an interloper in both.

The Commons and court might seem overly concerned about the succession at this time. Henry's four sons were still a few years short of adulthood, and even if suitable marriages were far from automatic each man still had plenty of time to father children. But common sense said that mortality was high and often unpredictable: an outbreak of plague could erase the royal house in a week. Moreover, any or all could fail to produce surviving male children. We see in retrospect that of these four brothers only one produced a legitimate child, and pure luck made it a boy.

No clear rules had as yet been codified and agreed upon, and had the House of Lancaster died out in the second generation there would have been a dispute over which collateral branch held precedence. To simply declare the Beauforts ineligible made little sense without discussing the other claims. Hindsight again shows the potential for dispute; in comparison, every member of the present-day royal family knows their own exact place in the order of succession. But nobody could have predicted the course of events that the fifteenth century would take.

As a final consideration it could be argued that if by some scarcely predictable sequence of events involving multiple premature deaths and childless marriages a Beaufort acceded as king, the stigma of their bastardy would have been raised and used against them by any would-be usurper and further succession disputes would follow.

From 1407 the Prince of Wales took an increasing interest in governing the realm. Prince Hal was not really the wild and uncontrollable youth that Shakespeare portrayed; his excesses while off duty were fairly typical for his age. Through his late teens he had served in the Welsh marches as the nominal head of the campaign to restore royal control over Wales, which had been an education in itself. At twenty he was developing his own ideas about ruling the country, and with a youthful arrogance he put them into action. He had as much reason as anyone else to believe that his ailing father might not live much longer, and so he gradually took more control. The legend which has Prince Hal reprimanded for trying on the crown in his father's lifetime might have originated from this tendency to assert himself in matters of state and to overstep the mark in the eyes of many. The king at times recovered at least partially but had little energy to overrule his son. There was never a formal regency, nor even any agreement that the prince would deputize for his father; he simply did so. The other council members mostly supported the prince; after all, the king could not be relied upon at this stage to rule on matters of government.

Bishop Beaufort had attended the council regularly throughout the reign and now his brothers John and Thomas also appeared. All three became increasingly identified with the Prince of Wales rather than the king, and their policies showed through the council's deliberations. Their cousin Thomas Chaucer became Speaker of the Commons for the first time in the 1407 parliament, a sign of growing Beaufort influence.

The government of Henry IV was faced throughout with an obvious need to balance the books without causing more discontent over taxation, a common problem throughout the reign and often cause for ill-feeling. Bishop Beaufort had laboured while chancellor to make ends meet. The council in 1407 were faced with demands for money from Prince Thomas, then Lieutenant of Ireland, but they made it clear that he would only receive the funds if he based himself in Ireland and performed his duties.

The early years of Henry IV's reign had put new strains on the already mismanaged royal finances, while the treasurers of the royal household, Thomas Tutbury and then Thomas More, were conspicuous for their poor management of expenditure and their tendency to leave bills unpaid. The 1403 rebellion increased financial demands, and the king was often criticised for not living 'of his own' as he had promised. Taxing the clergy was much resented despite Arundel's approval and appeared on the manifesto of the 1405 rebellion. From that point a more responsible approach to finance was attempted. Bishop Bubwith of Salisbury became Lord Treasurer in 1407 and as both an associate of the Beauforts and a highly experienced administrator he was a valuable counsellor.

Unlike his predecessor, who often insisted on his royal prerogative, Henry IV tried to work with Parliament as much as possible – an astute policy when the basis of his own accession was so uncertain. Henry played by the rules with the parliamentary process and was commended for it, but this came with a price tag of its own when he was obliged to ask the Commons for money. By the established practice, when new taxes were discussed Parliament would often expect matters of their own concern to be addressed first. It was by no means unthinkable that Parliament could be hostile to requests for money, and the king or his ministers could find themselves in the middle of hard bargaining.

With the deepening civil conflict between the Burgundian and Armagnac factions presenting too good an opportunity to ignore, the Prince of Wales felt that the time had come for intervention in France. Burgundy decided against fighting the English and had in March 1407 entered into a formal truce. John the Fearless eventually regained Paris and allied with the estranged Queen Isabeau, although his enemies blockaded the city. There could be no better time to resume the war with France.

There was serious discussion in the council in 1409 over a formal alliance with Burgundy in conjunction with a campaign. But at this point Henry IV suddenly left his sick bed and reasserted his authority. There was an explosive row, mostly over the king's resentment of what he thought was his own marginalisation. The quarrel prevented decisive action on France for a time, but in 1410 the king agreed to name a new council, and this tended to favour Prince Hal and his close associates. There were new additions such as Bishop Chichele of St David's and Richard Beauchamp, Earl of Warwick, both of them close to the Prince. The Beauforts were still present, but their treatment was inconsistent.

During this uncertain period John Beaufort took part in one interlude that delighted both the court and the multitude. The tournament was a prominent feature in chivalric culture, with knights pitted against each other in friendly displays of the arts of war for popular entertainment. In 1409 the Seneschal of Hainault came to England with a party of knights in search of glory on the field of combat at Windsor, and John Beaufort was among those the seneschal challenged. Unlike most of the other English combatants, whom the Hainaulters bested, John gave his opponent a hard fight, winning much acclaim from the crowd and emerging as a popular hero.[20]

A year before, when John Beaufort had returned to Calais, he had discovered that many of the garrison had gone on an ill-conceived raid into Picardy and were trapped by a French force. He had to rally the soldiers' wives in the town to go forth and rescue them.[21] He had laboured nine years for a more responsible attitude to the keeping of Calais and had shown the Burgundians that the town had a vigorous defence. His efforts indirectly contributed to a policy, not always adhered to but clearly understood, that Calais had to be maintained for both the economic well-being of England and as an important foothold for English ambitions in France. His heirs would be similarly involved in the keeping of Calais as a valuable outpost.

John had accomplished much in his lifetime and could have seen a longer career as a military man and lieutenant of his half-brother the king. But on Palm Sunday, 16 March 1410, John

Beaufort (I), Earl of Somerset and eldest son of John of Gaunt and Katherine Swynford, suddenly died. He was taken to the hospital of St Katherine-by-the-Tower in London suffering from what was probably an infectious disease, possibly plague, and died there. He was only thirty-eight according to the inquisitions made after his death.[22] John was buried in the abbey at Tower Hill, although his widow later had his remains brought to Canterbury Cathedral, to lie in the plot next to her and her second husband.

John Beaufort had four sons and two daughters, and through him alone the Beaufort line continued to the next generation. Of his brothers, the outwardly celibate Henry had only a bastard daughter and Thomas's only son had died young before his wife predeceased him in 1413. Joan, Countess of Westmorland was still producing child after child, creating her own political dynasty. John's eldest son had the king as his godfather in 1401 and was named Henry after him. Henry (II), aged nine, was now the second Earl of Somerset. He would never reach his majority, but two of his brothers would succeed as earls and then dukes in due course.

When Archbishop Arundel was relieved of the office of chancellor in 1410 it was generally expected that Bishop Beaufort would take the Great Seal again, but to everyone's surprise Sir Thomas Beaufort, who had just joined the council, was appointed instead. Not only was this a departure from the tradition that a senior prelate held the role – only seven laymen were chancellor before the sixteenth century – but Thomas was a military man without the appropriate background for this office. It appeared that Thomas was representing his brother, who had important duties of his own. He probably took the appointment against his own wishes, and most certainly relied heavily on the clerks of the Chancery to conduct the duties themselves. At the time there was some ill-feeling over ecclesiastics in government, and Thomas was a known critic of the wealth of senior clerics. He was also, as both a knight of the royal household and a close associate of the prince, acceptable to both sides of the divide. He might have had some difficulty working with Lord Scrope, given the part that he had played in the execution of Scrope's uncle the archbishop.[23] A year later Thomas was also raised to the peerage as Earl of Dorset. It was the designation that his brother John had briefly held, but at a lower degree. The king (or his son) probably understood the gap left by John's death, and trusted in the Beauforts' loyalty. Thomas was then made Admiral of England for life in March.[24]

For the time that the prince held the reins of government the agenda of council gave high priority to making financial ends meet and preparing to defend against France and Scotland should truces break down. Prince Henry understood the importance of keeping Calais and pushed to repay the loans from the Merchants of the Staple and to bring the troops' pay up to date. In this he had the full support of his two surviving Beaufort uncles, and dealings with the Commons were aided by Thomas Chaucer, who was speaker in the last three parliaments of the reign. Bishop Beaufort succeeded in bringing the 1410 parliament into a receptive frame of mind by his sermon on the respective obligations of rulers and subjects.[25]

On observing the dramatic turns in French politics, Prince Henry urged intervention in France. Council agreed to the truce with Burgundy, which gave Calais some breathing space, but then the English prepared military action to exploit the division. There were talks with the Duke of Berri of the Armagnac faction, but these faltered on such unacceptable terms as recognising Glyndwr's rule in Wales and the status of Normandy. A dialogue went on with Burgundy but no commitments were made. In September 1411 the Earl of Arundel led an unauthorised force that fought its way to Paris and aided the Burgundians in routing the Armagnacs at St Cloud.

Almost as a prelude to his campaigns as king, on the prince's initiative English armies once again crossed the Channel. Acting as if he had the power to decide, he prepared a new expedition that featured an alliance with the Burgundians. It appears that the Burgundians spoke to young Henry separately and there was even discussion of his marriage to John of Burgundy's daughter. There were other talks with the Burgundian faction headed by Bishop Chichele and other associates of the prince.

But in June 1412, when a Burgundian embassy requested to parley with the King of England *and his son*, King Henry was furious. Once again the prince had taken the initiative without consulting his father and the king instantly relieved the council of all their powers and responsibilities. He reinstated Arundel as chancellor and excluded the prince and the Beauforts from government for the rest of his reign. King Henry then prepared to lead the planned expedition himself, but soon had to admit that he was too ill even to stay on a horse. Still, he would not allow the Prince of Wales to command it.

The king then made two important changes to the planned campaign. He first decided that Prince Thomas would lead it instead, and created him Duke of Clarence on 9 July. As a result of his treatment by the council over Ireland, Thomas was not well-disposed towards his elder brother, the Beauforts or the other council members, and so took his father's side in the dispute. King Henry also decided that the campaign would aid the Armagnac faction instead. This side had recently made new overtures that included guarantees over the rule of Aquitaine and other territorial gains, which on paper were too impressive to turn down. For Prince Henry, almost certainly on advice from Bishop Beaufort and other counsellors, the Burgundian alliance was a better bet. The Duke of Burgundy was also Count of Flanders and close to both Calais and the Channel. Given the importance of the wool trade to both powers, Burgundy would be a more suitable ally than an enemy.

The crisis between king and prince gave rise to a controversial question. The king was clearly too ill to perform his role as monarch, and Prince Henry, an astute and energetic young man, was certainly ready to take active command. Many years later, Bishop Beaufort's enemies would claim in Parliament that he had approached Henry IV at this time and suggested that he abdicate. Beaufort then asserted in answer that he had ever been loyal, although he did not specifically deny this particular act.[26] In reality there were many about the court who felt that abdication would be the only solution to such an impasse. It is possible that Beaufort, as the king's eldest surviving half-brother and a respected man of the cloth, would have undertaken to suggest this action. It is also likely that Henry, not willing to see the situation for what it was, interpreted this as treason and went on the defensive.

The Beaufort brothers were servants of the Lancastrian monarchy, but their king's incapacity had caused them to adapt to the leadership of their nephew in order to ensure good government, and in doing so they had become identified with the prince's party in this division between father and son. If the bishop advised Henry's abdication it was done in good faith, but the king certainly took it the wrong way. For the remainder of the reign Bishop Beaufort was in disfavour, and it was fortunate for him that this period was short. In 1412 he was relieved of the chancellorship, which was returned to his rival Archbishop Arundel.

In August the new Duke of Clarence married Margaret Holland, widow of John Beaufort. Both had practical reasons for this: Clarence needed the revenues of John's estates and Margaret, widowed for only a year and a half, had a large family to provide for. Her eldest son Henry was only ten and Clarence had the use of his estates in his minority. The new match was childless, but this new generation of Beauforts was at least protected. Clarence referred to young Henry Beaufort (II) as *nostre treschier filz*[27] and provided for his stepchildren's upkeep, although the incomes from John's estates were mostly used to pay the dead earl's debts, with Clarence making use of the rest. Given the deepening division between prince and king, the Beaufort brothers could only have resented this appropriation of their relatives' wealth by a member of the other faction. When Bishop Beaufort objected to Clarence's acquisition of Margaret's third in dower, Clarence showed little cooperation.[28]

In September, not long after his marriage, Clarence set out with an army and landed in the Cotentin, among his lieutenants the Duke of York and Thomas Beaufort, Earl of Dorset. Thomas Beaufort was now in the important command that his new title suggested, and his military career showed promise as the French wars resumed. The English marched on towards Blois only to find that John the Fearless had not only defeated their Armagnac allies but rallied the other princes of France against the English invasion. The campaign ended with the French buying off the English and Clarence leading the army to winter quarters at Bordeaux. There was good news for the English campaign when the Calais garrison took advantage of the end of the Burgundian truce to seize the fortress of Balinghem, which strengthened the Calais march further.

The English had gained little from the *volte-face*. This confused foreign policy was doing their cause little good and was based more on Henry IV's paranoia than on any sound strategy. It was in some ways a relief when Henry IV died on 20 March 1413 after a final reconciliation with his eldest son. The reign had begun with promise, but the means by which Henry had encompassed the crown laid him open to further rebellion. It was his tragedy that as soon as he had defeated his challengers his illness prevented him from ruling effectively. He had however established the House of Lancaster as the royal dynasty; his son would reap the benefits.

Henry IV's reign was the making of the Beauforts, who gave their fullest support to the regime once it was established. Although it must be said that they depended on the patronage of Lancaster all along for their wealth and position, they gave service that aided this house in its survival and the furtherance of its aspirations, and Henry trusted them as his close relatives.

The loss of John Beaufort, 1st Earl of Somerset was a serious blow, but his achievements did not go unnoticed. The way that the remaining Beauforts found themselves in receipt of the king's wrath in 1411 was due to the wish to give their king good government, even if it might have involved asking for his abdication. The quarrel between Henry IV and his heir had ended with the young man identifying his Beaufort uncles as his own supporters, and in his reign and the next the Beauforts maintained prominent roles in government. The brothers had been loyal servants of Henry IV, but the end of his reign had seen them in royal disfavour.

3

THE KING'S UNCLES

It is far too easy to think of Henry V as Shakespeare wrote him, the charismatic, dutiful, magnanimous king, dreadful in war and just in peace. To an extent this image is accurate, but it is coloured by the propaganda that grew about him at the time. A king should be a puissant and able leader of men in war, and just and affable in ruling his subjects, and this does broadly describe Henry V far more closely than it does his two predecessors, but to what extent was he performing a role rather than expressing his true nature? Shakespeare briefly touches on this at times, writing how Henry V was a terrible king to have as an enemy, a 'dread' king who had little compassion.

Typical of his family, Henry V was tall, handsome and charming. He was energetic, charismatic and shrewd. His time as his father's lieutenant in the campaign to regain Wales had shown him a responsible commander. He was a lover of books, acquiring a reputation for not returning the ones he borrowed, and took an interest in matters of religion. It was remarkable how far he altered his lifestyle and personal manner once he was king, becoming strict in discipline, orthodox in religion and far from merciful in dispensing justice. He forsook all women until his marriage, and then lay only with his wife. As a king Henry V was beyond reproach; as a person he was not the easiest to endure.

Having learned statecraft during his unofficial leadership of the royal council, and no longer impeded by his father's interference, Henry addressed the business of kingship with a young man's confidence and drive. He had several supporters from the previous reign and his two surviving uncles, Bishop Henry Beaufort and Thomas Beaufort, Earl of Dorset, figured highly in his service. He also put his confidence in the Earl of Warwick, the Earl of Arundel and Lord Stanley, granting them respectively the captaincy of Calais and the lieutenancies of the Welsh marches and Ireland.

Once he was king, Henry V relieved Archbishop Arundel of the office of chancellor and replaced him with his uncle Bishop Beaufort. Arundel had always served the regime well but had even displeased Henry IV with his personal agenda at times, and the new king had known his opposition in the previous council. It was Beaufort who welcomed the first parliament with an address on the theme of 'stable counsel before deed' or how 'consultation precedes every action' (*ante omnium action consilium stabile*), which he hoped would characterise the new reign.[1]

Thomas Beaufort had reached Guyenne after the abortive campaign under Clarence. It was here that he showed his value when the Duke de Berri invaded soon after the death of Henry IV. Leading the fightback and regaining castles taken by the French, Thomas then made a truce with Berri before returning to England.[2] For a military man he was much in need; in July 1414 the king confirmed him as captain of the castle at Calais and separately as Admiral of England. Thomas had plenty of expertise to contribute.[3]

Henry was all too aware of issues that cried out for attention. The entire question of royal finance was a disaster area, poorly apportioned and politically sensitive when the king needed much more money to fight his oncoming wars. There was also the perceived threat of Lollardy, whose followers attacked the doctrines and material wealth of the Church. The Great Schism, the long-running split over rival popes, had recently become acute and attempts to resolve it had failed. Glyndwr was more manageable now that he had seen his dream of an independent Wales shrink to the small mountainous area that he still controlled, but the Welsh rebels were still intriguing with the French and it would be a mistake to ignore them.

The most serious problem concerned unfinished business in France. The claim of the Plantagenet kings to its throne, the defence of Calais and Guyenne and the status of other French possessions could not be resolved by diplomacy; Henry knew he had to take action. He was an ambitious young king with grandiose projects in mind. In his third year on the throne he renewed the war of conquest.

Mindful of complaints over the misuse of funds designated for Calais, including during his own captaincy, Henry annulled every grant made in relation to the town and appointed reliable officials. He first appointed his brother Thomas, Duke of Clarence as captain and in 1414 Richard Beauchamp, Earl of Warwick to succeed him. No doubt with help from the Beauforts, he had learned the importance of keeping the town secure and its accounts up to date.

The succession was still as vague as ever at this point while Henry V was still unmarried and without heirs of his body. His brother Clarence, married but without heirs other than his Beaufort stepchildren, was at least heir presumptive. The other two brothers, John and Humphrey, in 1414 awarded the dukedoms of Bedford and Gloucester respectively, were young men eligible for marriage.[4] The Earl of March was still in the order of possible successors and without heirs himself. The House of York also had a claim should all the sons of Henry IV die childless. Edward, Duke of York had not erred since 1405, but circumstances could cause him to advance his own candidacy. His brother Richard, Earl of Cambridge was married to Anne Mortimer, sister of the Earl of March. Henry V did nothing to clarify the position of the Beauforts as stated in 1407. It would then have been Henry Beaufort (II), the underage second Earl of Somerset, who was then stepson of the heir presumptive, who would have been king. This was thought unlikely ever to arise, however, given the size of Henry IV's family.

Henry V began his reign by attending to issues arising from his father's usurpation. He released the Earl of March from house arrest, a statement which affirmed confidence in his own legitimacy. His younger brother having died some years before, March was active in this reign, riding with Henry in the French wars. Henry also had the body of Richard II reinterred at Westminster Abbey. Rumours had persisted for some years that Richard was still living, which Henry tried to scotch – unsuccessfully, as it turned out.

Archbishop Arundel, determined to strike at the roots of Lollardy, wished to begin the new reign with a clean sweep. It is not certain if Henry V shared his enthusiasm for this war against heresy while Prince of Wales, but on his accession he adopted a strict orthodox stance, his hair cropped in a manner that made him look like a priest himself. Lollards disliked him, dubbing him the 'Bishop's Prince' while Henry outwardly supported Arundel's campaign to root out the Lollards, even though his friend Sir John Oldcastle was one of the first arrested. Oldcastle, who definitely held such views, escaped from the Tower in 1413 and spent four years on the run before he was finally captured and burned. This policy gave Lollards an interest in who held the throne, if only for their own survival, and compounded their heretical beliefs with thoughts of sedition. Tales of Richard II still living fuelled this; Richard at least had been fairly tolerant of Lollard knights at his court. A planned rising in London at Epiphany 1414 was savagely put down as the Lollards gathered and ended with several consigned to the flames.

Bishop Beaufort was not much involved in this hunt for heretics, but had serious concerns over the state of the Church, including Lollardy. Henry Beaufort was a man of the cloth as much as he was a politician and royal servant, and in terms of conventional religion he was an important player, especially in the new trend of Conciliarism which sought to heal the Great Schism where calling councils of eminent churchmen was urged. Since his time as chancellor of Oxford he had taken an interest in the movement.

Henry V's labours to conquer France might seem unnecessary to modern eyes but it must be remembered that he could not simply ignore France. The claim to the French crown was really secondary to the issue by which the French wars had begun, and the threat to English territories in France persisted. Edward III had revived his claim to the French throne through his mother partially for its propaganda value, and by 1361 it was only a bargaining chip in what he hoped was a final settlement. But if the Royal Arms of England was an indicator of how seriously the claim was taken, it was still unchanged when Henry V landed in France with the Lions of England quartered with the Lilies of France on his surcoat and shield, just as Edward III had done. According to the Treaty of Brétigny in 1361 Edward III had signed away his claim to the French crown in return for recognition of his French possessions and other concessions, but this agreement was voided when the French's king's hostage violated the terms of the treaty. Since then the French had regained territory and without any resolution to the original dispute a series of truces maintained the peace from one year to another. In the reigns of Richard II and Henry IV, French piracy harmed cross-Channel trade and French support for the Glyndwr rebellion had been ominous.

Events in France between its warring factions had opened new opportunities. In 1414 the Armagnac affinity, supported by King Charles VI in a more lucid phase, drove the Burgundian supporters out of Paris and placed John the Fearless and his faction on the defensive. Henry knew that this was the best time of all to campaign in France.

Although in the previous reign English policy toward France lacked coherence, the new king and his supporters favoured returning to the Anglo-Burgundian understanding that made far more sense to English interests. There were talks with the Duke of Burgundy's envoys in which a marriage between Henry and the duke's eldest daughter was suggested, but John had second thoughts about being too closely identified with a foreign invader. The prospect of marriage to the King of France's daughter instead was also discussed. There was eventually a military agreement with Burgundy, but it was far short of an alliance.

There were talks with the Armagnac faction at the same time, but these were unproductive and the French court was becoming more hostile and belligerent. There is the oft-cited story of the Dauphin sending Henry a gift of tennis balls, insinuating that he favoured a comfortable and idle lifestyle, which Henry countered with a gift of cannon balls. The factual basis for this story is uncertain, but the attitude of the Armagnac faction makes it plausible. In reality the English were playing the game of making demands that the other side could not reasonably grant, including enlarged territories and the marriage of Henry to King Charles's daughter.

The Armagnacs were willing to grant Henry Normandy and Aquitaine but not the complete sovereignty of either, and were willing to consider sanctioning the royal marriage. But in June 1414 Bishop Beaufort told the Armagnac envoys that his king would either receive Normandy and Aquitaine together with such other territories as Anjou, Maine, Touraine, Poitou and Ponthieu, all of which had been held by previous kings of England, or he would come and take them by force. Henry had been preparing for war all along, and was ready to show his hand now that it appeared that the other side were to blame.

Financing a war was never a welcome proposition for the Commons, the customary one-off tax usually obtained, if at all, by horse-trading with the members on issues of their concern. When as chancellor Bishop Beaufort opened the first parliament of 1414 with an address on the need of the king to regain his rightful possessions in France the Commons were partially swayed, but they called for negotiation first. The talks with the Armagnac side having broken down, Beaufort had little difficulty raising a subsidy from the second parliament of the year. There were also loans raised from many a place. Bishop Beaufort, often a supplier of royal finance, lent £1,963 *6s 8d*, while London merchant Richard Whittington produced £2,000 for the campaign. Other individuals and bodies also contributed.

Henry set a course for Harfleur on the northern mouth of the Seine. He had decided on an invasion of Normandy and needed a more convenient entry point than Calais. He was also concerned over the Channel pirates who used Harfleur as their principal base and sought to kill two birds with one stone. In the summer of 1415, the armies mustered to sail. Shortly before the departure date the Earl of March, obviously fearful of the likely consequences were he implicated, revealed a plot to kill the king while at Southampton. Together with Lord Scrope and Sir Thomas Grey, Richard, Earl of Cambridge, brother of the Duke of York, was arrested and all three were promptly executed. Cambridge left a four-year-old son, also named Richard. The invasion force sailed on 11 August and landed near Harfleur, where a hard-fought siege gained the town, and Thomas Beaufort finally accepted its surrender on 22 September. He had already made a name for himself on this campaign, and in the first two engagements of the reign he would make his most significant contributions to the cause.

When Henry marched away with his army on 6 October he left Thomas Beaufort in charge of the town. The English needed Harfleur for future campaigning in Normandy, and should the campaign go badly the English could retreat there to evacuate. It also gave the English control over the entrance to the Seine. Thomas therefore kept what had been hard won, treating the citizens fairly as the king had ordered. He won some popularity there too; they called him the 'little king'.

The king wished to turn Harfleur into another Calais, a reliable landing stage for English armies in Normandy, his main theatre of war.[5] Edward III had made Calais an English town over the course of his reign, replacing most of its population with English settlers, but Henry V did not embark on such a long-term project. He did order that all the inhabitants declare their allegiance to him or depart the town, and large numbers of English workers were sent to rebuild the fortifications, but this attempted 'ethnic cleansing' was not as rigorously pursued as in Calais.

Having lost so many troops in the siege of Harfleur and the accompanying outbreak of dysentery, Henry abandoned plans to take further territory on this campaign and settled for a 'show of force', a march to Calais that would show the inadequacies of the Armagnac resistance. After seeing to the defence of Harfleur, the king led his reduced following first northward along the coast and then eastward up the left bank of the Somme while seeking a crossing. They would meet the enemy in force at a place called Agincourt.

The Battle of Agincourt on 25 October was hailed as a stupendous and crushing victory over superior numbers. English losses were a fraction of the 8,000 or so French dead, and of the greater nobles only Edward, Duke of York and the new Earl of Suffolk were killed. It did the Armagnac faction severe damage, with the deaths of Constable Charles d'Albret, the dukes of Alençon, Bar and Brabant, and nine counts. Among the captured were the dukes of Orleans and Bourbon and the counts of Eu, Richemont and Vendôme. But the tangible gains of the battle itself were limited to the handful of captives taken to Calais, some heavily ransomed and some, like Orleans, held prisoner in England for many years. Thomas Beaufort remained to maintain the English foothold when Henry's expeditionary force returned to England. The French campaigns of this reign would be the high point of his military career.

The success at Agincourt made it far easier to extract funding from Parliament the following year, at which Henry was also granted a life subsidy from the wool trade. This was the last parliament of the reign over which Bishop Beaufort presided as chancellor, but he had secured parliamentary assent for taxation to fund the wars. He had also mollified opposition with the understanding that such taxation would end as soon as the king regained enough of his French possessions for them to pay for themselves. Even after Beaufort had resigned, the king received his money for war.

Henry V spent 1416 in England, preparing a more ambitious campaign for the next year. Thomas Beaufort was doing him good service keeping Harfleur during this period, and the king made sure that the town was well supplied by ships from the Cinque Ports. He also spent much time and money on a state visit by Sigismund, soon to be Holy Roman Emperor, whose support he sought. Sigismund was enthusiastic and did all he could to persuade John the Fearless to join them in an alliance, but Henry would carry on campaigning in France largely without support from the either ruler.

The French might easily have overrun Harfleur but for the garrison there of some 1,400 men under the command of Thomas Beaufort. In order to increase the English foothold he led forays into the hinterland, but the French lost no time in seeking to reverse English gains. On 9 March 1416, Beaufort with his lieutenants Sir John Fastolf and John Blount rode out with about 1,000 men on one such raid and at Valmont encountered five times that number of French soldiers under the leadership of the Count of Armagnac. Many English were killed or simply ran away, and Beaufort himself was seriously wounded, but he managed an effective retreat while the French were plundering the baggage train. Mounted French troops caught up with the English fleeing on foot the following morning, but Beaufort's men stood and fought, killing many and making it back to Harfleur with 800 prisoners. Once arrived he hanged about fifty English soldiers who had run at the first engagement. Both sides claimed victory, but the threat of a counterattack on Harfleur receded for a time.

The most serious problem, as Thomas made known by his messengers to England, was the shortage of supplies to Harfleur, and he advised that the English force would need to withdraw if this were not remedied, as foraging could support neither town nor garrison. The French had taken to blockading the harbour.[6]

On 16 August, John, Duke of Bedford led an expedition that fought off a French naval attack on Harfleur. Both fleets were large, the French reinforced by Genoese allies, but the English could claim victory. This enhanced the reputation of Thomas Beaufort, who still governed a town occupied by the English. In November, Thomas was appointed Lieutenant of Normandy in preparation for gains in that province which he was expected to hold in the same way.[7]

In those years the Great Schism once again became relevant, for now it became enmeshed in English policy towards France, when since 1378 rival popes in Rome and Avignon had split allegiances between nations. While France and Scotland now supported the Avignon Pope Gregory XII, England and the Holy Roman Empire endorsed Pope Boniface XIII in Rome. Even the Burgundian and Armagnac factions came to recognise different pontiffs.

The Schism weakened the entire Church while the popes had little power to rule on doctrinal issues and often pandered to the lay rulers for fear of losing their allegiance; it is unlikely that Henry IV would have dared to execute Archbishop Scrope had the papacy not been so ineffective. Even the legitimation of the Beauforts in 1397 was quite irregular, and the pope in Rome might not have been so obliging in different circumstances.

Over the previous few years a new heresy had spread from central Europe. Partially as a result of Bohemian scholars attending Oxford in Wycliffe's day, a movement similar to Lollardy had appeared in Prague when Jan Hus, the rector of its university, had proclaimed doctrines akin to those of the English Lollards. There was some correspondence between English and Bohemian heretics, but the two movements were unrelated. This did not stop conventional Christians from suspecting a shared leadership between the Lollards and the Hussites, as these new heretics were called.

Bishop Beaufort while chancellor of Oxford had certainly heard of proposals from the French urging that both popes be deposed and a new one elected. In March 1409, cardinals of both papacies met at Pisa and discussed ways of ending the Schism. They agreed that such a course was the best solution, but their efforts were soon undone. Their chosen pontiff, Alexander V, died within the year and his successor, who styled himself John XXIII, cast doubts among the cardinals as to his eligibility. Worse still, neither of the existing rival popes accepted the authority of the Council of Pisa to depose them, and both had substantial support.

Despite this, decades of weakness and discrepancy in the Church had led senior churchmen to form councils of their most able representatives to solve matters, and by early 1414, the second year of Henry V's reign, invitations had been sent to the English Church to participate in a new gathering at Constance. King Henry was interested in this, both as an opportunity to further his interests and due to his growing concerns on the spread of heresy in England. Sigismund, King of the Romans and later Holy Roman Emperor, had similar issues, in particular over increased Hussite influence throughout central Europe. At the opening of the Council of Constance Henry sent Bishop Hallam of Salisbury, who also had been at the Council at Pisa, but the bishop died at Constance. A large English delegation had remained throughout, including the Earl of Warwick and Sir Walter Hungerford, both having come from a diplomatic embassy to Sigismund.

There was also some concern in England over the uncertainty that followed the Pisa gathering. Several English bishoprics had since fallen vacant and the king and council were reluctant to fill them while there was doubt over the papacy. Constance was an ideal opportunity to clear the mess. The council, now in its third year, had discussed a single papacy, the Hussites and issues related to crusading in northern Europe, and also wished to correct the many abuses that had grown in the Church. Bishop Beaufort was as able a churchman as he was a politician. His duties as chancellor, where he worked political miracles, had taken up his attention since his nephew's succession, but now he prepared to go to Constance.

Bishop Beaufort had been on bad terms with Archbishop Arundel ever since the business in 1407 over the exclusion of the Beauforts from the succession. Both attended the king's council regularly, but their concerns were different, and while the archbishop was engaged in hunting down Lollards Beaufort maintained his valuable role in the king's civil administration. But when Arundel died in 1414, the king appointed Bishop Henry Chichele of St David's his successor as Archbishop of Canterbury. Chichele had also long served on council, had ridden in arms on the 1411 campaign and was involved in the Anglo-French diplomacy of 1413. The king preferred this pious and studious prelate to his Beaufort uncle.

Henry Beaufort was a very ambitious man. Did he think that he would be Archbishop of Canterbury one day? It was a logical progression, and the only step upwards he could envisage at that point. He might not have another chance at the role, for Chichele was likely to remain in this office for many years. He did so until his death in 1443 when Beaufort was near the end of his own career. Beaufort might have felt resentful, given his service to Henry to date.

In our modern times we do not consider ambition a negative trait. It is all in order to rise as far as possible and to amass great wealth; the only objection arises when one plays most foully for it. 'Ambition' in medieval and early modern times had sinister connotations and was a lure that led the righteous astray; it was the fault by which Shakespeare had Macbeth brought to his destruction. It was the opposite of the Christian virtue of humility, whereby all should know their place and not question God's decision to put them there. Yet many in those days, clerical and lay, desired to improve their rank and fortunes. Du Boulay called the fifteenth century an Age of Ambition.[8]

But would Beaufort really wish to exchange Winchester for Canterbury now that his place was assured with great wealth and powers as the king's banker? He showed no interest in promotion when the archiepiscopate of York became vacant twice in the early 1420s. His resentment, if he held any, was at seeing his junior associate promoted above him, but although the route he later took was not defined by precedent there was more than one way of gaining seniority in the Church. In fact the death of Arundel increased Beaufort's influence as a churchman for a time, as many of the new episcopal appointments were granted to his associates. Courtenay was related by marriage, Kemp was another protégé, and Caterik his chancellor at Winchester before his appointment to replace Chichele at St David's. Even Chichele himself had risen by associating with Beaufort.[9]

Beaufort had spent several months after Harfleur overseeing the office of treasurer along with his own after the Earl of Arundel contracted an ultimately fatal illness at the siege. As chancellor he read out the news of the victory at Agincourt outside St Paul's. His sermons to Parliament continued to help set the mood for each session, and did much to maintain their support for the king's campaigns. He then aided the king in other matters for a year and more.

But on 23 July 1417 Beaufort resigned the chancellorship, announcing that he would make his pilgrimage to the Holy Land. He then went to Constance, briefed by his king to resolve the deadlock, for it was Henry's main interest to redirect Sigismund's attention towards the French wars. So far the council had initiated action against the Hussites, having Hus himself condemned and burned and resolutions on reform passed, but otherwise it had made little headway.

The English delegation had acted in line with Sigismund's representatives, although after the death of Bishop Hallam in September they were in disarray and the council had fallen into a deadlock over procedure. Having secured the abdication or deposition of what had become the three rival popes, there were objections over the order of discussion. Sigismund insisted on certain reforms before the appointment of a single new pope, and the council was now in fundamental disagreement. When Bishop Beaufort appeared in his pilgrims' attire his arrival was timely. Sigismund and others met him on the way in the hope that he would clear the log-jam.

Beaufort's mental rigour and training in canon law was well applied and contributed towards the council steering round the procedural obstructions. Partially through his efforts the assembly arrived at a point where a new pope could be elected, and Sigismund's face was saved. A council composed of an agreed combination of representatives then finally decided on a single pope. Cardinal Odo Colonna, from the powerful aristocratic Colonna family of Rome, gained their assent after three days on 11 November 1417 and took the name Martin V after the saint's day. His address to the requirement for reform was modest, but he would assert the power of the papacy more strongly than any pope had for over a century. Despite further dispute over his replacing the incumbent popes, his elevation was the effective end of the Great Schism and the Church could finally hope to function again as a single body.

Henry Beaufort had contributed significantly to the success of Constance by the time he resumed his pilgrimage, winning respect throughout the Christian world. In recognition of this, Martin V rewarded him with a cardinal's hat. This was truly an honour, and he is known to history as Cardinal Beaufort. But his first holding of this dignity was brief, for on Beaufort's return from Jerusalem in 1418 his nephew the king immediately ordered him to give it up. Beaufort was in Venice by Palm Sunday 1418, whence he set sail for the Holy Land. Some time later he returned to Normandy, and on receiving him there the king made it clear that his red hat would not be tolerated in England. Attention has been drawn to the absence of this altercation in most historical sources,[10] but the king was apparently livid at the *fait accompli* that his uncle had brought on his return. He was certain that this was the new pope's way of imposing a degree of control over the English Church, and Chichele was apparently encouraging him in this belief. Having been ordered to give up the position, Beaufort then went on a second pilgrimage to Santiago, having promised to do so after being brought safely through a storm on the return journey from Palestine.[11]

The practice of a cardinal holding a see was not then established in England, for it was expected that cardinals once appointed would live and work about the papal Curia. Bishops Langley and Hallam had been created cardinals, but by the anti-pope Benedict XIII, and both creations were totally ignored in England. Beaufort had been granted wide powers as papal legate, and Chichele advised that this would expose England to demands for papal taxes, provisions to English bishoprics and other intrusions into the affairs of the English Church. Chichele's concerns were at least in part valid given that Martin had plans to tighten his rein on England.

The English were hostile to foreign authority over their affairs, which they termed *praemunire.* In 1351 the Commons had passed the first of several statutes that forbade papal intervention in English ecclesiastical affairs, and the kings in particular objected to the pope making appointments to English sees as these were traditionally in their own gift. But Martin V showed every intention of asserting his authority in England, and Beaufort could easily have become his instrument. Given the general instability in papal affairs over the previous half-century the English were understandably wary, and in 1418 it was too early to see that the Great Schism was truly over. It was felt that making a bishop of England a cardinal while he held his English see would produce a conflict of interests – a view that was both perceived and confirmed in hindsight. Over a century later Cardinal Thomas Wolsey found that to be both papal legate and Henry VIII's chancellor prevented him from acting effectively for either, and he met his downfall as a result.

Related to this was the nonsense it made of the English ecclesiastical hierarchy. As tradition permitted, the king had appointed Henry Chichele to the most senior position while Henry Bowet was Archbishop of York from 1407. If Beaufort, holding third place in seniority, was now a cardinal he could claim precedence over both archbishops. (Indeed, when he later regained the dignity he would insist on this precedence.) Perhaps he could have opted for the papal Curia and resigned his English diocese. He now had an international reputation, and Pope Martin did not forget him, as was later shown, but he would have given up much to decamp to Rome. Meanwhile, he was one of the richest men in England and still prominent in the court, although now without any formal position other than membership of the king's council.

It is possible that Beaufort considered his chances of becoming pope one day, but we do not know how realistic he was being over this prospect. When the cardinals placed their votes at

Constance for the new pope he gained a number in the first round but was not a contender in later votes. He might have won respect among the cardinals for his performance, but he was still an outsider in papal politics and had no powerful sponsors, while Pope Martin came from an influential Roman family with a network of associations in the Curia. Nonetheless, he might still have considered himself a future pope. Many men of lesser intellect and ability had been archbishop and pope before, and he lacked only the necessary support. He might have felt slighted given his protégé Chichele was archbishop and his younger brother Thomas was now a duke. It made a difference in terms of precedence, which was an obsession of the time; becoming a cardinal would have restored the loss.

Beaufort would be a cardinal again ten years later, but for now his ambition was halted and whatever designs he might have had in Rome now went into abeyance. He did resume his role of king's banker, lending Henry £20,000 of his personal wealth in order to offset his plans to tax the clergy, which lessened the pressure on Parliament as the king sought funding for his campaigns. For over two years he remained in disgrace over the affair of the red hat, and on his return to England he mostly confined himself to diocesan business. He was replaceable in royal service – Thomas Langley had promptly taken up the Great Seal, as he had in the previous reign – but the standing he had with the new pope was obvious.

Henry V had taken two years to prepare his second, more ambitious campaign. Rather than disembarking as expected at Harfleur, in August 1417 the army landed on the left bank of the Seine and laid siege to Caen. Once this town surrendered several others were besieged and captured, including Bayeux, Alençon, Falaise and Cherbourg. Normandy had once been a possession of the kings of England, and Henry won much acclaim by his efforts to regain it. He was also mindful of its proximity to Paris.

Thomas Beaufort had given important service in his two years tenure of Harfleur, and now he played a significant part in this campaign of 1417. On 18 November 1416 he had been created Duke of Exeter, the first Beaufort to attain the ducal dignity. This creation was only for life; dukedoms were not automatically hereditary at the time. He was granted an annuity from the Treasury of £1,000 and a further £40 from the revenues of the County of Devon.[12] In his grant of this dukedom to his uncle, the king was aware of pitfalls. The last to hold it had been John Holland, Earl of Huntingdon. Holland had been stripped of this dukedom by Henry IV and later executed for his part in the 1400 conspiracy. His son, the new Earl of Huntingdon, was loyal and diligent in Henry V's service, but may have been irked by Thomas Beaufort holding a title his father once had. The king made it clear that Thomas would only have the title for life.

As Duke of Exeter, Thomas was at the forefront of the English conquests all through the campaign. He had remained at his post at Harfleur throughout the intervening period, except for a pilgrimage to northern England in 1417 during which he aided Bedford in repulsing the so-called Foul Raid and driving the Scots from Roxburgh.[13] His contribution to the war cannot be overstated; the French might have retaken Harfleur but for Thomas' unflagging defence and methodical campaigning in the area.

Throughout the next two years Exeter showed himself a valuable commander. In May 1418 he gained the surrender of Evreux after a siege of four days, after which the king sent him to Rouen, the principal city of Upper Normandy, to demand its surrender. The defenders, who wrongly believed that the King of France, the Dauphin and even the Duke of Burgundy were on the way with a relieving army, not only refused Exeter's demands but sent a force out from the walls against him, which the English routed. Once Henry had heard of these events he concentrated his efforts on

Rouen itself, where he laid siege until the inhabitants were reduced to eating cats and finally despaired of any rescue. Exeter spent the winter maintaining the siege from the north.

When the defenders of Rouen finally presented the city keys to Henry on 19 January 1419 he handed them to his uncle Exeter, who rode into the town and up to its castle, and draped the banners of the English forces there and on the gates. Exeter was then appointed Lieutenant of Rouen.[14] In 1419 he took Lillebron and Château Gaillard, a fortress that dominated the border between Normandy and the Ile-de-France.[15] The English were now dangerously close to Paris.

Despite these victories it had to be acknowledged that the conquest of all France could have taken a lifetime for the English king to accomplish, with financial and military costs England could ill sustain. For all his territorial gains Henry could never expect to occupy the whole kingdom without the support of many of its nobles. He also needed the acceptance, if not the support, of the French people.

The feud between the Burgundian and Armagnac factions had done serious harm to the French defence. When the Armagnacs rode out to meet the English invasion in 1415 they gave no military roles to any Burgundy supporters. John the Fearless had found the English invasions somewhat to his advantage, particularly after so many of his opponents were killed or captured at Agincourt, but he was as concerned as the Armagnacs over the prospect of an outright English conquest. Henry's attempts to woo him to his side had not resulted in any decisive action, but at least Burgundy and his following had not strengthened the French defence that year.

In August 1418, John and his following besieged and then occupied Paris. He not only put many of the rival faction to death, the Count of Armagnac included, but gained control over the government of France. When Armagnac died, his supporters looked to the adolescent Dauphin Charles as their figurehead, perhaps in the forlorn hope that he would be successful as king, even though his manner was not encouraging. Many simply wanted an end to the destructive civil war, knowing the English were its real beneficiaries.

In 1419 an extremely ill-conceived act of treachery altered the political landscape. When John the Fearless attended a meeting of reconciliation on 10 September with the Dauphin and leading Armagnacs on the bridge at Montereau he was murdered. By design or not, the meeting abruptly turned into a violent exchange and ended with the duke's skull cleft with an axe. His son Philip the Good, who inherited the dukedom and other titles, was soon moved to an accord with the English. This did not exactly mean that the new Duke of Burgundy and his following would fight on the English side – the Burgundians still conducted their own war of vengeance, and not always in cooperation with the English – but it certainly meant that Burgundy and his supporters, strong in northern France, ceased to resist the English. The English now gained entry to Paris, where the most powerful guilds favoured Burgundy.

It was Philip who brokered the Treaty of Troyes, designed to end the French wars of succession. His allies included Isabeau, estranged queen to Charles VI, who had sided with Philip's father, and the French court was persuaded to sign a peace agreement with the English in 1420. While the mad king Charles VI remained on the French throne, Henry V, who married his the French king's daughter Katherine de Valois, would be regent and eventually king after him. Queen Isabeau obliged by 'remembering' that Dauphin Charles was the result of her extramarital affair some sixteen years before and repudiated his claim to the succession. On paper the treaty was a fair agreement which would have been a final settlement to the French wars, leaving Henry as King of France on the death of Charles VI in a few years. But when the Armagnac faction refused to agree to any of this and threw themselves behind the Dauphin Charles, the war was set to continue.

The English at least now had access to Paris, and most of northern France was under the control of either the English or their Burgundian supporters. Thomas Beaufort, Duke of Exeter was Governor of the English in Paris from 1420, and deputised for Clarence in the same role over all occupied France. During his time there he notably defended the city from an Armagnac attack in June 1420.[16]

While the surviving Beaufort brothers were prominent in royal service their sister was conducting a phenomenal project of social climbing for her own children. Joan Beaufort, Countess of Westmorland had presented her husband with at least nine surviving children and was now seeking to provide for all of them. Her eldest son, Richard Neville, was approaching manhood. In 1415 she agreed to the marriage of one daughter, Eleanor, to Henry Percy, son of Hotspur, since restored to his grandfather's earldom of Northumberland the same year.

In 1420 her eldest stepson and husband's heir, Sir John Neville, died. He left a small son, named Ralph after his grandfather. As the elder Westmorland was now becoming senile he grew more pliable and Joan took advantage. By tradition the Neville and Percy families shared the responsibility for keeping the border regions, but as neither the Earl of Westmorland nor his heir were personally able, Sir Richard Neville was now the likely candidate and at twenty he took over the post of Warden of the West March from his dead half-brother. He needed material resources to maintain his role, and Joan made sure – without any legal basis – that he had the incomes of the Westmorland estates. Her husband had made over to him the honour of Middleham in north Yorkshire. Joan was now using her influence in court and with the noble families to find provision for her brood.

The six children of John Beaufort (I) were also growing up. Living in the household of their stepfather Thomas, Duke of Clarence, the four sons were approaching an age where they could expect to take part in military and state affairs and be considered for dynastic marriage. The eldest, Henry Beaufort (II), second Earl of Somerset, would have been bound for the French campaigns had he not suddenly died on 25 November 1418.[17] The second son, John (II), then became third earl aged just fourteen.

In a family marked by dramatic ascent, perhaps the greatest of all occurred when one of John Beaufort (I)'s daughters became a queen. In 1406, King Robert III of Scotland had concerns over the safety of his twelve-year-old son James in an unstable kingdom and decided to send him to France for his education, but in March the ship bearing the boy was waylaid by pirates who delivered him to Henry IV. James would spend eighteen years in captivity, most of it as an absentee king as his father died soon after his capture. Henry V treated him as an honoured guest and even brought him on campaign in France, where James fought on the English side in the French wars, even against Scotsmen at Melun.

Henry was making the best use of James while he had him. The Scots fighting on the French side were accordingly in revolt against their king, as could be interpreted. Now, as some settlement on his release was under discussion, a dynastic marriage that could ease Anglo-Scottish relations was considered. The House of Lancaster had no eligible females and the Beauforts provided the best remaining option. Of this rising second generation the council decided on Joan (II), daughter of John (I) and niece of Bishop Beaufort and the Duke of Exeter. Plans for this marriage were made, but it would take time to come about.

Not necessarily related to this diplomacy, James himself wrote a long poem known as the *Kingis Quair*. It speaks of how James saw a young lady walking in the garden below his window in the castle and fell for her:

And therwith lest I doun my eye ageyn
Quhare I saw, walking under the tour,

Full secretly new cummyn her to pleyne
The fairest or the freschest yong floure
That ever I sawe, me thought, before that houre
For quhich sodayne abayt, anon astert
The blude of all my body to my herte[18]

And so it continues, rich in classical references, where Venus, Cupid and Minerva appear with their related imagery, as does many a device of the literature of courtly love. The walled garden was a well-used component. It is obvious that Geoffrey Chaucer was James's prime influence; he used the same rhyming pattern as *Troilus and Criseyde*, and his imagery resembles a surfeit of Chaucerian forms.

Poetry and real life are not the same. The reality was negotiations over the arranged marriage, designed to bind the Scottish king further to England. It is not known when James wrote this poem, but it was likely between 1418 and his release in 1424. It is even possible that he himself did not write it; on the other hand, Bishop Beaufort may have had his niece walk in the garden where she could be seen as a way of gaining James's approval for the match. Whatever the real course of events, James did think highly of Joan. His poem was a fantasy based on courtly love themes, but Joan was thereby immortalised by this beautiful if idiosyncratic literary outburst.

Margaret Beaufort (I), Joan's younger sister, would marry Thomas Courtenay, Earl of Devon at some point after 1423. Her son, also called Thomas, would succeed to the earldom decades later.[19]

In 1420, the three surviving males of the Beauforts' second generation had reached an age where their active careers as young aristocrats could begin. John (II), third Earl of Somerset and Thomas Beaufort (II) went to France in the retinue of Thomas, Duke of Clarence and fought at the siege of Melun, a stronghold on the Seine just below Paris. The youngest son, Edmund (I), although only a year younger, did not play such an active role in the campaigning. When their mother, Margaret, Duchess of Clarence, joined her second husband in France Edmund remained with her, no doubt impatient for his own chance to fight. Melun was a promising beginning for both older sons, but the following year their stepfather would commit one of those flamboyant military gestures common in the Hundred Years War, his belligerence causing him to cast sensible procedure to the wind – much to his own cost.

On 22 March, Easter Saturday 1421, Clarence and his following were crossing the Loire on their return from a successful raid into Armagnac territory when he learned from his prisoners of a pro-Armagnac army at nearby Baugé and decided to follow up his success with a headlong attack. His army included many seasoned captains, and also his teenage Beaufort stepsons, both learning the arts of war under his tutelage.

Several of the party told Clarence that he would best wait until the archers caught up because the Armagnac forces, including a large Scottish contingent, outnumbered the English. Ignoring this, he ordered a prompt attack. Initial success due to the element of surprise was quickly reversed when the ground proved too marshy to make good a charge on horseback. Among those killed were Clarence himself, Lord Roos and Sir Gilbert Umfraville, these last two accomplished veterans of the wars and supporters of Lancaster. Those captured included the Earl of Huntingdon and both young Beauforts. It was the first major defeat for the English since Henry V had renewed the war.

Captures were part of the usual traffic of medieval warfare. Once a man of coat armour surrendered, he would usually be kept in moderate comfort until ransomed or exchanged according to his social standing. It was part of the game-playing culture of chivalry and did not apply to common soldiers. Both King John II of France and young Geoffrey Chaucer had been ransomed in the wars some sixty years before, although the king brought a far higher payment than the squire. Individuals on both sides had such unwilling guests in their households, sometimes for years or even decades.

For John Beaufort (II), third Earl of Somerset, this was a terrible situation. The young man was raring to follow his father and uncle in a career as a soldier but now he was held in Armagnac territory against his will, awaiting a ransom or a suitable exchange; hardly a bright start. The two young Beauforts were feasted well that night, obviously to their chagrin, and now waited in a state of enforced leisure under guard for the expected settlement that would allow their return to the fight. Weeks passed and no such settlement materialized; those weeks would become months, and the months would become years.

The king was much saddened by this defeat and the loss of his brother, although he said little of it other than requesting that Clarence's remains be returned. Through the following year he fought on, the war having moved south of Paris. He was elated to hear that his queen was delivered of a son on 6 December, and it seemed that apart from Baugé the news was encouraging all round. He had made great strides in the gaining of French territory, and although south and central France still recognised only the Valois monarchy, the English cause had made serious progress.

After nine years, much of it spent in tent cities or on the front line of the fighting itself, Henry V had known almost unadulterated success as a soldier-king, but a more subtle enemy curtailed his reign when he was struck down by dysentery at the castle at Vincennes on 31 August 1422. Surrounded by some of his senior captains, as the end was approaching he dictated codicils to his will to Thomas, Duke of Exeter.

The Beauforts had rendered valuable service to their nephew throughout his reign, counting themselves among his most useful supporters and instruments of his will. Thomas, Duke of Exeter was simply one among many able commanders, but his activities at Harfleur made all the difference between the two major campaigns when he maintained the gains of the first. Bishop Henry Beaufort had done much to provide the finance for this grand project, steering funding through a Commons that could be very sceptical, and maintaining the civil government while the king fought his wars. As a churchman Beaufort had done much to end the most serious problem that the papacy had posed, although the king must have understood that his uncle had an agenda of his own. There was some ill-feeling between the two over the business of his appointment as cardinal, but king and bishop were reconciled in the closing years.

Henry V led from the front. A medieval government could not function much better, as the king brought decisive and broadly successful leadership. There were deeds and victories, and only a few rebellions and conspiracies, for which Henry compared well with his two predecessors, and the Beaufort brothers performed their roles diligently under their nephew's direction. But when Henry V died, the vacuum saw a struggle in which Bishop Beaufort was an important contender.

Rather than his father, it was young Henry V who had set the agenda for the Lancastrian monarchy. Henry IV had sought stable government in England, and once his son began the enterprise to make himself and his line kings of France as well as England his subjects would labour in the enterprise for the next forty years. The Beauforts themselves had given their full support, and would continue to further this ambition in the new reign despite the troubles it would bring.

4

THE BISHOP AND THE GOOD DUKE

When King Henry V's counsellors convened at Westminster at the beginning of September 1422 they were well aware of the perilous and uncertain times that lay ahead. Their king had died in Normandy a week before and his son who had automatically succeeded him was nine months old. It would be a long regency, and difficult to manage.

Henry V had run the country and the French war in a decisive manner and there had been little scope for dissent. But now the absence of such an indisputable authority gave some influential men the opportunity to assert their own will, and the entire Lancastrian endeavour, both the monarchy in England and the ongoing conquest of France, was in danger of falling apart. The two surviving Beaufort brothers had important roles in this time of uncertainty, and both sought to manage the disruption that followed.

At that September meeting, Thomas Beaufort, Duke of Exeter appeared before the rest bearing the codicils to the dead king's will, itself made the year before, having come straight from France with others present at the death to ensure that the will was carried out. The counsellors included his brother the Bishop of Winchester, Archbishop Chichele, Chancellor Bishop Langley, Bishops Kemp and Stafford, the Earl of Warwick and Henry's two surviving brothers John, Duke of Bedford and Humphrey, Duke of Gloucester. As they listened to the terms in the codicils there were murmurs of unease.

As agreed upon at his birth the previous December, Henry of Windsor, only son of Henry V and Katherine de Valois, was now King Henry VI, but none had expected him to succeed at such an early age. Exeter himself had been delegated responsibility for the protection and upbringing of the infant king and other nobles charged with attending him more closely, at least one of them in his presence at all times.

Bishop Beaufort was directed to execute the will itself. While the council agreed to most of the specifications, it was Henry V's decision as to who would take charge of England and France in the interim that produced cause for concern. His two surviving brothers were appointed regents of his two kingdoms, to continue his policies until young Henry was of age. Bedford as Regent of France was the expected and accepted choice, but to hear Gloucester designated his counterpart in England was a shocking revelation to some, Bishop Beaufort in particular.

The two brothers were fundamentally different in their manner, although they shared some characteristics. John, Duke of Bedford, aged thirty-three, was one of the dedicated English soldiers of his day. He had been Warden of the East March towards Scotland at fourteen, where he was credited with diffusing the 1405 rebellion. He almost certainly relied on the counsel of the Earl of Westmorland, but nonetheless he was introduced both to fighting and intriguing while very young. By the time he gained his dukedom in 1414, John was a seasoned commander of men in his own right. He had since been a soldier in France, apart from when he deputised for his elder brother in England on the 1417–18 campaign. He was known for a hot temper, which he learned to control through self-restraint and prudence. Although a practical man he was no stranger to culture, and the Book of Hours that he commissioned is one of the most beautiful illuminated manuscripts to survive the entire Middle ages. It was said that he always placed duty over pleasure.

Humphrey, Duke of Gloucester, a year younger, was handsome and charismatic, a man of letters, a lover of literature and a charmer. He had seen his own share of military activity in the previous reign, having performed noted service at Agincourt, after which he survived serious wounds, although his efforts as Warden of the Cinque Ports to protect the Channel and maintain the provision of Harfleur were his most significant contributions. His reputation as 'the Good Duke' may not have been as much deserved, but he was very well liked for his pleasant manner. He was particularly known for the library he built and stocked at Oxford (since absorbed into the Bodleian), his founding of Greenwich Park and his patronage of St Albans Abbey, where his remains now rest. His two illegitimate children were named Arthur and Antigone, testament to his literary pursuits.

In December 1419, with Henry V still on campaign, Humphrey had been sent home to replace their brother Bedford as the king's lieutenant in England, when he was created 'Guardian and Lieutenant of England'[1] with the power to summon both council and parliament. By the accepted practice the choice fell to him by virtue of his status as Prince of the Blood, but none questioned his ability to govern. In 1421 his brother the king took him again to France, where he first played an important part in further campaigning but afterwards returned to England as the king's lieutenant once again. But in 1422, after Henry's death, several among the council voiced serious doubts regarding his fitness as Regent of England in the long term; it would be at least fifteen years before the king gained his majority and the Lancastrian regime would suffer without effective government. Duke Humphrey was not the man to guide the country in that time, said Bishop Beaufort and others, and Bedford was of the same mind.

Perhaps Humphrey's manner gave the impression of someone who did not take such duties seriously, as one with grandiose ambitions but little capacity for the labours needed to accomplish them. The evidence does not declare Humphrey a total incompetent, and it may have been partially issues of politics, for those in public life never fail to make enemies. However, it is clear from hindsight that the duke was given to impulsive and ill-conceived actions that caused difficulties for others and could have easily damaged English interests.

It was debated whether the council could interfere with the dead king's codicils, or whether Henry V could bind his counsellors posthumously to such stipulations; some even questioned whether Henry really did dictate the codicils. The pragmatists prevailed, and the outcome as agreed by the council and then by Parliament altered the position ordained for Gloucester. A will cannot bind the council, they finally decided, opting instead for Beaufort's model of a regency council.

In 1422, Duke Humphrey was reappointed 'Protector and Defender of the kingdom of England and the English Church and principal counsellor of the lord King' but this title was mostly hollow. He would still be regent, but only while Bedford was not in England. He would head the council, but now he would submit all decisions for their approval. Bishop Beaufort was only one of the counsellors, but his influence was strong; many on the council were his relatives or associates. Exeter, Warwick, Westmorland, Northumberland, March and the Earl Marshal sat as lay magnates, while the ecclesiastics included Chichele, Langley, Kemp and Stafford as well as Beaufort, and there was also Thomas Chaucer. Deeply resentful, Humphrey would count his uncle Bishop Beaufort as a sworn enemy for the rest of his life.

For Bedford in France and Gloucester (and his restraining council) in England there were serious matters to address. As ever, the finances of Calais were in a critical state and the Scots threatened the northern borders. Calais was in part appeased by a duty of one mark on every sack of wool and more than £4,000 was raised by seizing the wool at Calais and reimbursing the merchants. The council ordained that the revenues of the port of Hull would pay for the northern marches and certain payments were made to the Earl of Northumberland so that some of the old debts were alleviated.

Only one plot was said to have threatened the new king at this time, and there is doubt it even took place. Sir John Mortimer, a cousin of the Earl of March, escaped imprisonment in the Tower by bribing his gaoler. When recaptured he was said to have told an accomplice of his plans to use the Earl of March as the figurehead for a revolt with help from the King of France, and that he would smite off the heads of Gloucester and other lords. He had a low opinion of his cousin, saying that March was 'but a dawe'. On these charges Mortimer was hanged, drawn and quartered at Tyburn in February 1423. The chronicler believed that he was executed for 'braking of the Tower' and does not mention the alleged conspiracy, which raises the possibility that the accusations were invented.[2] This incident might indicate some unhappiness with the new regime, but there were no further disturbances. The Earl of March escaped blame for the affair, and his death without issue in 1425 removed one alternative claim to the throne that had niggled since 1399.

For Bedford the brief was to complete the conquest of France. Since the Armagnac faction refused to accept the Treaty of Troyes in 1420 the fighting had continued and Bedford inherited the ultimate goal. Now in overall command of the French war, he had an impressive crowd of commanders such as the Duke of Exeter, the earls of Warwick and Salisbury, Lords Willoughby and Scales,

Sir John Fastolf, Sir John Talbot among others. As long as the campaigning was adequately financed Bedford could continue the war, and in the next seven years the English territory in France grew larger than ever. Bedford did all he could to gain support from those in Normandy. He sought to prevent the occupying forces from pillaging and in 1434 he ordered the execution of Richard Venables, a company captain who had turned to brigandage and plundered the villages of Normandy. He introduced a standard currency in Normandy and founded a university at Caen which he hoped would come to rival the one in Paris.

By the terms of the Treaty of Troyes, if Henry V had lived six weeks longer he would have been King of France when Charles VI died. However, the child king Henry VI's accession caused little complaint at the time. After the death of the Count of Armagnac the Dauphin Charles became the focus of resistance to Troyes, but he had been forced out of Paris and south of the Loire to set up his court at Bourges. Poverty stricken while many of his estates were out of his reach, and far from impressive as a weedy young man in tattered finery, the 'King of Bourges', as the English dubbed him, rallied little enthusiasm for his cause.

First in 1423 at Cravant and then on 17 August 1424 at Verneuil, Bedford soundly defeated Armagnac followers and their Scottish allies; even the French described Verneuil as a second Agincourt, where the Dauphin's field army was shattered and could not easily be rebuilt. Bedford's efforts were winning territory to the south of Paris and brought the frontier to the Middle Loire.

Relations with Philip the Good, Duke of Burgundy were far from straightforward. Philip had joined with the English after the murder of his father, and although the alliance was more to his advantage than to his English partners it was the cornerstone of English policy, for without it the current situation would be simple conquest by an occupying army and therefore less palatable to the French. But Philip actions over the war were inconsistent and he could very easily decide at any time that the alliance no longer suited his purposes. Bedford made supreme efforts to keep Philip on side, even showing his commitment by marrying Philip's sister Anne in the first year of the new reign; completing his dead brother's ambition became his life's endeavour. Bedford also drew the Duke of Brittany into an English alliance.

The biggest stumbling block to Bedford's success was his brother Humphrey. Smarting from the way he was prevented from being an effective regent, the Duke of Gloucester set about building his own empire in the Low Countries. He must have known all along that he was offending the Duke of Burgundy but he proceeded, and in the process almost wrecked the entire English strategy.

Philip, who was also Count of Flanders, was then consolidating his hold over the region that is now Belgium and the Netherlands. In 1420 he arranged the marriage of his niece Jacqueline, heiress to the counties of Hainault, Holland and Zeeland, to her first cousin John, Duke of Brabant. There had been discussion over marrying Jacqueline to Bedford, but Philip, who held her wardship, decided otherwise so that he could gain their combined territories if the marriage was childless. For some years there had been a dispute over the succession to these lordships, with Jacqueline's rival supported by Sigismund, but when Philip succeeded his father he decided to back the Duke of Brabant. However, Brabant did not make it easy. Not only did he lease Holland and Zeeland to the other claimant but he treated his wife in an unreasonable manner, even rationing her supplies of soup and wine, it was said, while his pro-imperial counsellors manipulated him into shabby treatment of her household. Within a year Jacqueline decided that she could stand him no more and fled to England.

Humphrey, in his role as Warden of the Cinque Ports, welcomed Jacqueline to England when she crossed from Calais. Each found the other's company pleasing. Jacqueline sought a papal dispensation to dissolve her marriage with Brabant, but when

Pope Martin prevaricated in Rome she claimed to have obtained her divorce from the persistent anti-pope Benedict III, expecting that Martin would feel pressured to agree to it. Duke Humphrey's marriage to Jacqueline in England late in 1422 took everybody by surprise. The estates and incomes Humphrey's father and eldest brother had granted him were modest, and this marriage would have gained him the equivalent of a small kingdom. It was also the most reckless and potentially disastrous act he could possibly commit at that juncture.

With Bedford making a supreme effort to maintain the alliance with Burgundy, the marriage could not have come at a worse time. Humphrey began preparing to regain his wife's lands by force of arms just as Philip was making overtures of peace with the Dauphin. For Bedford it was a diplomatic nightmare when in February 1424 Humphrey marched an army from Calais across Flemish territory against Philip's expressed wishes. On installing himself at Mons, Humphrey assumed the comital titles of the three provinces while ignoring advice from all sides. Worse still, his activities proved very popular in England, particularly among Londoners, who disliked the Flemings. There was a tendency in England to talk of 'the war in France' as opposed to the 'war in Flanders', and the latter had more popular support. In one conflict Burgundy was presented as an enthusiastic ally while in the other he was the enemy.

Philip the Good responded by giving his full support to John of Brabant. Humphrey and Jacqueline were soon driven out of Hainault by combined Burgundian and Brabançon troops, and while Humphrey returned to England the Burgundians captured Jacqueline, who soon escaped to Holland, and 'there long tyme helde wer a yenes the Duke and put him dyverse tymes at the worst'.[3] Humphrey's claim on the three counties in right of his wife dragged on for several years and he made two more attempts to regain them, but when Pope Martin finally ruled the marriage as invalid in 1428 Humphrey swiftly abandoned both the claim and Jacqueline.

As if by a miracle, Philip decided to retain the English alliance for the present. Despite this major interference in his plans, he shelved his attempts to make peace with the Armagnacs – at least while it suited him.

During his dubious marriage, Humphrey had taken a mistress. An English girl named Eleanor Cobham, daughter of a minor baron of the duke's entourage, had been assigned as one of Jacqueline's ladies-in-waiting while she was in England. Eleanor and the duke plunged into an affair, and once his marriage to Jacqueline was invalidated he married her. It was said that she was very beautiful and that he cared for her, but one in his position needed to marry for reasons of state or personal ambition. Whereas his marriage with Jacqueline would have given him wealth and power and made him a prince of the Low Countries, this second union gained him nothing but her; she was not even an heiress. Eleanor scandalised the senior nobles and their wives by her haughty manner as a parvenu. She was made a Companion of the Garter and gained other honours, but was snubbed by most of the court. Some years later she would prove to be her husband's downfall.

While Humphrey was away on his continental adventure Bishop Beaufort deputised for him, allowing the council to function without the usual tension between bishop and duke. The government had succeeded in raising funds to pay the debts of the Calais garrison and had finally resolved the captivity of James I of Scotland through a ransom of 50,000 marks, a seven-year truce and James's marriage to Beaufort's niece Joan (II). After two decades, James I of Scotland finally returned to his kingdom. Whether he really had fallen in love with young Joan Beaufort having seen her from his window is not known for certain, but it is likely that the settlement for his release was conducted in a more mundane manner.

On 2 February 1424, the marriage between Joan and James finally took place. The two were married by Bishop Beaufort himself at the Priory of St Mary Overy at Southwark and stayed at the nearby Winchester Palace as the bishop's guests before the journey to Scotland. This was an ideal conclusion to the long-running matter of James's imprisonment, both for the nation and for the Beauforts. After the death of her stepfather Clarence, Joan was in wardship to the crown; the Regency Council settled the matter on the king's behalf.

One of the problems solved by the marriage was Franco-Scottish cooperation in the French wars. Since 1296 the 'Auld Alliance', an ongoing accord whereby the Scots and French fought together against the English, had seen Scottish troops fighting in France throughout the wars, and this would end as one of the terms for James's release. He did renew the Auld Alliance a few years later, but after Verneuil the Scots did not fight the English in France again.[4]

There is no mistaking the part of Bishop Beaufort in the proceedings. He had recently been engaged in restoring a transept of the wedding venue, which is now Southwark Cathedral, and which had been gutted by fire in the 1390s. His niece was not the daughter of a king, but she was the nearest available female to the English crown.

Joan (II) Beaufort, daughter of the first Earl of Somerset, was crowned Queen of Scotland at Scone with her husband on 21 May. The years James had spent at the English court had taught him much about English institutions and he made better use of the Scottish Parliament than any king had before. He savagely broke the power of the Albany and Lennox families, a move long overdue after their unchecked licence over the previous years, but James I's reign once he returned to Scotland was turbulent.

The English Church had concerns over the papacy as it emerged from the Council of Constance, and although Bishop Beaufort's international standing made dealings with Pope Martin much clearer business was still fraught with problems. Committed to end not only the abuses that had grown during the Great Schism but also much older limitations on papal authority in England, the pope insisted on the right to appoint bishops to English sees, which had long been the prerogative of the English kings. Martin thought highly of Bishop Beaufort, but even if he was keen on pleasing the pope Beaufort knew there were problems over acceptance.

In 1424 there were four vacant sees, and as both Archbishop Bowet of York and Bishop Bubwith of Bath and Wells had died that year there was concern. The papal Curia nominated Bishop Fleming of Lincoln as Bowet's successor, which the council vetoed out of resentment to this interference. There was also some alarm, voiced by Bedford, over Martin's improving relations with the Armagnacs.

The pope was reluctant to alienate Beaufort, who was a useful supporter. In the event Beaufort sought a working relationship over this business, although it was eventually Bedford's intervention that resolved the matter. The duke conceded papal provision of bishops to sees in Lancastrian France, while some discussion over appointments to the English bishoprics took place. Kemp would be Archbishop of York and Stafford was appointed to Bath and Wells, both with papal assent, while as part of the agreement the pope's nephew Prospero Colonna gained the archdeaconry of Canterbury.[5]

As a postscript to the matter, in 1427 the council requested that Simon Sydenham become Bishop of Salisbury, while the pope decided on Beaufort's recommendation of his own nephew Robert Neville, then only twenty-two and still a student at Oxford. Neville finally gained the see, but only after Beaufort had himself fallen from his high point and probably as a concession to ease his exit from government. It is also likely that Martin was then reviewing the matter of the cardinalate for Henry Beaufort as a way of maintaining his own influence in England.

On 16 July 1424, Bishop Langley resigned as chancellor. He had kept the Great Seal since Beaufort had laid it down in 1416, and the elderly man certainly found the office wearisome, although he remained a reluctant member of council for some time afterwards. His successor could only be Bishop Beaufort, who was now at his most influential, and whose third and final term as chancellor would be his most contentious.

The initial crisis had passed. The loss of Henry V had jeopardised the Lancastrian monarchy, but his counsellors had succeeded in maintaining stability, solving some major problems and keeping the French war of conquest on the rails. Now they needed to maintain the status quo until Henry VI was old enough to rule as king, and this was not as easy.

Beaufort had already opened Parliament in May with another of his political sermons ('Glory, honour and peace to all those who do good'). Employing his usual strategy of twisting biblical texts to sell policies to the Commons, he stated that subjects owed to the king obedience, sound counsel, provision of sustenance, and determination to end corruption and ambition.[6] He used the image of the elephant as his example, with its patience, steadfastness and keen memory a model for Parliament. Using such imagery he emphasised the importance of remaining true to the Lancastrian mission and giving Bedford the material support he needed for his campaigns.[7]

This sermon was not as effective as some of his previous offerings. There was still ill-feeling against the Burgundians and the Commons was not too pleased about financing interminable wars. Duke Humphrey was very popular in London, where the Flemings were resented for their preferential treatment, and many hoped for concessions once he was secure in Hainault. By association, and for his opposition to Humphrey's adventure,

Beaufort was highly unpopular. There had recently been threats to his person.

The kings, as ever, needed large amounts of money both for governing England and waging extensive wars in France, and their established incomes did not always cover such requirements. Custom dictated that kings could request a one-off tax by sanction of Parliament, but the Commons would expect concessions for doing so. There were times, such as from 1422 to 1427, when no such subsidies would be granted. This made the practice of loans from individuals and bodies an important feature of royal finance, with Bishop Beaufort the principal creditor to the Lancastrian kings. He was not the only one; Archbishop Chichele lent a total of £14,218 in eleven years. Richard Whittington and other London merchants also contributed, and various towns and cities chipped in.

But lending money had a serious constraint in the fifteenth century: charging interest was a sin, and known as usury. With Christians unable to participate in the profession, Jews were in much demand as moneylenders. It was once believed that Beaufort's lending was usurious, although Harriss has shown that it had more subtle returns than mere financial profit.[8]

As Bishop of Winchester, Beaufort was one of the richest men in England. The estates of the bishopric were extensive, and their production of wool for export, still the most lucrative business concern in England, brought revenues that many would envy. The bishop's estates brought him about £4,000 a year as a conservative estimate and revenues for the wool exported on top of this were considerable.[9] Beaufort therefore had plenty of money at his disposal and could make large loans to the crown. But instead of doing so to make more money, the main benefit that Beaufort reaped as the king's banker was his influence over policy, where the council were more amenable to the bishop having his own way while they were mindful that he often picked up the bill and could be less generous if he wished.[10] In the 1430s Beaufort softened the council's attitude with loans while he was under attack from Humphrey.

Unlike many who showed their generosity to the crown, Bishop Beaufort always made sure that his loans were paid back and in each separate agreement it was stipulated what source of royal income was earmarked to pay it off. Sometimes it was from the customs duties raised at Southampton and on other occasions he was granted part of a subsidy. In the 1430s Beaufort would take custody of the crown jewels as collateral, which was often resented. While those who loaned money to the king might not see it repaid, Beaufort always made sure that the method of repayment was used until the loan was returned to him.

Beaufort had placed three loans to Henry IV and six to Henry V, but in the reign of Henry VI he made a total of forty-six awards. Most of these were over £1,000 and some above £9,000. He was granting such loans within a year of his death and repayments were made to his estate for some years afterwards.[11]

Beaufort was performing a service to the crown here. His income was greater than he or the see required, and the king's finances had to be balanced. It was not without benefit, however, for in the process Beaufort was strengthening his own hold over policy. His control over the cashflow gave him leverage, and unease over royal finances may have swung the council to his side at times. Unlike a modern financier, he did not make a penny on the loans themselves but instead received other favours and political power. He would later lend a total of £7,666 3*s* 4*d* to finance the 1443 campaign in France, and insisted on having his nephew John Beaufort (II) placed in command as a condition.[12]

There is a reference to a ship that Bishop Beaufort owned, *St Mary of the Tower*, which was taken when he allowed it to be used at the siege of Mont St Michel in 1423. By 1437 he was calling for its restoration. Beaufort's ownership here is puzzling, as ships named 'of the Tower' traditionally belonged to the king.[13]

Thomas Beaufort, Duke of Exeter was officially the infant king's protector and tutor, but as soon as he had made the necessary provisions in 1422 he returned to his duties in France, fighting and governing in the conquered regions. There was little else he did for his charge, apart from engaging a troupe of boys to entertain the infant king with interludes that Christmas.

Thomas Beaufort had spent a lifetime soldiering, and his perseverance been vital. He might not have been the best commander while on campaign, but his expertise lay in the maintenance of defences and conducting sieges, both of which called for steady and unrelenting effort rather than field strategies, and this made him a successful rearguard to his nephew's aggressive campaigning. It was said of Exeter that he would not tolerate swearing, lies or the telling of tales in his household, nor would he accept rewards or gifts.[14] On the other hand, he was particularly generous to the poor.

Thomas was appointed to the Council for the Regency and also as Chief Justice for North Wales, but his military career was nearing its end, as was his life. In 1423, in his late forties, illness saw him delay his departure on the campaign to retake Melun. Three years later, on New Year's Eve 1426, he died childless, all his titles rendered extinct, and his nephew the third Earl of Somerset inherited his estates.[15]

At this time Joan Beaufort (I), Countess of Westmorland was labouring to advance the standing of her children. As her stepson Lord John Neville was designated heir to the earldom of Westmorland she had the task of arranging for the sustenance of her own issue, but when Lord John died in 1420 he left a small son to inherit the earldom. The Earl of Westmorland was traditionally engaged in the defence of the western border region, but as her husband was becoming senile and his grandson still a child, Joan sought to ease her own eldest son, Sir Richard Neville, into the position of Warden of the West March towards Scotland and to share with the Earl of Northumberland the defence and policing of the border with Scotland. In such circumstances it was easier for her to appropriate for Richard the lands due to her step-grandson, and many of the Westmorland estates in County Durham and Yorkshire were illegally diverted to his use. This continued after the first earl died in 1426, and years later the two branches of the family would almost come to blows over the misappropriation of the estates. Using her connections and every other device available, Joan found places for all her children. She used the influence of her brothers Exeter and Bishop Beaufort, and took advantage of at least one wardship. As long as the House of Lancaster had few available marriage partners, Joan could provide a tenuous family connection to the monarchy; she was, after all, Henry VI's great aunt.

Joan's most successful move was to secure for her eldest son the most eligible heiress of the time in Alice, daughter and heiress of Thomas Montague, Earl of Salisbury. Old Salisbury was killed by a cannonball at the siege of Orleans in 1428 and young Richard eventually inherited his earldom. This was far from certain – Thomas Montague had taken subsequently taken a second wife, Thomas Chaucer's daughter Alice, but no children emerged to challenge Richard Neville's inheritance. A relative on the Montague side contested the inheritance but could not succeed against Joan and her illustrious brother the bishop.

Joan's other sons all gained noble titles or the equivalent. The second son William secured the barony of Fauconberg by marriage to its heiress, Joan. The extinct Latimer barony, which had once been in the Neville family, was resurrected for George. Through another heiress Edmund gained the barony of Abergavenny, the only Neville peerage to survive to the present day. As the son who entered the Church, Robert was assured of the patronage of his uncle Bishop Beaufort, through whose offices he was recommended to the see of Salisbury, which he only gained after the dispute of 1426. In 1437 Robert was translated to Durham, one of the most powerful lordships of northern England. The daughters too married into the higher nobility, so that Neville girls became duchesses of Norfolk, Buckingham and York and Countess of Northumberland, while one more married Lord Stanley. All the families into which Joan married her daughters had suffered forfeiture in the previous three reigns, so they were seeking to re-establish themselves. Union with the Middleham Nevilles was a desirable move, but it is hard to tell which side gained the most from each marriage.

One match had far-reaching consequences. Richard 'Plantagenet', somewhat in limbo since his father Richard, Earl of Cambridge's execution for treason, had been left under the care of Sir Robert Waterton. Probably at Joan's urging, Westmorland purchased the boy's wardship in 1423 and with it power over his marriage. It was understood that Richard would inherit the dukedom of York from his uncle, who had been killed at Agincourt.[16] On the Earl of March's death without heirs in 1425, Richard inherited many estates and a claim to the throne after the House of Lancaster. Almost certainly with this in mind, Joan married him to her youngest daughter, Cecily Neville. They created the House of York, the focus for the Yorkist faction in the civil wars that eventually supplied three kings of England; two were a quarter Beaufort in lineage, and the third was one of their sons.

It is not known how close Bishop Beaufort was to his sister. Whether he or Exeter consciously used their influence to promote these matches is not clear, but it was at least desirable to associate with such important figures. It is certain that Bishop Beaufort gave his patronage as an ecclesiastic to Robert Neville, and he also showed much interest in the marriage of his niece Joan. Perhaps in the latter case he was motivated for reasons of state, but the marriage was nonetheless to the advantage of the House of Beaufort too.

Meanwhile John Beaufort, third Earl of Somerset, and his brother Thomas remained prisoners in France. The capture of a senior noble in the French wars was a serious business on either side; his captor could grow rich on the ransom. There were many French nobles confined in England from the Agincourt campaign onwards, including the Duke of Orleans, who spent a quarter-century in captivity after his surrender at Agincourt itself. Of course John and other high-born prisoners lived in fairly comfortable conditions until their release, but they were still forbidden much.

Such captives had other uses. They could be used to bargain during negotiations and could be exchanged for prisoners of equivalent rank. Like many hostages, they could be indoctrinated and might take a favourable viewpoint once freed; James I, for instance, returned to Scotland educated in English ways and values. But young Somerset was unlucky. Time was passing and no terms for ransom or exchange had been agreed.

In the early years of his enforced sojourn, his brother Thomas was with him. Also taken at Baugé, the younger man was still in France in 1427 when a petition went to the Duke of Burgundy requesting release for the two.[17] Thomas was freed soon after, to be plunged straight into active service on his return to English territory. But he was lower in status than his brother John, and could be ransomed more easily.

Bishop Beaufort as chancellor was then regarded the most powerful man in the kingdom. While Gloucester was still on his reckless grand project in the Low Countries, Beaufort could comfortably pursue stability in England and material support for Bedford's efforts. But many of his affiliates on the council were now dead, including the ecclesiastics Bowet, Bubwith and Wakering, his brother Exeter and his kinsman Westmorland, while Langley attended less often. Bishop Stafford as treasurer was his close associate at that time and the two worked well together. The council even voted Beaufort a salary of 1,000 marks for him to deputise until either Gloucester or Bedford returned to England, while making it clear that this was not a precedent.[18]

But Beaufort was unpopular in some quarters, as is often the case for those in government. Londoners blamed him for losses in their trade with the Low Countries, mostly favouring Gloucester. The bishop's policies extracted certain duties that they resented and it was felt that the alien merchants who came to London had preferential treatment. In 1425, an unpleasant incident in the capital almost caused serious civil disturbance. Some people had been arrested on Beaufort's orders and charged with treason, allegedly based on accusations from the bishop's own men. Protesters then gathered in July at Wine Crane's Wharf, almost opposite Beaufort's own palace in Southwark across the river. Some were heard to declare that they would throw the bishop in the river to teach him to 'swim with wings'.[19] Nothing came of the demonstration, but many archers from Cheshire and Lancashire were thereafter visible around the bishop's home.

Discontent was still brewing the following October, with the Londoners wary of the armed men in the bishop's livery, when Duke Humphrey returned to England. He had not given up his attempts to gain Hainault, Holland and Zeeland but a lull in the fighting allowed him to return to resolve some personal business. From his own residence at Baynard's Castle, a fortified house near St Paul's, he proceeded to the Tower of London with his following. At its gate, to his extreme affront Gloucester was informed that Bishop Beaufort had instructed the guards not to admit him. Beaufort had put Richard Woodville, chamberlain to the Duke of Bedford, in charge of the Tower and ordered him not to admit anyone 'stronger than he', later specifically telling him that Gloucester was not welcome.

The duke was extremely annoyed, as would be any noble in an age where degrees of social standing were so important. Woodville was a lowly esquire, although he was only following orders. But Gloucester was protector, and Beaufort as chancellor was theoretically subordinate to him. Gloucester demanded an audience with one Friar Randolph, imprisoned in the Tower since 1419 for his alleged role in a plot to kill Henry V by magic. He was almost certainly seeking information on Beaufort's believed involvement in the plot, as he later presented a number of spurious accusations over this business. Woodville again refused.

Gloucester was acting outside the powers the council had allowed him in 1422. He had never accepted the restrictions on his regency, nor was he aware of specific areas prohibited to him. Beaufort had a valid concern: if Gloucester had entered the Tower, he and his following would have had access to the royal armoury, which included firearms and artillery. Given Gloucester's popularity with the Londoners, it could have turned ugly for Beaufort. Moreover, whoever held the Tower could control London. Beaufort made no attempt to solve the dispute, and neither did Gloucester. His anger aroused, the duke spoke to the mayor and aldermen, who took little persuasion.

On 29 October, the bishop's men found the gates on the south end of London Bridge barred to them. There was also a gathering of citizens who had taken to the street against those they called the 'king's enemies'. A rumour circulated that Beaufort was about to seize the king's person at Eltham, and the Londoners decided to intervene. The archers took their place at the gates, and an uneasy stalemate followed.

There were attempts to mediate, first by Archbishop Chichele and then by Duke Pedro of Coimbra, Gloucester's Portuguese cousin who was then visiting London. There was a truce, but no lasting solution. Beaufort wrote to Bedford in France, requesting that he come back and deal with this matter 'for, by my troth, if you tarry we shall put this land in adventure with a field'.[20]

Such a letter shows how serious matters had become for the bishop. To call back Bedford could easily jeopardise the English war effort in France while it was making progress. The political tensions were leading to instability, and both sides had private followings. Uncertainty over the minority and Gloucester's refusal to accept his restrictions gave too much scope for division and could easily turn into violence after months of unrest. Perhaps the bishop was overreacting, but only a little. Bedford returned, spurning an opportunity to deal the French another important blow.

It was pure luck that the situation had not turned violent before the Duke of Bedford arrived at Westminster on 10 January 1426. Beaufort had met his nephew on the way and the two stayed at the abbey while Gloucester occupied the royal apartments at the palace itself. While the truce was still holding Bedford made overtures to his younger brother to discuss the matter, but Gloucester refused to meet with him, and then refused to attend two councils. He would only meet Bedford in a parliament, he declared, for he believed the Commons would support him.

By this time Humphrey had collected a dossier of accusations against Bishop Beaufort spanning the past twenty years and was preparing to present them before a parliament that he expected would be hostile to the bishop. He was sure of his own popularity even though his adventure in the Low Countries was not going well; a force led by Lord Fitzwalter on his behalf had just invaded Zeeland and been defeated by the Burgundians.[21]

Bedford was always close to his uncle, but he had some hard thinking to do on this matter. Bishop Beaufort had been disobedient towards the regent, who was his superior. Given the danger of the regency falling apart, it would be an unwelcome precedent to endorse insubordination. One could argue that the division of power during the regency was vague and the basic idea behind the agreement of 1422 was to limit Gloucester's brief as much as possible. But he was acting in a partisan manner, and not putting the country's needs before his personal agenda. As a final consideration, it is true that Beaufort had acted in his own interest but he had every right to prevent the unrest from escalating, which could have been the outcome had Gloucester's supporters gained entry to the Tower. In the end it was political considerations that forced Bedford's decision.

Bedford agreed with his brother but ordered a parliament convened at Leicester, far from Gloucester's support base. Meeting on 18 February, it was called the Parliament of Bats. While delegates were ordered to leave their weapons at their lodgings, a number came with bats or clubs hidden in their clothing. Even this was disallowed, and some contented themselves with carrying concealed rocks instead. There was no violence, but the atmosphere was ominous.

Gloucester had prepared a series of charges going back to the reign of Henry IV. He brought up the allegation that in 1408 Beaufort had tried to force Henry IV's abdication, which might have been the case, although it would have been understandable in the circumstances.[22] He also raised a more serious accusation, also some twenty years old. A man had been found attempting to murder Henry V, then Prince of Wales, in his bed at Westminster. He had confessed his intent while in the custody of the Earl of Arundel, who immediately had him drowned in the Thames in a sack. Gloucester claimed that Beaufort was involved in this business.[23] Thirdly, the alleged plot by Joan of Navarre in 1419 was linked with the bishop. Joan had been accused of seeking to kill her stepson Henry V by witchcraft and was imprisoned. She was released three years later, and it is likely that there had never been any such plot, but her alleged accomplice Friar Randolph was still in the Tower and Humphrey probably wanted him to give evidence.

In reality the duke was clutching at straws. He had not obtained the information that Friar Randolph was said to have possessed, and was simply making wild accusations. Beaufort stated that all charges were 'unsubstantiated', and Gloucester for all his efforts could offer no evidence to offset his uncle's denial. Parliament heard the bishop standing before the boy-king swearing an oath:

> I consider my name and reputation completely tarnished in various men's opinion... I call upon God as my witness ... that I have been and am a loyal friend and loyal subject to you my sovereign lord... and also I have been a loyal subject to my sovereign lord your father, during his entire reign, and... in like wyse I was a trewe man to Kyng Henry the Fourth.[24]

His lengthy statement was heard and submitted to a small committee, effectively most of the regency council. While Beaufort probably did adhere to the widespread belief in 1408 that Henry IV should give up the crown while his illness was causing instability in government, there is no evidence at all that he was ever involved in plotting against Henry V. The Beauforts depended heavily on the House of Lancaster and had no reason to want Henry dead. Despite all such considerations, when the committee delivered their judgment on 7 March it was surprisingly Bishop Beaufort who felt that his wrist had been slapped. They obviously chose to follow Bedford's line.

While no grounds could be found for proceeding over the bizarre allegations that Gloucester had raised, they decided that it was Beaufort who had exceeded the bounds of propriety. Duke Humphrey was still Protector of England when his elder brother was in France, and Beaufort's action was insubordination. They recognised that given Humphrey's position – the third-highest person in the realm after the king and Bedford – it was not so easy to censure him. Eventually they agreed that both sides would forgive and forget all that had happened in the past months. Both Gloucester and Beaufort made public statements resolving to quarrel no further. Beaufort apologised for his improprieties, and Gloucester was obliged to publicly accept his uncle's innocence. The two shook hands, and the crisis was over.

On 16 March Bishop Beaufort resigned as chancellor; he could not serve on a council dominated by a resurgent Gloucester. His associate Bishop Stafford was also forced to give up the office of treasurer, and soon Archbishop Kemp and Sir Walter Hungerford took their respective places. The parliament then resolved some other issues, including that of papal provision to the see of Salisbury. There was a point of contention over the papal candidate Robert Neville, recommended by his uncle Bishop Beaufort instead of Sydenham. Partially in order to placate Beaufort, the choice finally fell on Neville. Despite this small victory, it was Bishop Beaufort who had lost face in the wider dispute. Few could easily side with him in the circumstances. In May he was granted leave to go on pilgrimage and he departed soon after, to the relief of all in government. He would never be chancellor again.

For a time Gloucester and his supporters rejoiced, but it was obvious that they had gained nothing from the business. In 1428 Pope Martin V finally declared against the validity of Gloucester's marriage to Jacqueline of Hainault; there had been no marriage to Gloucester and Jacqueline was still married to John of Brabant. Rather than contest the decision, Gloucester married Eleanor Cobham, signalling an end to his claim. Philip the Good, Duke of Burgundy took Jacqueline into his court and appropriated half the revenues of her lordships. Gloucester then tried to have his own powers in England defined, but very little authority was conceded.

Henry Beaufort's political career was far from over; in fact, a dramatic new phase was beginning under a different master. He had left on his pilgrimage at Shrovetide in 1427 but once he had crossed to Calais there was an unexpected development. On 25 March, in St Mary's Church, there was a ceremony where the Duke of Bedford placed on Beaufort's head the cardinal's hat that he had been forced to relinquish a decade earlier.

It is likely that Bedford had agreed to remove his veto on this issue to convince Beaufort to back down in the quarrel with

Gloucester, but no evidence exists. Beaufort was out of reach to those who would object to this elevation, including Chichele and Gloucester, and once the role was resumed as a *fait accompli* it could not easily be reversed. He was now Cardinal Beaufort again, and embarked on his new career as a prince of the Church, an international role that would take him on crusade. Perhaps he entertained once more the thought that he might be pope one day, but he must have known that it was a long way off.

It was not an easy time for those concerned over the state of England and France in 1422, with the sudden loss of Henry V threatening the entire status quo. Indeed, everything the Lancastrian monarchy had achieved could easily have crumbled. For the Beauforts, committed as they were to the cause of Lancaster, there was a need to maintain stable government in England and to prosecute the conquest of France, and they worked towards this goal. They were not alone, but they did play important roles.

History does not show Humphrey, Duke of Gloucester in too favourable a light, and it is understandable that Bedford, Beaufort and others sought to muzzle him. A firebrand and an adventurer seemingly oblivious to the damage he could do, Duke Humphrey was not the man to deputise for the king. The business over Jacqueline of Hainault had placed the entire French strategy in jeopardy, and he took little notice. He wished for the power and trappings of regency, but few could trust him to carry out the everyday business of running the country.

But it would be simplistic to see the feud with Bishop Beaufort as the conflict of stable, sensible governance against reckless adventuring. Beaufort was high-handed, confrontational and stubborn. He could have been more conciliatory towards Gloucester, while the latter was not easy to deal with when thwarted. The bishop had expected Bedford to agree with his stance but issues of before and after, and a poor definition of powers, led to events turning against him.

Beaufort was not at all popular with the multitude; he advocated unpopular courses of action and his moneylending activities were resented. But these were not the easiest of times and even during better days those in public life made enemies. No regency ever ran smoothly, and this one was particularly long. Beaufort advocated the policies that he felt were needed, unpopular as they may have been, while Gloucester was identified with spectacular anti-Flemish activities and impractical ideas.

The regency council had achieved much in five years. They had maintained political stability in England, made sense of the financing of Calais, concluded the matter of King James in Scotland in a fairly favourable settlement, established a workable dialogue over papal provision and facilitated the expansion of English territory in France, at the same time maintaining the Burgundian alliance despite Gloucester's interference. All of these owed something to Beaufort, and he bequeathed to his successors a functioning government and a military campaign in France that was in the ascendant.

But there was still a long minority ahead, and much scope for the undoing of these successes. The feud between the restored Cardinal Beaufort and his nephew Gloucester was not resolved, and would flare up again later.

5

THE CARDINAL'S CRUSADE AND THE CORONATION CAMPAIGN

By the spring of 1427 it seemed as if the political career of Henry Beaufort had been shot down in flames and that he had embarked on a new calling as an international churchman and papal servant, even a crusader; in theory he was just one step away from becoming pope. But this spectacular new career did not last, and Cardinal Beaufort would later return to prominence as an English statesman.

Of course it took more than acumen and organisational ability, and certainly more than simple piety, to attain the papal throne. Various aristocratic families and other factions dominated the College of Cardinals at different times; Pope Martin was himself the candidate of the Colonna family, and a newcomer would struggle to navigate the political complexities. But the council at Constance had given Beaufort the reputation of a respected international ecclesiastic and he might still have been a contender if he found the right support. Henry Beaufort was a man of inflated ambition with an ego to match, and he might well have reasoned that service to the incumbent Martin V might gain him the necessary prominence to become a feasible candidate when the papal chair was next vacant.

It had been the prospect of losing his Winchester see that had forced Beaufort to relinquish such ambitions along with the red hat back in 1417. He knew that the wealth of the bishopric had gained him power and he would never give it up. Any agreement made at this time would surely have stipulated that he must keep Winchester, but it was not the end of the debate in England over cardinals holding bishoprics.

The entire question of whether one could be a cardinal and a bishop in England at the same time was only properly raised at this point. Two archbishops in the previous century had been cardinals, but whereas John of Thoresby had succeeded in holding both designations Simon Langham's occupation of the two positions had incurred the wrath of Edward III and he duly resigned his archiepiscopate to go to Rome. Hallam and Langley, both created cardinals after attending councils, were never recognised as such in England due to the inconclusive nature of the gatherings. Strictly speaking, an English bishop was also a greater feudal magnate and often a government official, and to act in the service of the pope at the same time left wide scope for conflict of interest. Even the most devout English Christians were chary of *praemunire*, and Gloucester was soon preparing to challenge his uncle's elevation. Beaufort managed to establish the precedent of cardinals as bishops in England, and was followed by seven others before the Reformation; the last two were Thomas Wolsey, Henry VIII's chancellor, and Reginald Pole, the last Catholic Archbishop of Canterbury during the reign of Mary Tudor. Even today, Catholic bishops holding sees in England are often also cardinals.

But the red hat that sat firmly on Beaufort's head caused many headaches for other prelates, not least for Chichele, who was trumped several times when Beaufort considered himself the senior ecclesiastic in England. There was periodic unease over this; in August 1429 Beaufort was summoned to Parliament as 'H. Bishop of Winchester *commonly called the Cardinal of England*'.[1]

But Beaufort had regained his cardinal's hat in a manner that his opponents could not easily challenge, and this time he would keep it.

So it was that on 25 March 1427, in St Mary's at Calais, Henry Beaufort finally felt the hat fit snugly on his head once more. Two papal bulls were then read to him; the first appointed him papal legate for Bohemia, Germany and Hungary in the place of Cardinal Orsini, and the other agreed to his keeping his English bishopric and other ecclesiastical roles, including his see and its temporalities. By papal licence he would have a cross borne before him everywhere he went. More significantly, he was instructed to join the crusade in Bohemia without delay. Pope Martin had agreed to Beaufort resuming the dignity of cardinal, and perhaps this was the price and the pope reminded Beaufort in the papal bull that the deep red colour of the cardinal's robe showed his willingness to shed his blood for the Christian cause.

Crusading, the practice of furthering the Christian cause by force of arms, was a much-lauded institution in Europe from the end of the eleventh century onwards. It reconciled the martial lifestyle of a medieval knight with Christian ideals – they used the same terms as they would to describe a pilgrimage – and material gains could come a crusader's way. Some of the first crusaders, active between 1095 and 1099, carved out lordships for themselves in the Levant from the territories they had conquered in the name of Christ.

Over the following two centuries it became obvious that good intentions were not enough. As the Muslims regained their lands, it became harder to raise armies. Many in Europe expressed their resolution to go crusading, some even enjoying the legal and canonical advantages of 'taking the Cross', but their timetables for setting out were often modified by practical considerations, being delayed from year to year indefinitely. Henry IV of England announced his intention to set forth and fight his way to the Holy Sepulchre soon after he gained the throne in 1399, but was forced to delay these plans while his monarchy was challenged by rebellion, and by the time the kingdom was quiet enough, he was too sickly to go. Worse still, the ideals of crusading were continually abused and concealed all manner of ulterior motives. There were crusades against the heretical Cathars of Provence and the excommunicated Emperor Frederick II. The Fourth Crusade of 1204 was supposed to liberate Jerusalem but was diverted en route to conquer the Christian Byzantine Empire instead. In 1270, the ailing Louis IX of France (later a saint) called for an army to halt the systematic destruction of the Christian East by the latest Muslim rulers, but the undertaking was diverted for commercial and political reasons; this Eighth Crusade ended a long way from Jerusalem at the unsuccessful siege of Tunis, where the French king succumbed to dysentery.

The Holy Land had been won and lost by 1291, but the ideal and the intention to regain Jerusalem for Christianity persisted for centuries to come. A crusade was the ultimate quest for a chivalrous knight, but chivalry often suffered from practical issues. Many still talked of crusading in the early fifteenth century as enthusiastically as in the twelfth, but few acted. The abuses were also repeated, as Cardinal Beaufort's own experience testifies.

Since the twelfth century there had been an ongoing crusade to the east of the German Empire where the Baltic and Slavonic pagans were said to threaten Christendom as much as the Muslims did, and at much closer proximity. The Teutonic Knights, one of the orders of warrior-monks of the time, led many campaigns into this region. After Lithuania had finally embraced Christianity in the late fourteenth century the threat seemed to be over, but the rise of the Hussite heresy practically reprised it all when, spurred by their heterodox beliefs, the Hussites took control in Bohemia and Holy Roman Emperor Sigismund urged action to end the heresy by force of arms. Hus himself had been condemned and burned at Constance, and Martin V was keen to suppress this latest threat. An organisation that radically attacked the authority of the Catholic Church to lay down standards for doctrine, belief and behaviour – and, worse still, criticised the Church's material wealth – was far more dangerous than any pagan enemy.

Even Sigismund had an ulterior motive for this crusade. He was King of the Romans, the customary title before his eventual coronation as Holy Roman Emperor in 1433, but was also hereditary King of Bohemia. It was his contention that he could not enter his own kingdom, but conveniently his enemies were heretics and he had the support of Pope Martin in warring against them. His first two crusades in 1420 and 1421 pitted him against the charismatic blind Hussite Jan Ziška and ended without lasting gains. A civil war between Hussite factions and Ziška's death in 1423 did little to aid the third crusade of the following year, and Prokop the Great proved an able successor. A fourth crusade to Bohemia was already underway when Beaufort was appointed its papal legate in 1427.

Cardinal Beaufort was not a young man when the pope charged him to join the campaigning army. To be over fifty was an advanced age for the day, and while some old soldiers might have relished the thought of campaigning beyond that age – if his brothers John and Thomas had still lived they would have done so for sure – this was not the life for one who had lived as an ecclesiastic, scholar and royal official. Of course he would not be fighting, but to travel with the army and live in tents for a year or more would have been hard going for a man of his years who normally lived in a palace.

Beaufort set about recruiting a small force, mostly from English-occupied France, although it is not certain to what extent he truly commanded it. His nephew Sir Edmund Beaufort accompanied this small army on crusade and it is reasonable to think that he and other career-soldiers took the military affairs upon themselves.

Beaufort stayed a while in the Low Countries on a visit to the Duke of Burgundy; the conflict between Philip and Humphrey, Duke of Gloucester over Jacqueline had certainly strained relations, and Beaufort was keen to preserve their important alliance. He later made his way east, reaching Nuremburg by 18 July 1427. Here he wrote a long letter to the Hussite leadership. Remarkably, its tone was basically conciliatory, with no hint of threat or condemnation. Lamenting the hardships and carnage of war, it offered 'the gift of peace'. It is only a pity that such a strategy could not change the other side's beliefs, and that harmonious coexistence was not an option.[2]

Ten days later, Beaufort finally reached the crusade near Tachov and was dismayed to find the army, commanded by the Archbishop of Trier, had been driven back by the enemy. Beaufort planted a cross in the road and exhorted the force to return and fight. They halted for a time but the retreat resumed: it was one thing to go forth and fight the good fight, but it was another to maintain a workable strategy.[3] Beaufort claimed to have orders to advance unconditionally. He did all he could to rally the crusaders, unfurling the banners of the pope and emperor. But the army was poorly organised and not primed for battle whereas the Hussites had developed the technology and strategies of the *Wagenburg* or war wagon. This involved chaining wagons together into a square. The crews, with crossbowmen and handgunners reinforced with howitzers, would then defend this mobile fortress, often effectively.

The crusaders had been heavily defeated at Tachov, and Beaufort soon relented and withdrew with the remainder. Rather than consider his duty discharged, the cardinal then returned to England with the intention of raising money and men for a proper crusade; there is no doubt that he took his mission seriously. He placed the projected crusade before the council but found them unwilling to support him while the French war was putting such demands on resources. His promotion to cardinal had also caused much ill-feeling, which Gloucester was already stoking. The council at least permitted him to recruit for Bohemia, but only if he would first gain an extension of the truce with Scotland.

Although few admitted it at the time, the English drive to conquer France had not shown the same impetus in the past few years. From Henry V's landing at Harfleur in 1415 it had been a relentless advance and the English could control most of northern France, albeit in part through their Burgundian allies. Baugé had been the only important defeat. The victory at Verneuil had opened Maine for occupation and Bedford was campaigning in Anjou and Poitou to link English Normandy with Guyenne and cut off the Dauphinists from the Atlantic coast. But 1426 had brought shock reversals when the Bretons repudiated the English alliance and seized Pontorson and Maine. The English recovered both the following year but the siege of Montargis was a failure. Bedford's commander, Thomas Montague, Earl of Salisbury, urged for the taking of Orleans which would consolidate the English hold on the crossing of the Loire. Rather than strike at Bourges, the Dauphin's capital, Bedford agreed to this as a first objective.

This strategy raises questions in hindsight. Orleans dominated the best crossing of the Loire, but there were other routes to Bourges, and Orleans took up much effort that could have been better used elsewhere. In September 1428 Salisbury himself was killed at the siege and his replacement, the Earl of Suffolk, gave the defenders respite by withdrawing the troops to winter quarters. The siege would persist, but there was by this time an element of complacency among the English. Since Verneuil it had been a relentless grind rather than a stream of spectacular victories, but they still had no reason to expect less than complete conquest.

Cardinal Beaufort had similar complacency on his side in his current project. The English were conscious of the 'threat' of heresy, and most saw Lollardy and Hussitism as one and the same. Gloucester had recently put down a Lollard rising in the St Albans area, or rather the plundering of a nunnery by suspected Lollards. Beaufort advocated the eradication of the heresy at its centre, but paying for a crusade on top of existing war taxes was not a welcome notion to the council.

Although King Henry VI was still far too young to rule his country he was now old enough to walk in processions and to undertake other ceremonial roles. In 1428 the boy king knighted several young men at a single session, among them Richard of York and Richard Woodville. Around that time Bedford was pressing for a timetable for the king's coronations in England and France. Given Henry's accession as an infant, both ceremonies were essential to his credibility.

The events of 1429 are well known, if often from the hagiography. Appearing from Lorraine, Joan of Arc rode at the head of an army that drove the English from the walls of Orleans, a major reverse without considering supernatural assistance. The Dauphin was near his wit's end when Joan appeared at his court; sending her to Orleans with an army was an act of desperation, but it worked and the Dauphinist defence was suddenly revitalised.

The death of Salisbury and the laid-back strategy of Suffolk had also aided the relief, as had the Burgundian withdrawal. English complacency may have also played a role. The besieging army was hardly prepared for this Holy Maid (or Witch as they believed) riding in the Dauphinist cause; the French defence had been sluggish since Verneuil and the English knew of no charismatic new leaders among their enemies. Also, the wind changed just as Joan arrived and enabled a long-delayed French attack across the river by boat; whether divine providence or simple luck, it made all the difference. The English were soon forced back.

The cardinal's embassy met James I and Queen Joan at the Scottish border. The truce agreed in 1424 was due to expire within the year and as the English did not want a new Franco-Scottish alliance they hoped that Beaufort, the queen's uncle, could negotiate an extension. He came back without any agreement, for he had little to offer apart from easing terms on the ransom still to be paid, which James had no intention of paying in the first place. The French were keen to renew their Scottish alliance, and the Archbishop of Reims was also visiting at that time.[4]

In 1430 there was a new embassy to Scotland, with Sir Edmund Beaufort at the head of his first important diplomatic mission. As Queen Joan's brother he could deal with the royal couple more easily than most. He also had more concrete offers than his uncle the cardinal had borne, being permitted to discuss granting Berwick and Roxburgh and proposing the marriage of King Henry to a daughter of James and Joan, all for a 'final pees' and Scottish neutrality in the French wars. The proposals were well received, but the Scottish estates nonetheless rejected them outright.[5]

Since the embassy to Scotland, the cardinal had been recovering his lost standing in English politics. It is believed that he intervened in the dispute over the inheritance of the earldom of Salisbury. After the old earl died at Orleans the earldom passed through his heiress to Richard Neville, Beaufort's nephew, and he finally gained it in 1429 despite a dispute to the inheritance from the Montague family. Beaufort was also involved in the partition of the lands between his nephew and the dowager countess.[6]

But while the cardinal was in Scotland his rival Gloucester was busy preparing a new attack. He first stirred up concerns about whether Beaufort's dual roles constituted *praemunire*. He also declared that a cardinal sitting on the royal council would create a conflict of interest. At first the council debated this, and it made sense given the long tradition of resisting papal intervention in matters of Church and State. With the approach of St George's Day, the feast day for the Order of the Garter, Beaufort, who was chaplain to the order, was quietly asked not to attend. It was eventually agreed that he could continue to sit on council but must absent himself when issues of the papacy were raised.

On the same day that the council gave Beaufort permission to recruit for the Bohemian crusade, the English commanders Talbot, Fastolf and Scales were defeated at Patay. Sir John Fastolf escaped, but the other two were captured when Joan of Arc headed the French force storming the castle. Suffolk had been captured at the fall of Jargeau shortly before. These events in France had little effect on the deliberations as it usually took at least a week for news of the French wars to reach London, but there was soon concern over what had happened. Tales of this 'Fiend' in the form of a young girl leading the dramatic French recovery jarred the English from their complacency.

Not only did Cardinal Beaufort's crusade seem inappropriate for the time, but the cardinal himself was hard pressed to maintain his position in England. As a result of Humphrey's new onslaught Beaufort needed all the friends he could find. Even after exchanging his role as chancellor for that of cardinal and crusading papal legate he would not give up what he had in England, and this may have prompted him to abandon the last two years' preparation for the crusade and aid the English cause in France instead. In July 1429 he offered his small crusading army of about 3,000 to reinforce the defence of Paris, to which the council agreed. Bedford was much relieved when this force arrived and the Dauphinists did not take Paris that year.

But once Beaufort had promoted this armed attack on Bohemia as a crusade, to divert it to a secular war seemed blasphemous; it even paralleled the infamous Fourth Crusade. It was a textbook example of what happened when more mundane motives hijacked the selfless intentions for which crusades were preached. The 'crusade' against the Hussites was itself far from pure in conception, but as a political action conveniently launched against heretics it qualified as a crusade and gained papal endorsement and widespread support. Furthermore, it was knights and nobles who were expected to crusade whereas Beaufort raised a force largely comprised of archers and soldiers who fought for pay.

There is the hint of an ulterior motive that Beaufort might have harboured all along. In the same way that Henry V had courted Sigismund's support in his French war it is likely that Beaufort saw potential in giving aid to Sigismund. The emperor-elect could be a powerful ally, or at least it would be desirable if he did not aid the Dauphinists; Philip of Burgundy had cause for unease over his presence in the Low Countries. Of course there is no evidence that the cardinal planned to make use of the crusade in this way, and it is also just as likely that Sigismund would not have shown much gratitude; he was hardly useful to Henry V for all the late king's efforts. But it must certainly have crossed Beaufort's mind that had the crusade been successful, he might have scored points in diplomacy with Sigismund. If so, he may have come to the conclusion that abandoning the crusade would not help his king at all.

Some said that it was the cardinal's original intention in raising this crusade to take the troops to France, but this is unlikely. There are better ways to recruit soldiers, and Beaufort could have raised them more easily for a French campaign. He had returned from Tachov annoyed at the defeat and had spent nearly two years on this project, but suddenly he was letting it go. If anything it was the triumph of Beaufort the politician over Beaufort the ecclesiastic. It may have been his own anxiety over Gloucester's campaign to drive him out of his Winchester see, or it might have been a final realization that his efforts in Bohemia would neither make much impression nor further his ambitions in Rome. Perhaps he saw his life's work as the conquest of France. From now on he would serve the King of England.

The pope was angry at the abandonment of the crusade and Beaufort was never called to act on papal affairs again. His dispensation to have the cross precede him was withdrawn and he was forbidden from wearing the legatine insignia in France. Martin showed his displeasure while writing to the Dauphin.[7] The grateful council gave the cardinal leave to raise a new force for Bohemia the next year, but he never went on crusade again. In furthering the English war effort Beaufort had sacrificed his new career as an international ecclesiastic and his possibility of ever being pope.

At Henry's first coronation on 6 November 1429, Cardinal Beaufort was prominent. Henry was almost eight, and although the ceremony was much belated Bedford planned it as a public stunt, in part as a prelude to his second coronation as King of France. It was a muted affair as expense had to be spared, but the nature of the dual monarchy was stressed. Once again that cardinal's hat interfered with the proceedings, and it was Beaufort who placed the crown on the boy king's head; as cardinal he claimed precedence over Archbishop Chichele.

Bedford then began preparations for the second coronation in France. Cardinal Beaufort and about twenty nobles accompanied the king, first crossing to Calais in April 1430, where the royal party remained for a month. The entourage then took a year to assemble in Rouen before setting off for Paris. Gloucester's regency had ended with the English coronation but he was now the king's lieutenant in England, and while seeking material for a new attack on Beaufort he dealt with important domestic matters surprisingly well.

Given the French revival the journey for the coronation was part military campaign and part propaganda spectacle. It was risky bringing the boy king to France once the war had turned unpredictable, and Joan of Arc was still leading the French recovery. It showed the importance of the French coronation to Bedford, designed as it was to affirm Henry's claim to France and cement his support there, particularly in Paris.

Beaufort sent his nephew Richard Neville, the new Earl of Salisbury, ahead to reinforce the young Beaufort brothers' efforts in Paris. It was a major concession to hold the coronation in Paris, as it was tradition in France that the king would assume the title when crowned at Reims, north of Paris in the Champagne region where St Remegius crowned Clovis in 496. But Joan of Arc and the Dauphin had taken Reims the previous year, and the Dauphon's own coronation there on 17 July 1429 was intended as a clear statement that he was King Charles VII of France. Paris, meanwhile, was relatively secure; Thomas Beaufort, Count of Perche and Edmund Beaufort, Count of Mortain headed an effective defence, which was an important responsibility given Joan had her sights set on regaining the capital.

In the time it took for the English royal party to reach Paris, much had changed once Joan was captured on 23 May 1430 at Compéigne, pulled from her horse by a Burgundian archer. This did not immediately end the French counter-offensive, but the Dauphin's aura of divine support quickly faded.

As a public relations event, Henry's coronation in Paris on 2 December 1430 was a poor show. Like its counterpart in England it was a spectacle on the cheap, and the Parisians made their feelings known. Planning was poor. The goldsmiths and other craftsmen, who expected many lucrative commissions before the coronation, were mostly disappointed, as were those who hoped for amnesties, largesse and other benefits usually granted at coronations. The food was even cooked in an English manner, to the dismay of the French. With no lessons learned from the Westminster coronation, it was again Cardinal Beaufort who placed the crown on the king's head, this time flagrantly upstaging the Archbishop of Paris. The cardinal believed himself the senior prelate, but this was hardly a good example of diplomacy when the ceremony was designed to present Henry as King of *France*.

Beaufort even had the English coronation ceremony used in place of the traditional French rite.

Almost everything went wrong for the English cause that day. The coronation banquet at the Hôtel de Ville could not seat all those who came, and as quarrelling broke out over places the Paris mob burst in and raided the tables for food. Even the poor complained of the meagre leftovers distributed to them. The silver-gilt flagon that held the communion wine was grabbed by one of the English, and the chapter would later take legal proceedings to regain it.[8] The crowning of 'Henri II' of France thus did little for his acceptance as king. Philip of Burgundy was conspicuously absent.

Joan of Arc had now been sold to the English, and Beaufort took an interest in her trial and condemnation. Burgundy had made a separate truce with Charles VII just before, and England's alliance with Burgundy hung by a thread. But the loss of the Pucelle had shaken the Dauphinists, and for a few years the war was again going the English way.

Legend has Cardinal Beaufort playing an important part in the trial and execution of Joan of Arc at Rouen. The English certainly wanted it to happen this way, for it would have vindicated their stance in this affair, but Beaufort's own part in the matter is complex. Bedford at least believed she was an incarnate fiend, a witch or an agent of Satan, but it is unclear if Beaufort agreed or if he was simply bent on eradicating this propaganda threat to the English conquest.[9]

Beaufort was not as prominent in the trial as thought, but his participation is certain. He was present in the party that met John of Luxembourg when he handed Joan over to the English. Beaufort was listed once in the records of the trial itself, as the most senior prelate present during the session on 24 May 1431, but he did not take the leadership role he would usually insist upon. He closely associated with Pierre Cauchon, Bishop of Beauvais, who headed the trial and who was intent enough on condemning Joan as a heretic, but otherwise remained in the background of the affair. He held one of the three keys to Joan's prison.[10] Beaufort was apparently intent on making sure that the French clergy condemned Joan for witchcraft and heresy rather than making her a martyr to the English, so his role called for discretion.

The matter had serious diplomatic constraints where the pro-English French clergy were concerned, and undue pressure from the English could damage their complicity. Cauchon wanted her burned, but when Joan did agree to abjure her belief that she was a divine appointee he was obliged to accept her repentance. Whether or not Beaufort wanted her to burn, he had to apply his diplomatic skills to calm relations, but only until she was tricked into apparently relapsing six days later.

When an English chaplain hectored Cauchon during the proceedings, saying that he was being too lenient to the accused, Beaufort instantly commanded him to hold his tongue. He had no time for insubordination, but also knew that the French could easily change their minds in the matter. With the assent of Cauchon and others he could eventually report to Bedford that the myth that God wanted Joan to save France from the English had finally been discredited. It was Beaufort who ordered that after the burning Joan's ashes be scattered in the river, for he knew the power of martyrs' relics.[11]

With the coronation and other business concluded, the royal entourage finally went home. The king, Bedford, Beaufort and many of the senior nobles of England had been in France for nearly three years when the royal party finally landed at Dover in February 1432. The cardinal, who preceded them with the mission of raising funds for Bedford's further campaigning, soon found himself under attack by his old enemy.

While almost all the great were out of the country for the French coronation Gloucester had far more power in England than ever before, and many conceded that he was fairly successful in his role. The first year passed without major incident, and his attempts at a new truce with Scotland had no lasting results but at least maintained good relations for a time. He was forced to deal with a rebellion led by one William Perkins, who called himself 'Jack Sharpe', and later found him in hiding at Oxford. This rising was said to have been inspired by Lollardy, but few details survive other than the subsequent execution of its leader.

There were some complaints, such as that of Lord Cromwell who complained that the duke had dismissed him from his office of chamberlain contrary to the original ordinances. But Gloucester was known for strong government, with many transgressors executed; his first biographer credited him with a 'firm and true justice'.[12] But even as he showed that he could perform a regent's duties with competence, the duke was preparing to renew his onslaught against the cardinal.

Gloucester told the council that Beaufort should have given up his Winchester see on becoming cardinal and should have to repay the revenues gained since. The Bishop of Gloucester spoke of a papal dispensation severing the see and city of Winchester from the jurisdiction of Canterbury that the Bishop of Lincoln had been told to obtain for Beaufort. That in itself was a valid instance of *praemunire*, and Beaufort was served with a writ as soon as he landed in November 1431. In addition Gloucester had purged the council of all committed supporters of either Beaufort or Bedford, among them Archbishop Kemp, the Earl of Huntingdon, Ralph Cromwell and Lord Tiptoft. He even added a charge of treason to the list of accusations against the cardinal.

Beaufort had tried to remove his own plate and jewels from the country, but Gloucester ordered them seized before he could.[13] Charged to appear before Parliament, he was informed of the charges beforehand and struck back quickly. He offered to lend the king £6,000 if he would delay collection on an outstanding payment of 13,000 marks, and offered a further £6,000 for the recovery of his own plate and jewels, which mollified the opposition. Gloucester was met with a general unwillingness to proceed with the charge of *praemunire*, and Beaufort even gained assurances from the council of immunity from any such action. Without the required support Gloucester was once again forced to abandon his attack.

Cardinal Beaufort again took his place on the council. His hat would always complicate issues, but he would never consider giving up his status in England – not completely. Cardinal or not, he would remain a powerful force in England and his feud with Duke Humphrey would not end for as long as they both lived.

6

WAR AND PEACE

King Henry VI was eleven when he returned from his coronation in France. There was still every expectation that he would grow into a king as illustrious as his father, but his minority was nowhere near its end and the same problems remained with little sign of resolution. The vendetta between Cardinal Beaufort and Humphrey, Duke of Gloucester was also far from over.

John Beaufort (I), first Earl of Somerset had produced six children who would be the entire second generation of the Beaufort family. Joan Beaufort (II) had risen the farthest, as Queen of Scotland, but it was already family tradition for the men to serve the Lancastrian kings as soldiers, administrators and counsellors. While Henry Beaufort (I) was now one of the most powerful men in England, the second generation had little opportunity to excel at this time. Henry (II) had died young and Baugé had been a serious early setback to John (II) and Thomas (II), sending both into a long and comfortable captivity when their military careers had just begun. John had already spent a decade as a prisoner and there was still no sign of his deliverance.

Cardinal Beaufort pressed for his nephews' release. The problem with the elder John, third Earl of Somerset lay with the fine bargaining details of the exchanging or ransoming of prisoners.

None were able or willing to pay the ransom and the English had no prisoners of equivalent rank that they would part with as an exchange. John therefore remained an unwilling guest in France for years to come. His mother, the Duchess of Clarence, gained custody of the Count of Angoulême in the hope of exchanging this prisoner for her son, but nothing came of it.

Cardinal Beaufort was in control of vast sums of money, and it is surprising that he did not attempt a loan for his nephew's ransom. Absence of recorded information makes speculation on this matter pointless, but John was later known to resent the widespread failure to obtain his release. Revenues from the estates of the Somerset earldom and other incomes should have been useful in raising ransom money, but even after so many years there was no sign of this. An earl was an expensive person to ransom, and John remained in captivity for an inordinately long time.

Thomas was much easier to deliver. His lower status made his release more straightforward and certainly less expensive, and after some negotiation by his uncle the cardinal he had been freed by December 1427 for 7,000 marks, 3,000 of which he brought back with him. Soon after his return he was created Count of Perche, a lordship that the Earl of Salisbury had held until his recent death. Thomas and his younger brother Edmund took part in the defence of Paris in 1429 and Thomas was certainly making up for lost time in the following years as a competent soldier. He died unmarried and without issue at the siege of Louviers in 1431.

The career of Edmund Beaufort took a while to get going, but he and his sister Joan were the two most successful of the second generation. With his elder brothers and sisters he grew up in the household of Thomas, Duke of Clarence and later trained for knighthood and command. At seventeen Edmund was approaching an age where he might take part in the fighting but was not present on the fateful campaign of 1421. It is not known where he spent the five years following his stepfather's death, but he almost certainly entered the service of a greater noble. This was probably the Duke of Bedford, given their later association and his subsequent military role, or perhaps the Earl of Warwick; he later married one of the latter's daughters. It has also been suggested that Edmund lived in the household of his uncle the Duke of Exeter and was sent to France after the household was broken up following the duke's death.[1] He is first mentioned in royal records on 25 February 1427 when commissioned to muster at Sandwich with the Earl of Huntingdon and other captains, where he was listed as a knight.[2]

There is oblique reference to a controversy in 1426 or 1427 when Katherine de Valois, Dowager Queen of England and mother of the king, expressed her wish to remarry to Edmund Beaufort. Parliament, at the urging of Archbishop Chichele and some other prelates, put an end to such plans but the matter begs questions. The business is discussed at length in Appendix V.

As the youngest of the first Earl of Somerset's sons Edmund was disadvantaged. He had no material resources of his own and military seniority largely depended on social status, but he was an able young soldier, very much in the style of his late father and uncle Exeter, and he got results. When Edmund arrived in France in April 1427 Bedford made him Count of Mortain.[3] This was another example of Bedford appointing his captains to the French nobility for the administering and defence of a part of Normandy, just as his brother Thomas was later made Count of Perche, but Edmund would have needed to show some ability to gain the appointment. Now that the English occupied such large areas it became the practice to hand out French titles and lordships to English commanders; the French nobles who refused to recognise the Lancastrian monarchy were dispossessed, and it was customary to grant the English captains titles senior to those they held in England, giving them a stake in the conquest. John, Lord Talbot was Count of Vendôme, for instance, and Sir John Fastolf held three baronies.

When Edmund took over Mortain, the county was theoretically worth revenues of 3,000 *livres tournois*, but its real returns were much eroded after long warfare. This was only the beginning of a long career in command; apart from the time he accompanied his uncle on the Bohemian crusade and his own diplomatic mission to Scotland, Edmund served almost continuously in France for over two decades. He was soon Captain of Gisors, Neufchâtel and Gournay, and Bedford made him Constable of the Army with a salary of 250 *tournois*. In 1431 he gave assistance to the Duke of Burgundy in the Louviers campaign.[4] His participation in the crusade to Bohemia was almost in imitation of his father's expedition to Lithuania some thirty years previously. In 1434 he was one of the lay ambassadors to the Council of Basel,[5] and in 1436 he was made Constable and Captain of Aberystwyth. Wales was comparatively quiet by this time, and the posting brought more material gains than responsibilities.[6] He has other mentions in the Chancery records, mostly over grants of the marriage of minors, but despite his status in Normandy as Count of Mortain Edmund did not attract much attention in England until the events of 1436.[7]

Cardinal Beaufort had been a lifelong supporter of Conciliarism, which advocated councils of churchmen to solve the Church's problems, and as soon as his duties concerning the double coronation were completed he travelled to the Council of Basel as an English delegate. Despite the successes of Constance and the widespread desire to hold periodic ecumenical councils, however, this gathering began the collapse of the movement.

The Council of Basel had begun on a note of optimism. It was felt that much could be accomplished, even reuniting the Eastern and Western Churches. But Pope Martin V had died in March 1431, soon after it began, and his successor Eugenius IV had a varying agenda. The council dragged on for several years, adjourning to Ferrara in 1437, but from the outset it was at odds with Eugenius, who tried to dissolve it against its will. Beaufort soon lost interest and returned to England in 1433. Surprisingly for one who had always advocated Conciliarism he gave his support to the pope in this affair and urged the young king to follow his lead.

Meanwhile Bedford and Gloucester were at loggerheads. Having returned to England, Bedford was now in charge again and restored to the council several people whom his brother had removed. Gloucester was pressing for yet more charges of *praemunire* against the cardinal, demanding that his wealth be appropriated to finance a new expedition he wished to undertake. Even the king, now in his early teens, was exhorting his two uncles to make peace. Bedford soon returned to France, again leaving Gloucester in charge, but ensured that the council had a tighter hold on his brother.

The two coronations in France, of Charles VII in Reims and 'Henri II' in Paris, had put paid to any hopes of a peaceful settlement. For the English to achieve peace would mean all of France recognising the Lancastrian monarchy and resistance in Charles's name ceasing completely. Once Charles had affirmed his own claim to the throne Bedford had no choice but to prosecute the war.

Once the Joan of Arc affair had ended in the flames and recent losses had been recovered, the English had reason to be optimistic. However, the attitude of Philip the Good was still Bedford's prime cause for unease. The matter of Jacqueline of Hainault had finally come to an end, with Philip taking half her revenues and Gloucester out of the picture. But once again Philip was making overtures to Charles, having agreed to another truce in 1430 independent of his English allies. In February 1430 during the coronation expedition Cardinal Beaufort had visited Philip and persuaded him to renew the alliance. Philip had agreed, but then entered into his truce with the Dauphinists and extended it another six years. His absence at the Paris coronation was also ominous.

Bedford's wife Anne of Burgundy died in 1432. This was a sad day for him, but within a year he had remarried to Jacquetta, niece of the Count of Luxembourg. This was still a match within the Burgundian sphere of influence but it angered Philip to hear that Bedford had married again so soon after his sister's death. Anne had been a calming influence when Bedford and Philip quarrelled.

In April 1433, Bedford and Gloucester visited Calais for peace talks. They waited a whole month but the French failed to appear. The Burgundians were also present, but seemed restless. They had established a secret channel of communication with the Duke of Orleans, who, although a prisoner in England since 1415, had his own political agenda. By 1433, the Burgundians saw little point in remaining on the English side. They had made their gains, and cooperation with a foreign power had proved highly unpopular, so they were looking for a pretext to break their promises. They had been poor allies for the English since Verneuil, but they remained vital if there was to be any widespread French acceptance of the Lancastrian monarchy.

Bedford had been the best possible successor to Henry V as leader of the English war machine, but by 1435 he was dying. Thirteen years of continually fighting the French on one side and preventing Burgundy from wandering away on the other had taken a severe toll on his constitution.

Philip certainly did not reveal his own agenda to his English allies when he pressed for the English and French to meet in conference at Arras in the summer of 1435. He had briefed his chancellor, Nicholas Rolin, to make peace with Charles even if the English would not; he was ready to change sides. At the same time Charles was arriving at the same place; the anti-Burgundy counsellor La Trémouille had been forced out of his court and Charles's mother-in-law Yolande of Aragon now found it easier to persuade him to seek an accord with Philip. One stumbling block still blocked Philip's plans, however. In 1420 he had sworn to uphold the terms of the Treaty of Troyes and was therefore committed to supporting the Lancastrian succession to the Kingdom of France. Philip was founder of the Order of the Golden Fleece, which demanded high standards of behaviour, and he did not wish to be seen as the breaker of a solemn oath.

The English were not at all enthusiastic over this conference; while they sought to consolidate their hold on Paris a ceasefire was not at all in their interest. They did make a big show of their appearance at the gathering, but it is unlikely that they expected to resolve the main dispute at Arras. Bedford, on his sickbed at Rouen, was unable to attend but dictated the brief that the title of King of France for Henry was non-negotiable.

Philip's third duchess, Isabel of Portugal, was accessible to the English as John of Gaunt's granddaughter and therefore Cardinal Beaufort's niece. While the cardinal corresponded with her, the English did not know that she was in receipt of a pension from Charles VII and was seeking to sway Burgundy towards his side at Arras.

Archbishop Kemp was nominal head of the English delegation and his party included the bishops of Norwich and St David's and the earls of Warwick, Huntingdon and Suffolk.[8] When the delegation moved from Calais towards Arras, Cardinal Beaufort remained behind in the coastal town; he had a brief beyond simply making peace with the Armagnac–Dauphinist faction. Aware of the developing situation, he was left free to negotiate with Philip separately, and the duke visited him several times. There was another hidden agenda as well; since Philip had imposed an embargo on the Flemings importing English cloth, Beaufort also had powers to negotiate separately with the Four Members, the main cloth-trading towns of Flanders. The cardinal was not due to arrive at the Congress until after such negotiations had broken down.

The delegates assembled in the Benedictine monastery of St Vaast on 8 August. The French themselves, fronted by the

Duke of Bourbon and their chancellor the Archbishop of Reims, sought peace too but had their own brief to end their civil war. A number of offers from the English – leaving France south of the Loire to Charles, keeping Normandy in full sovereignty – met with little enthusiasm. One suggestion was the marriage of Henry VI to one of Charles's daughters, but this too saw little progress. The French suggested an English evacuation of all France, but this was far from realistic to expect. A permanent peace could not be made while King Henry was still a minor, and a truce was not too attractive to either side. The English could only be satisfied with the acknowledgement of Henry as King of France, and the French were neither briefed for such a step nor for a complete surrender. Talks had certainly broken down when Beaufort sped from Calais in a last attempt to save the Burgundian alliance, which he knew was in more serious danger.

Since Henry V's day the English had believed wholeheartedly that their king was King of France. Rather than use the claim as a detail in bargaining as Edward III had done in 1360, they refused to consider any retreat from their position. Now that Charles VII had felt the crown on his head he was similarly committed, and Arras was the meeting point of their collision course. This precluded any agreement on the English holding Normandy as it could only be in full sovereignty, and not as a vassal of the French king. The English were accused of inflexibility, but they saw neither the need nor the justification to abandon their claim. On 1 September Cardinal Beaufort led the English withdrawal from the congress.

Although many English saw the peace talks themselves a useless charade, they were soon conscious of the danger their fundamental policy had fallen into. Once the English delegation withdrew, Philip and Charles's representatives could hardly be more cooperative. Rolin cynically presented an argument that would release Philip the Good from his oath in the Treaty of Troyes, explaining that his duke had sworn specifically to assure the succession of Henry V to the crown of France on the death of King Charles VI and that Henry V had died a few weeks *before* the King of France; nothing in the oath provided for Henry VI taking his father's place in the succession.

To complement this spurious pronouncement Charles's agents produced their own argument that no king of France could alienate the royal succession. Charles was willing to do penance over the earlier murder of John the Fearless. Philip kept Ponthieu, the Mâconnais, the counties of Boulogne and Auxerre and some of the towns on the Somme, all gained in his time of association with the English. It was Burgundy who profited most from Arras.

During the talks the Burgundian delegation was seriously split over this change of allegiance and some such as Jean of Luxembourg condemned it as a mistake, but Philip decided to proceed and the French civil war of three decades was over. Even to use the term 'Armagnac' to describe alignment would invoke severe penalties. The Duke of Burgundy and all of his faction were the loyal subjects of Charles VII, and none would question their allegiance. In England the boy king wept on receiving a letter from Philip that simply addressed him as 'Henry, King of *England*'. Some said in retrospect that Philip should have stayed on the English side, for it was to his benefit to keep the French monarchy weak; a generation later the recovered Valois monarchy would destroy the Burgundian state that Philip had left to his son.

Could Beaufort and his fellow delegates have made a success of Arras? The timing was not the best for the English, given their activity in Paris. They were also still sure that they were winning and saw little need for concessions. But to show so little care over the disposition of the Burgundians was a colossal mistake.

For all that the English had done to maintain the Burgundian alliance they could never rely on it, for Philip had simply fought his own war with the Dauphinists and kept to the alliance only when it suited him. After Verneuil he had given the English precious little aid in the field, even withdrawing his troops from Orleans in 1428 when they could have aided the taking of the city. While the English, most of all Bedford, laboured to keep Burgundy on side at all costs, they almost certainly knew that Philip would decide sooner or later that the alliance could do him no more good. That day had arrived.

Did Cardinal Beaufort, by his dramatic walkout at the Congress of Arras, commit the worst gaffe in the entire Hundred Years War? Beaufort had met with Philip shortly before, and probably knew of his talks with the Armagnacs. Perhaps he could read the writing on the wall and knew that the Anglo-Burgundian accord was doomed; his two secret briefs show awareness that the alliance was unstable. Beaufort had always been a strong advocate of the pro-Burgundian policy, but perhaps even he knew it was coming to an end. He might have walked out simply to save face.

It could be argued that the English had little to gain from Arras in any case and were annoyed at Philip's calling the conference at that time. They might have laboured to keep the Burgundians from defecting at that point, which was prudent given their importance in Paris, but it is hard to say how much longer they could have maintained the alliance, especially after Philip had gained Jacqueline's lands. The gathering at Arras was simply a staged opportunity for Philip to change alignment, and could not have brought peace whatever else happened.

Many of the English did not share Bedford's concern for the alliance, nor were they so well disposed towards Burgundy. When he died at Rouen on 14 September that year John, Duke of Bedford probably knew that his life's work was all for nothing. Philip formally returned to the allegiance of the Valois monarch eleven days later.

Cardinal Beaufort and John, Duke of Bedford had been an effective double act throughout the reign, Beaufort supplying funds and support for his nephew to fight the wars in France while he himself helped to maintain the governance of England. Bedford's death must have been a sad blow to the cardinal. When his will was read twelve years later it showed that he had made provision for masses said for his soul and for some members of his family. Those specified were Kings Henry V and VI, Beaufort's parents and siblings, and also John, Duke of Bedford, the only individual outside this family and royal grouping that Beaufort chose to honour after his death.[9]

The outcome at Arras had left the English position seriously damaged. The writ of Henry Plantagenet now only ran in Calais, Normandy, Maine and Guyenne, and not everywhere in these territories, while Paris was not as easily held without the support of the Burgundians. After Arras there were popular risings when Dieppe was suddenly taken, and Fécamp, Harfleur and other important towns were also quickly lost. In February 1436 the Constable de Richemont and the Bastard of Orleans besieged Paris. The English commander, Lord Willoughby, found the city cut off and without even the support that the pro-Burgundian elements had given them. He tried to coerce the Parisians into compliance, but this and near starvation only added to the plight of the English garrison. There was rioting and over 400 English soldiers deserted during the siege when their pay was not forthcoming. In April the French gained entry to the city by a rope ladder that some Parisians let down for them and took possession of a gate. Willoughby obtained safe conduct to leave Paris with his men some days later.

Bedford's death left a serious void. Among other roles a new Captain of Calais was needed. The position initially went to Sir Richard Woodville as Bedford's lieutenant, but on 1 November 1435 Gloucester secured the post despite already being Warden of the Cinque Ports. He received the lordship of the Channel Islands three weeks later.

In the eyes of Cardinal Beaufort and his allies, there was one more ominous development concerning John Duke of Bedford's death: despite his two marriages Bedford had begotten no legitimate children. King Henry VI was still a minor and his marriage was not even on the horizon. Humphrey, Duke of Gloucester was now next in line to the throne.

The political fallout of the failure at Arras settled in part on Cardinal Beaufort, who was always identified with the pro-Burgundian policy. It was thought that his perceived standing at the papal Curia would serve the English cause, but the legate Cardinal Albergati had strongly opposed the English claim to France at Arras. Not only was there a new pope who wished for Charles's support at Basel but the regard that Beaufort had gained among the Curia dimmed after he abandoned the Bohemian crusade. The Londoners and others affected by the cloth embargo in the Low Countries maligned him as well. In reality there was little that he could have done given the duplicity of Burgundian policies, and it is in part due to his efforts that the alliance lasted so long. Gloucester did not exploit the issue to attack his uncle at this point, but he did bring it up to advance his own position.

While Paris was under siege a new problem emerged. Philip the Good had returned to the Valois fold, and as soon as the campaigning season began in 1436 he went on the offensive against Calais. He might at first have wondered if it was a good idea to alienate the English, who supplied wool to his Flemish textile towns, but he had plans to deal with this and by defecting he had left himself little choice but to declare war on England. He engaged in a secret meeting with the Four Members over his planned attack on Calais, knowing that the Flemings resented the restrictions imposed by the Staple. A spy at the meeting relayed the information to the English but at quite short notice.

At the end of June an army composed of the Burgundian lords and their followings, swelled by levies from the Flemish and Picardian towns, entered the March of Calais. They forced the surrender of the smaller castles of Marck, Oye and Sangatte, destroying each by fire. Gloucester as Captain of Calais was raising an army in England to defend the town but was nowhere near ready to set off. By that time Cardinal Beaufort had produced a force of about 4,500, mostly archers, and despatched them to recover Paris under the leadership of his nephew Edmund Beaufort, Count of Mortain. With the agreement of the council Gloucester urged the diversion of this host to Calais and Edmund, then at Winchelsea, set forth to lift the siege.

With his lieutenants Lord Camoys and Sir Richard Ashton, Edmund landed with his army near Boulogne and ravaged its suburbs. He also ordered a raid on Loos. Driving a herd of cattle to supply the besieged he led his troops to Calais. It is said that he did not lose a single soldier en route.[10]

By 9 July Philip the Good had encamped near the walls of Calais and was seeking to breach the defences of the town itself. Calais was not only surrounded by a double wall and double moat, but then by marshland that made catapults and cannon difficult to place. During the summer such marshes were comparatively dry but flies were then a constant annoyance. A garrison of professional soldiers was a permanent fixture, hence the severe expense the kings of England required for its upkeep. The Burgundians prepared to turn their cannon on the town walls and Philip ordered the blockading of the harbour by having twenty ships loaded with rubble scuttled in it.

But Edmund and his force fought hard. They had the ships emptied of the rubble at low tide and used it to build. Edmund then attacked the half-hearted Flemish troops and put them to flight. With the men of Ghent becoming mutinous, Philip realised that little more could be done. When Gloucester and his army arrived at Calais soon after, the invaders withdrew. The real danger having passed, Gloucester could only order a raid into Flemish territory.[11]

Despite the poor quality of the troops Philip brought to Calais the English possession was in genuine danger in 1436. Philip had systematically destroyed some of the castles of the March and Guines was heavily damaged despite holding out. The defences of Calais itself were daunting to any attacker, but the presence of so many cannon shows how seriously Philip was taking the siege. Edmund had ordered the hanging of William of Bulleyn, who had mysteriously walked free to the town after the taking of Oye and was considered a traitor. The *Brut* mentions one more traitor and it is likely that Philip had men planted in the town who would open a gate at an opportune time; such was a common strategy in medieval sieges.[12]

It would have been a psychological blow to the English to see Calais threatened. In typical manner the English had not been as vigilant as they could have been, exemplified by its captain being the absentee Gloucester. Then again, years of nominal alliance with Burgundy had lulled the English into a false sense of security.

It is erroneous to say that by saving Calais the English lost Paris, for Paris had already fallen before Edmund Beaufort's force had set sail. The original plan might have been to send this force to lift the siege on Paris but events overtook them, and then they could only have attempted to win the city back – no mean feat once the French had taken possession. At least this army made a difference given the last-minute diversion. Calais was still in English hands more than a century later, and not until then did the French make any new attempt on it.

Gloucester won much acclaim for saving Calais, but it was also recognised that Edmund Beaufort had played a vital part in maintaining the defence at the most critical time. Edmund was gaining prestige, often on opportunities gained through his uncle's patronage. He was a delegate at the Congress of Arras and Constable of Aberystwyth Castle. By 1436 he had married Eleanor Beauchamp, widow of Lord Roos and daughter of the Earl of

Warwick by his first wife. Edmund had acquitted himself well in serving his king and reprised the prestigious acts of his father and uncle as military commanders. During the defence of Calais he was sent the Garter. There was a popular ballad of his relief of Calais, which is reproduced in Appendix VI.

There is a story concerning Edmund's marriage, but the details are lost to history. He married Eleanor without royal licence; he almost certainly had the agreement of Warwick, but the circumstances were uncertain given the decree ten years beforehand that the king had to consent to the remarriage of any widow. The king nonetheless indicated his retrospective assent and pardoned Edmund for the act,[13] and the couple went on to have ten children. Edmund's appointment as Constable of Windsor Castle for life two months later shows him very much in favour; this was a prestigious grant, although he avoided visiting in person while under a prophecy concerning his death beneath a castle. He was also granted the lifelong annuity of 500 marks his late mother had held.[14]

Cardinal Beaufort renewed his efforts to obtain the release of Edmund's elder brother John, Earl of Somerset, still imprisoned in France after sixteen years. The Count of Eu, a prisoner in England since Agincourt, was of equivalent social rank, but Henry V had stipulated before his own death that Eu must not be released until his son was of full age. After the cardinal had pulled some strings to have the count transferred to Edmund's custody, and with the minority of Henry VI due to end soon after, Edmund set about a year-long process of negotiation. John finally returned to England in 1437.

John Beaufort (II) was not the best example of his family. His years as a prisoner had not only harmed his physical health but it was likely that his mental condition had suffered too. He harboured a deep resentment for being left in captivity for so long. It was hard to raise the necessary ransom for him or find a suitable exchange, but some might say that more effort could have been made. Once free he was appointed Captain of Cherbourg; as a noble and Prince of the Blood he was in demand for such a role. In 1439 he was engaged in an unsuccessful attempt to recover Meaux, but the following year he prevented a French army from relieving Harfleur while his brother Edmund was besieging the town.[15]

As soon as John returned to England he apparently used his feudal resources to raise further monies to pay the outstanding portion of his ransom. The Abbey of Crowland felt the force John's methods in relation to his nearby manor of Deeping in Lincolnshire when his local officials meticulously levied tolls and charges for impounding strayed livestock and also barred the abbot from passage on their embankment. The returned earl was far from popular in some places.[16]

There were misgivings in 1437 over Gloucester taking his dead brother's place as Lieutenant of France with Cardinal Beaufort, Kemp, Cromwell and others feeling it would give him too much power. His track record was not encouraging where sustained efforts were needed and so these counsellors laboured to make the Earl of Warwick the new lieutenant instead. They succeeded, but had trouble persuading Warwick to accept the position; the ageing earl felt unsuited for such an active role.[17] He replaced the young Richard of York, who had briefly held the office and was becoming an active commander in the post-Bedford era.

That year also saw the minority of Henry VI come to an end. He was only sixteen, so this was expecting much of him even at a time when boys were expected to grow up quickly. It had been a long and costly minority, and everyone looked to the young king with high hopes for the return of decisive government. After Bedford died it was decided to prepare the handover of the reins and in the following two years Henry was introduced to the ways of kingship. At this time none of his failings were apparent and he was expected to develop in wisdom and martial virtues. It was of course accepted that an inexperienced young king would need wise counsellors and at least some of the council of regency would now act in this capacity.

The royal council was in part a continuation of that of the regency. Gloucester and Cardinal Beaufort were its two most senior members, and Archbishops Chichele and Kemp also remained, as did the earls of Huntingdon, Northumberland and Stafford, Lord Cromwell and several of the bishops. The five new appointees included Richard Neville, Earl of Salisbury, who as Joan Beaufort's eldest and the cardinal's nephew hints at continuing Beaufort influence, but really he had a standing of his own, having been Warden of the West March. The new council was certainly appointed under advice, and was in fact fairly balanced and conservative in nature. It might have tended towards Beaufort's influence, but it did not initially include Somerset or his brother.[18]

On the death of Bishop Langley in 1437, Robert Neville was again advanced somewhat by his translation to the see of Durham. Considering the controversy of ten years ago this shows the lasting power of the cardinal, for this was an important consolidation of the Middleham Nevilles' hold over the north: the Bishop of Durham was all but king of the county itself and several outlying territories.

Life for Joan Beaufort (II), Queen of Scotland, had taken a dramatic turn in 1437. She had produced eight children and her six daughters had all married into the princely families of Europe, save for one who married the Scottish Earl of Morton. She had twin sons in 1430, one of whom died at birth and while the other would go on to become James II. Her husband had been a vigorous reformer who sought to limit the powers of the nobles. In the course of his policies James had made many enemies, in particular Walter Stewart, Robert Stewart and Robert Graham. On 20 February 1437, these three decided to murder the king while he lodged with his queen at the Friary in Perth.

Joan witnessed the sordid killing and barely escaped with her life. Just as the assassins rounded on her one of them said it unnecessary to kill her too, stating dismissively that 'she is but a woman', and Joan got away in this moment of indecision. She then turned her efforts to revenge. Although an unpopular choice as both a woman and English, Joan gained the regency for her son and took revenge on her husband's killers. She then had to contend with the appointment of the Earl of Douglas as co-regent, and she took the dramatic step of forming an alliance with Sir James Stewart, Black Knight of Lorne, whom she married in 1439 and with whom she had three sons. Joan spent the following decade intriguing and was at times imprisoned by her enemies. She struggled with Sir William Crichton and Alexander Livingston, gaining and then losing custody of her son. Joan died in 1445 and her son assumed personal rule four years later as James II.

There was no resolution in sight over the continuation of the Lancastrian dynasty, Henry VI himself the sum total of the house's third generation. Gloucester was heir presumptive but there were many, Cardinal Beaufort among them, who cringed at the thought of him as the next king, although it remained a real possibility at this stage.

But even then there was no clear candidate to follow Gloucester, the king's senior by over thirty years. His two children were illegitimate and after a decade of marriage to Eleanor Cobham no issue had appeared. In an age of uncertain lifespans, if the king and Gloucester failed to produce at least one son between them within wedlock, who would come next? The House of Lancaster would be exhausted, and no clear order of succession was established beyond it.

Some felt Richard of York would come next in line as he was the only other remaining Plantagenet, but there was scope for dispute. Where did the stain of his father's treason leave him after the plot of 1415? It was also uncertain whether the crown could pass in the female line. Some said it could, for the kings were pretenders to the throne of France through Edward III's mother Isabella Capet and there were several nobles related to the kings on the distaff side who could be put forward as candidates. John Holland, Earl of Huntingdon could then place his claim through his mother Elizabeth, daughter of Henry IV. There was also the vague but perceptible claim of the Beauforts themselves. If the Lancastrians and the other Plantagenets were exhausted then the issue of John of Gaunt and Katherine, their bastardy erased by Act of Parliament, might be considered. This made John, Earl of Somerset a contender, followed by his surviving brother Edmund, Count of Mortain.

But all these candidacies could have been challenged, possibly by force of arms, and the succession would have been very messy indeed. Only the incumbent King Henry and then Humphrey had clear claims, and it is even possible that some would find ways of challenging the latter. After 1407 did any of the Beauforts believe they could be kings? If they did, none of them voiced this idea for it would have been dangerous, but one could wonder how seriously they took such a possibility. There was no attempt to define the order of succession beyond the House of Lancaster, politically sensitive as this was. Most simply hoped that King Henry would marry in due course and present an heir to his throne, preferably with other sons to follow, and then live long enough for to rule out another long regency.

There was little good news over the French wars now. Arras was clearly the end of an era and many, Cardinal Beaufort included, came to the conclusion that once the Burgundians had crossed over there was no possibility of a final victory and the best ending was an honourable peace where the English kept what they held. Beaufort had every reason to conclude that England would eventually be bankrupt if it continued what was now an unwinnable war.

But this war had been an important part of the lives of the English aristocracy for generations, and it was hard for many old soldiers to envisage abandoning ground they had long fought over once it was lost. Sir John Fastolf believed it could still be won, as one influential captain of the wars who advocated returning to Edward III's policy of *chevauchées*, highly destructive raids into French territory. Now Gloucester set himself up as advocate of those who would only be satisfied by total victory, and he championed the wishes of the ageing campaigners to whom cutting losses was unpalatable. It is unlikely that Gloucester attempted the arithmetic, but he was never one for such mundane details.

But the French war was not only unwinnable but unstoppable while Charles was in no mind to consider peace. There was a French attack on Rouen in 1436 which Talbot repulsed, soon retaking the castles the French had occupied. Through 1437 there was further fighting when Talbot stormed the walls of Paris without success. In 1438 the French invaded Guyenne in strength but were again beaten back. Despite all this, even to maintain what the English held was expensive.

In 1439 the debate was still unresolved. In April that year the Earl of Warwick died in harness; his appointment really did suit a younger man as he had maintained. The young king, with little understanding of the real situation, himself favoured peace and endorsed the cardinal's search for it. Through lack of experience and a poor grasp of affairs generally he was unable to see the real issues involved. In February Cardinal Beaufort made further use of his family connection by making a new truce with Burgundy, where the duchess acknowledged her '*tresami oncle*'.[19] Philip the Good saw no advantage for the war to continue and again called for a tripartite conference.

The Duke of Orleans, a prisoner in England since his capture at Agincourt, was on the agenda. Henry V had ordered that he not be released on other than exceptional terms, but contrary to Gloucester's reminders the council used him in the bargaining because they thought he might be able to aid the peace process. He took part in talks with the Duke of Brittany in 1438.

In June 1439 the delegations of England, France and Burgundy met at Gravelines, near the north-eastern limit of the Calais March and nearest they could come to neutral ground, where they built a small town of wooden buildings for the purpose. The king first made Archbishop Kemp head of the delegation, instructing that no concessions on territory or sovereignty be made and that Orleans should be ransomed for 100,000 marks. Then he made Cardinal Beaufort his plenipotentiary with a wider brief altogether. This change of mind probably happened when after Beaufort spoke with him privately, knowing how pliable his royal great-nephew could be.

The conference soon reached stalemate. The English believed that the French were playing games and generally prevaricating, and the French decided that the other side was simply playing for time. When the initial proposals were deadlocked Beaufort discussed a new package with the Duchess, which examined the possibility of Henry renouncing the title of King of France and keeping Calais, Normandy and Gascony. There would be a long truce in which a permanent peace could be made, and Orleans could go home without payment. Although the two agreed verbally they could not reach a written statement over it; Beaufort was unwilling to take on the responsibility of giving away the French crown. In July the conference agreed an adjournment until 11 September and the English delegates went to try the proposals on the king in England.

But Gloucester, dominating the king's council on this issue in the cardinal's absence, persuaded Henry to condemn the proposals outright. The king was pressured on both sides and in Beaufort's absence Gloucester had the best chance to turn him against the idea of relinquishing his French claim. The terms Beaufort raised were closer to his own views, realistic for the status quo after

Arras, but with the French not at all keen on conceding territory it is unlikely that they would have finally agreed to them either. A French army just having taken Meaux, Charles and his ministers lost interest in the peace talks and their envoys did not bother to return.[20] Beaufort did salvage one success from the meeting at least, concluding a commercial treaty with his niece the duchess, but the main talks had failed.

But negotiations had not closed and Beaufort continued to pursue peace. He still believed that the Duke of Orleans, disappointed by the talks at Gravelines, could be of use while freed, and pressed for this. He finally saw Orleans released on 12 November 1440, but at a serious political cost when Gloucester again exploited the decision and launched yet another attack on his uncle. He condemned the move in council, saying that the French duke could not be trusted to work for peace. He did bring a ransom of 40,000 marks, of which the Duchess of Burgundy helped raise the initial third, but Orleans really did little after his release and the ransom was the only real gain for the English.

Initially leading the opposition to Orleans' release, Gloucester widened his offensive against Beaufort. He renewed accusations of *praemunire*, usury and holding his English see while a cardinal, to which he added that Beaufort had taken advantage of the king's 'tendre age' to his own advantage and had even tried to give away the claim to the French crown. This was mostly a repetition of his previous attacks, but some of it had popular agreement. The cardinal and his supporters issued a counter-manifesto, but felt themselves on the defensive.

Gloucester now gained growing support from discontented elements. The council appointed him Chief Justice of South Wales as an attempt to appease him and there was also talk of him going to France again to fight. Disliked as he was at court, Gloucester was now too powerful to ignore. Early in 1441 he produced a second manifesto, now calling for peace like his rivals, but on favourable terms. The other side tried with a new statement, but their position was not very strong.

In June 1441, Gloucester was brought down in a spectacular manner. It is not known for sure if Beaufort was responsible for this but one could suspect it. The affair in part resembles a modern political scandal but holds elements that would strike minds of that age with irrational terror.

Throughout the society of the fifteenth century there was widespread fascination with the occult. Popular culture was riddled with this, from charms to cure toothache and placing pine cones in windows to consulting witches and wizards. It was much in evidence in the French court: Charles VII, while still Dauphin, was known for a fascination with prophecies and horoscopes, as were many of his courtiers. Many on both sides believed Joan of Arc to have been a witch. In 1440 the Marshal of France, Gilles de Rais, who had ridden with Joan on campaign, was burnt as a sorcerer, alchemist and Satanist. If he had first developed this interest while at Bourges he was one among many; quite a few prominent members of the Armagnac faction claimed to have made pledges with Satan.

In 1419 when Joan of Navarre, widow of Henry IV, was accused of plotting to kill Henry V by magic, she was imprisoned for three years and then returned to court as if nothing had happened. Given that this affair also involved Friar Randolf, it is possible that Gloucester himself had some interest in it. It is debatable as to whether the practitioners believed themselves scientists of the Hermetic Art from ancient Egypt or were instead at least flirting with Satan himself, but they trod dangerous legal ground as the 'dark arts', or 'nygromancy', was considered a means by which the Devil recruited his foot soldiers and worked evil in the world. As in the witch craze of later centuries, common sense was always the first casualty when a supernatural agency was suspected.

It emerged that Gloucester's wife, Eleanor Cobham, privately encouraged such practices. She had taken into her household as chaplain Master Roger Bolingbroke, an Oxford scholar whom she knew to have studied magic, and Bolingbroke associated with two other academic ecclesiastics, Thomas Southwell and John Hume, who shared his interests. It is not known whether Eleanor knew the other two personally, but she did at the same time consult with Margery Jourdain, the 'Witch of Eye', a wisewoman who lived near Westminster. Nor is it known if the three magicians associated with Margery, but as witches and wizards used different magical systems this was unlikely.

It was in 1441 that Hume inexplicably informed on his fellows. On his arrest Bolingbroke became extremely cooperative with the cardinal and implicated Eleanor in a Satanic conspiracy. He might have done so to save his own skin – he might have been offered a deal – but this did not save him from being hanged, drawn and quartered in November that year, nor Margery from the stake. Southwell would die in the Tower. Despite finding sanctuary at Westminster Abbey, the duchess was arrested and confined.

At her subsequent trial Eleanor claimed that she only consulted magic in order to conceive a child, for her husband was next in line to the throne and had no legitimate heir. The books found in her house were all of a medical nature. Now in her thirties, she might have felt that the hour was growing late for childbearing and turned to more desperate action. Unfortunately there were also found wax images in human form and others made of metal. It is hard to see how these could be used for such purposes, and with Bolingbroke now testifying that she was plotting to kill the king by magic her defence crumbled. Worse still, it was revealed that she had tried to establish by astrology and prophecy how long Henry VI would live, and that was itself deemed treason. She was sentenced to walk the streets of London for three days in penance, barefoot and in her shift, and was then imprisoned for life.

It could not have been much better for Cardinal Beaufort if he had engineered the breaking of the scandal himself. Perhaps he or one of his visited Bolingbroke in his cell and persuaded him to turn evidence, or perhaps he forced Hume to 'out' his associates in a similar way. There is no way of knowing, and so much remains unanswered on this affair. We are not sure if Eleanor was seriously trying to make her husband king by magic or was just bending the rules by consulting those of a dubious disposition and was in reality a victim of politics.

It was all but the end for Humphrey, Duke of Gloucester. He was forced to divorce his wife immediately and had to distance himself from her, but he only barely avoided the wrath of King Henry, outraged at this satanic attack on him. For a number of years Gloucester kept a low profile. He would appear on the political stage one last time, but his fall in 1441 was decisive.

Cardinal Beaufort and his associates had good reason to rejoice at the fall of this troublesome duke, but little was gained from the business. There was still an unwinnable war and an unobtainable peace to contend, and the king, still a vague and naïve youth, was not providing the leadership needed. Years of indecisive action, as before, still lay ahead.

Beaufort himself was now an old man, tiring of public life and seeing his influence at court dwindle. On the death of Joan, Countess of Westmorland in 1440 Henry Beaufort was the last of the children of John of Gaunt and Katherine Swynford. Apart from Queen Joan of Scotland, the second generation had known slow advancement up to this point while his nephews John and Edmund were making their own impressions but were yet to reach the last generation's prominence.

Cardinal Beaufort's career was now quietly fading, and although he had accomplished much he had seen his labours for victory in France come to nothing. He was personally unpopular for his efforts, but in those years he had faithfully given Bedford his full support. Henry Beaufort was a realist, though, and after 1435 he knew that the Lancastrian dream in France could no longer be fulfilled, and his subsequent policy of seeking peace while holding onto the remainder held by the English was pursued by his political successors to its ultimate failure. As the cardinal's star dimmed there was no peace. England would lose the Hundred Years War.

The cardinal's constant fights with his nephew Gloucester were partially political, certainly in the phase from 1439 to 1441. For most of the time Gloucester believed himself the rightful regent while Beaufort was sure that his nephew was unsuitable for the role. But for all that Gloucester's accusations were motivated by spite and jealousy, there was some truth in accusations that Beaufort was manipulating the young king.

Beaufort himself was committed to his mission to maintain the dual monarchy of Henry VI until the king was old enough to take charge, and to deliver England and France to his king mostly undamaged. However, his efforts would come to nothing.

7

THE FALSE PEACE AND THE LOSS OF FRANCE

Whatever satisfaction Cardinal Beaufort felt on witnessing the Duke of Gloucester's spectacular fall, it probably compensated only a little for the worsening state of affairs he was observing in England and France. Now that the English were losing the war in France and unable to make peace, all the effort and acumen that Henry Beaufort had applied over the previous four decades was proving worthless.

During the fifteen-year minority of Henry VI many contented themselves with the belief that the boy king would eventually attain his manhood and rule as successfully as his father. The assumption 'like father, like son' is seldom confirmed by experience but it was still taken as read in this era, and when a young man failed to live up to his family's expectations it drew comment.

Young Henry was nothing like his father. His performance in 1439 over the peace conference must have been cause for concern, and each year of personal rule that followed indicated a poor fit for kingship. At first this could be put down to his 'tendre age' and the naivety of adolescence, but as he approached his twenties many about him were forced into a disturbing rethink.

There have been attempts to revise assessments of the character of Henry of Windsor, who has traditionally been presented as simple-minded and given to bouts of insanity, easy prey to those who could manipulate him. Some say that he did show some presence of mind in affairs of state, but it is hard to banish the image of an obvious simpleton, qualified as it may now be, and he certainly did not succeed in dispensing astute and decisive government.

Henry for much of the time appeared vague, obsessive, cranky and unable to make well-informed decisions. Attired in tattered clothes, he performed extreme acts of religious piety, declining to eat from anything but a red plate that reminded him of the Five Wounds and hectoring the ladies of his court for wearing low-cut dresses, which he considered shameful. He tended to act on the last piece of advice he was given and could be easily manipulated into changing his mind. He was far too quick to forgive even the worst offences in an obvious caricature of Christian compassion, often when severity was thought the best policy. His bouts of madness, a condition he probably inherited from his French grandfather, only began in his thirties, but each episode did his cause serious harm. Henry is famed for funding both Eton College and King's College Cambridge, although such pious acts, typical of medieval monarchs, did not exactly compensate for his failings in ruling his countries. The fall of the Lancastrian monarchy is often attributed to the shortcomings of Henry VI and there is at least some truth in it. The best compliment he has received in recent times is a movement in English Catholicism that has resumed the campaign for his canonisation. Henry of Windsor might make a suitable saint yet, but he was a disaster as a king.

Rather than the cardinal and the council it was members of the royal household who had the king's ear after the minority ended, particularly William de la Pole, Earl (later Marquis and then Duke) of Suffolk, Steward of the Royal Household since 1435. Following the deaths of his father and elder brother on the Agincourt campaign William had inherited the earldom and had a long career as a soldier, in command towards the end of the unsuccessful siege at Orleans and afterwards captured by Joan of Arc at Jargeau. He was later keeper of the captive Duke of Orleans, and became Chamberlain of England in 1447. Yet the cardinal in the twilight of his career had few misgivings as to Suffolk's rising influence. The duke was of a similar mind to him over the French situation and also married to Beaufort's great-niece Alice Chaucer, widow of Thomas Montague, Earl of Salisbury.

Charles VII, King of France had found a new vigour. In 1441 he led an army that took Creuil and Conflans and then laid siege to Pontoise, the last important English fortress in the Île-de-France. In 1442 he invaded Guyenne, temporarily occupying some towns but failing to gain Bayonne.

By the early 1440s the English had lost most of their best commanders. Bedford, Salisbury and Warwick had all died and an ageing Fastolf retired from the combat around this time. Suffolk now mostly concerned himself with matters in England. There was still John, Lord Talbot, who after long and successful service was created Earl of Shrewsbury in 1442, although even he was hampered by advancing years. A younger generation of greater nobles now came to prominence, including Edmund Beaufort, Count of Mortain and his elder brother John, Earl of Somerset, who had found his feet since his release. A third new commander was Richard of York, then lieutenant in Normandy with Talbot in his service; both showed their worth by aiding the recovery of the Guyennois lands. But for all their efforts to fortify and re-provision Pontoise, it finally fell. Talbot at least regained Harfleur in 1440, for which service he was granted his earldom.

There were in fact quite a few promotions handed out to English nobles in those years and Henry Holland, Earl of Huntingdon knew the king's generosity on becoming Duke of Exeter. Edmund Beaufort finally gained the English peerage he needed when in

1442, like his father and uncle before him, he was created Earl of Dorset. Finally there was recognition of his worth: he was certainly himself an able soldier and loyal servant of the king, and he was then lieutenant in Maine. The following year Edmund was again raised in dignity, this time as Marquis of Dorset, the designation once again revived for a Beaufort and now considered an acceptable English peerage.[1]

Neither of these awards brought Edmund any estates, for the king had no lands to grant. In 1442 he was awarded an annuity of 600 marks 46*s* 8*d* from the Exchequer, specified to be paid until the king could grant him lands and incomes to match that amount. On his promotion to marquis he gained a further annuity of £224 6*s* 9*d*, paid from the revenues of Carmarthen and Cardigan. In the latter award it was recognised that 'in consideration of his being a younger brother and inheriting nothing by the demise of his ancestors' he needed a sizable income to maintain his dignity and obligation.[2]

Edmund's elder brother John was apparently not pleased by this promotion, which made Edmund senior to him in precedence, but this did not last long. Since his release John had been much in demand. By 8 November 1438, within months of regaining his freedom, he was Captain of Cherbourg, an office he still held in 1443. In 1441 he led an army that prevented the French from relieving Harfleur, which Edmund was besieging. In these commands he was successful enough, or at least was not responsible for any noted failures, but he must have suffered from the long lull in his military career after his capture.[3] John was now finding recognition as a Prince of the Blood and was admitted to the Order of the Garter. He married in 1441 to Margaret, sister of John Beauchamp of Bletsoe and widow of Sir Oliver St John. This was not a marriage that brought much wealth or social advancement, although his bride was a relative of the Earl of Warwick. In 1442 his only legitimate child, Margaret, was born.[4]

John's years of captivity were not as lonely as may be believed. While in France he had produced an illegitimate daughter who was granted denization when he brought her to England. Known as Tacine of Somerset and also Thomasina or Thasnya, she was married to Reginald, Lord Grey of Wilton by 1447. Somerset also had a bastard son named John, born after his death in 1444 and himself dying in 1453, who was mentioned in Cardinal Beaufort's will.[5]

John was obviously making up for lost time, but the following year brought disaster and disgrace for him, and his own end. In April 1443 the council agreed on an ambitious campaign. French attacks on Guyenne, the oldest English possession in France, brought a new sense of urgency, and this expedition was designed to do widespread damage and to eventually defeat the French king's force in the field, bringing a victory of the magnitude of Agincourt and Verneuil, and an army of the size of the 1415 campaign was envisaged.[6] Some such as Fastolf had urged a return the devastating large raids of yesteryear, and at least this 'sharp and cruel war' would take the pressure from Guyenne and possibly prompt the French into talks on peace, or at least a truce.[7]

Cardinal Beaufort, who provided a massive loan for the expedition, made it a condition for his aid that his nephew John take command. If anything it was an enterprise dominated by Beaufort family members, for Edmund and Richard Neville, Earl of Salisbury would be his lieutenants. It was also decided that the force would land at Cherbourg, where John was still captain, and progress along the western edge of Normandy.[8]

John was accordingly designated Captain General of France and Guyenne. When he insisted that he should be elevated to a dukedom as the appropriate dignity for such a command, the king instantly agreed and John was again senior to his brother as the first Duke of Somerset. He would have the right to keep any castles or towns he took in this campaign and was also made governor of Anjou and Maine, which upstaged his brother further.

There was serious objection to all this from Richard of York, then lieutenant in Rouen, a role which Somerset had previously held for a time and for which the Beauforts resented York. He complained that Somerset's promotion undermined his overall authority in the war, and this made sense because a single command was necessary to ensure stability. His other complaint was more practical: his payment to continue the defence of Normandy was already much in arrears, so he found it increasingly difficult to perform his role, and now the Exchequer was diverting funds to this Beaufort-inspired expedition. The new dukedom gave Somerset precedence over all dukes *except* York, but this was small comfort to Richard.

When the expected expedition did not set sail in June there was concern in Westminster; campaigning seasons were limited to the summer months. John appears to have spent more time recruiting, which seemed to be proving harder than expected, and he also complained that he was quite ill, and only the politics involved prevented rethinking over the campaign leadership. As June slipped into July he showed no sign of setting forth and even the king urged him to embark.

Finally in August 1443 Somerset, Dorset and Salisbury landed at Cherbourg with about 8,000 men. From there Somerset led the army on an eccentric path of his own while refusing to reveal his strategy to anyone, even his brother Dorset, and in retrospect it appears unlikely that his plans had much coherence. After a haphazard march the force besieged and took Le Guerche in neutral Brittany. The English then engaged in a damaging raid through French lands, acquiring the castle at Beaumond-le-Vicomte and a few other towns and strongholds. But suddenly, without the envisaged battle with Charles's forces, Somerset disbanded the army declared the expedition over.

Funeral effigy of John Beaufort (I), 1st Earl of Somerset.

Wimborne Minster, resting place of John Beaufort and his duchess Margaret Beauchamp. (Courtesy of Bellminsterboy under Creative Commons)

Above: John of Gaunt (left of centre). (Courtesy of the British Library)

Left: John, Duke of Bedford (kneeling, left) in the *Bedford Hours*. (Courtesy of the British Library)

Edmund Beaufort, Duke of Somerset at the court of Charles VII in 1445. (Courtesy of the Bibliotheque Nationale de France)

Humphrey, Duke of Gloucester. (Courtesy of the British Library)

Above: Tomb of Richard Beauchamp, Earl of Warwick. The image of John, Duke of Somerset is presented as a 'weeper' on the base, second from left. (Courtesy of J. Guffog & J. Hannan under Creative Commons)

Below: Antony van Wyngaerde's sketch of London in 1534. Cardinal Beaufort's Winchester Palace is the large property on the lower left.

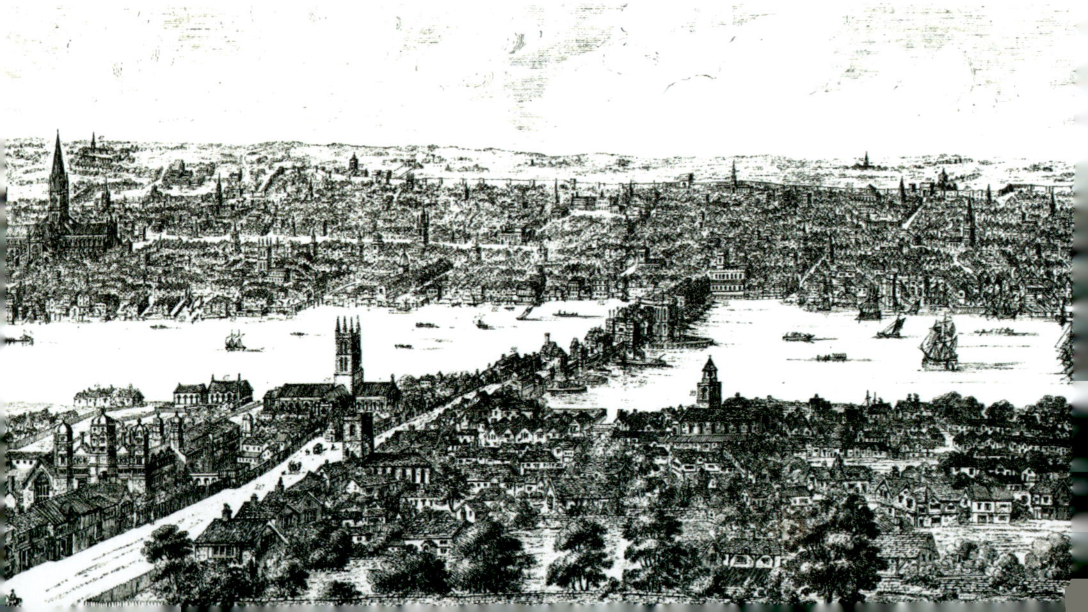

Right: A later painting depicting Cardinal Beaufort interrogating Joan of Arc by Hippolyte Delaroche, 1824. (Courtesy of the Rijksmuseum)

Below: Tomb effigy of Cardinal Henry Beaufort. (Courtesy of PJP O'Sullivan under Creative Commons)

The execution of Edmund Beaufort (II) at Tewkesbury. (Courtesy of Ghent University Library)

Margaret Beaufort. (From *The Sisters of Lady Jane Grey*, 1912)

Left: The arms of John Beaufort, Earl of Somerset, prior to his legitimation. (Courtesy of Sodacan)

Right: The Beaufort Arms. The Royal Arms differenced by a bordure. (Courtesy of Sodacan)

The marriage of Katherine de Valois and Henry V. Rumours abounded that Henry Tudor was the offspring not of Katherine and Owen Tudor but of Katherine and Edmund Beaufort I.

Above: Beaufort devices above the main gate of St John's College, Cambridge, founded by Margaret Beaufort, which include the Yale and the Beaufort Portcullis. (Courtesy of Andreas Praefke)

Left: The Yale of Beaufort, from the Queen's Beasts at Hampton Court Palace. (Courtesy of Man Vyi)

Questions were asked over why such an expensive and prestigious campaign gained so little and ended so quickly. The English promptly sold Le Guerche back to the Duke of Brittany, hoping to keep his neutrality. The Duke of Somerset returned to England in disgrace, a laughing-stock in some quarters and the subject of anger over taxes and redirected monies in others.

Later assessments of this campaign see it as more successful than believed.[9] It did ease the pressure on Guyenne for a time, and the French were moved to talks on ending the fighting. But such a large expedition had little to show for the expense and politics, and this called John's strategy into question. Multiple campaigns on such lines would have done the French cause much harm, but the expenditure required for such large-scale *chevauchées* would have been unsustainable. The real gains of the 1443 campaign were not so tangible, and the English had hoped for some more lasting advantage. Somerset was the focus for the disappointment that followed, although some of it was deserved, as many could not understand why he had ended the campaign so abruptly and with so little accomplished.

John Beaufort, first Duke of Somerset died soon after his return, on 23 May 1444 at his home at Wimborne in Dorset. It was whispered that he had committed suicide, but this was never proven and the fact that he had long complained of illness makes death by natural causes just as likely. The Crowland Chronicler recorded that he was excluded from the royal presence following allegations of treason and also believed in his suicide, but John was far from popular at Crowland Abbey.[10] He was a flawed character, living out the frustration of his long imprisonment and spurned ambition. His infant daughter Margaret gained the bulk of his estates save for those he held in tail male, and the Somerset earldom went to his brother Edmund.

The title of duke, unlike other ranks of peerage, was still not considered as necessarily hereditary, and Edmund did not inherit it at first; he was still known for a time as Marquis of Dorset. There was similar case concerning the earldom of Warwick when Henry Beauchamp, who had succeeded his father in 1439, was made a duke in 1444 but his brother-in-law Richard Neville inherited the earldom in 1449 without the dukedom. Edmund would not become Duke of Somerset until 1448, and when he did it was not by inheritance. Acceptance for the principle of hereditary dukedom only came about in the following decade.

The second generation of the House of Beaufort had been somewhat unfortunate, but Edmund Beaufort was the most able of the men, and his elder brothers' deaths allowed him to finally come into his own. Gaining the earldom of Somerset would increase his standing, which was already in the ascendant. His eldest son, Henry, was created Earl of Dorset in his place.

Over the previous two decades the Middleham Nevilles, the children of Joan Beaufort's (I) marriage with the Earl of Westmorland, had asserted themselves in northern England, pushed on by her drive to gain the best for them. Between 1420 and 1425 Joan had appropriated various estates belonging to the earldom of Westmorland for her eldest son, Richard, eventually Earl of Salisbury; such an act had been contrary to the laws of inheritance but the second Earl of Westmorland could do little to prevent it while still a minor. As Warden of the West March towards Scotland Richard was in need of a large income, and it was some time before he gained access to the estates of the earldom he had acquired.

But in 1434 Westmorland, now a grown man, demanded his birthright. Supported by his younger brothers, he set about a challenge to his uncle Salisbury. The sources speak of unrest in northern counties but are far from specific; it is likely to have been a matter of sharp words rather than any actual fighting. It was nonetheless a matter of concern for Salisbury, who persuaded the council to warn Westmorland not to act when Salisbury was in France in 1436.[11] It was only in 1442 that Robert Neville, then Bishop of Durham, settled the dispute, strangely in favour of the senior branch. Salisbury was ordered to hand back Raby, Staindrop and other possessions in County Durham, but this stung far less now that he held the estates of the Montague earldom of Salisbury.[12] Cardinal Beaufort intervened early in the dispute when it was discovered that a box of legal documents had been deposited at Durham Priory by the first Westmorland and, with Bishop Langley, the cardinal had pressurised Prior Wessington to hand it over. These papers might have vindicated the senior Nevilles' claim, but predictably they now vanished forever.[13]

This matter did not turn into the kind of private civil war that would later characterise the north of England; Westmorland had little power to raise a following nor much influence in Westminster, and reports of conflict between the two branches appear to have been exaggerated. However, it is illuminating in showing how Cardinal Beaufort used his influence in the favour of his nephew and his sister's family, even resorting to underhand methods. By the time that Joan Beaufort died in 1440 Salisbury was an important magnate in his own right, and the Middleham Nevilles were all comfortably positioned.

The failure of the 1443 campaign in France was effectively the end of Cardinal Beaufort's long career. For all his remarkable energy, expertise and commitment over five decades, the years had mounted and by 1445 he had attained his threescore and ten. His itinerary in the last few years shows him moving as before between his palaces of Wolvesley, Farnham and Southwark, but his visits to London became fewer. Travelling in such times was difficult for one of such advanced years.

Many of his associates, such as Bishops Langley and Bubwith, Bedford, Warwick and Thomas Chaucer had either died or retired from the council long before. Others, such as Kemp and Stafford, had ceased to associate so closely and Beaufort did not have so many personal supporters on the new body. When Archbishop Chichele died in 1443 he was replaced by John Stafford and no attempt was made to nominate Beaufort to Canterbury. It was probably felt that he was too old by this time, or else none wished to restart the *praemunire* controversy. Kemp was now a cardinal too, but the debate was not really over. If Beaufort himself wished to be archbishop he no longer had the support in the English Church to advance his candidacy, and it is unlikely that he still had the energy to fight for it. Perhaps to be a cardinal gave him all the seniority he ever wished for, and the Winchester estates all the wealth he wanted.

Cardinal Beaufort's attendance at council gradually became less frequent from 1436. He was attending roughly one meeting in five in the early 1440s, and fewer after the military disaster of 1444.[14] He still came to some meetings, and his last loan to the crown was made in 1446, within a year of his death.

We have mostly seen Cardinal Beaufort as a political figure and for a time as a papal instrument, but he was an active ecclesiastic and left his mark on Winchester itself over his long tenure. He refounded the celebrated almshouses at the Hospital of St Cross near the cathedral, often considered a masterpiece of medieval architecture, where Beaufort provided for a porter's lodge and a tower, on which his image is fashioned. St Cross was a twelfth-century foundation, where a number of old men were provided for as brothers of the Order of the Hospital of St Cross, distinct in their black robes. In 1445 Beaufort founded a second organisation in the cathedral precinct, whose brothers wore a claret-coloured robe with a silver cardinal's badge. He provided for new building work, and both orders continue to the present day.

There were other charitable foundations, which was by no means unusual for ecclesiastics and lay lords in those days and often, as in Beaufort's case, involved ulterior motives: the recipients of his charity were expected to remember the cardinal and specified members of his family in their prayers. His will arranged for ten thousand consecutive masses to be said for his own soul, commencing immediately on his death. Beaufort had also amassed an impressive collection of purported holy relics. In 1448 Henry VI, who had inherited many of these items, presented a drop of the Holy Blood and a piece of the True Cross to Eton College among other prestigious artefacts.[15]

After the 1443 campaign Suffolk was also calling for an honourable peace as the only remaining option, but the French were still not of a mind to settle while so much of western France was occupied by the English. Charles was certainly uneasy over a possible alliance between the houses of Burgundy and Anjou, which would ease the pressure on English-held Maine, but when the English came to offer peace he could tell that their resolve was weakening.

Suffolk led a delegation to Paris in February 1444 but soon found there was little to be accomplished. Sovereignty over Normandy and Guyenne could not be negotiated and all he gained was a two-year truce. But as a separate brief the meeting did agree to the marriage of Charles's niece Margaret of Anjou to Henry VI. The betrothal was announced on 24 May and Suffolk stood proxy for his king at the marriage ceremony at Nancy in February 1445. She came with no dowry. Charles had just vetoed the wedding of the sixteen-year-old Margaret into the Duke of Burgundy's family and this new match did the French cause more good than the English. She was the daughter of Count René of Anjou, titular king of Naples and Jerusalem. The marriage was expected to solve the burning issue of the English succession, but this hope was far from realistic.

Peace was still elusive. There were secret talks at Tours in the summer that year once the English had agreed to surrender Maine to René of Anjou by 30 April 1446 in return for a twenty-year truce. Suffolk, who later took the blame for this concession, had come to the conclusion that nothing could be gained from the French without such a large offering and it is certain that the king agreed with him. This was not only a bad strategic decision in the long term, as it left Normandy poorly defended to the south, but it was widely resented by those who had fought for the territory and those who had estates and lordships there. Sir John Fastolf was angered by the loss of his own barony in Maine. Twenty years was a long time for a truce to hold, and the fundamental issue – who sat on the French throne – was not resolved.

In later years Margaret of Anjou would be hated by many English. At first the circumstances of the marriage saw her reviled in England, but her own knack for survival left their mark on English affairs for over a generation. Developing a shrewd, politically astute disposition, she eventually learned how to manipulate her husband and navigate court politics. She was always close to Suffolk and to an extent Somerset, and had lobbied for their dukedoms, both granted in 1448. The king was only too pleased to honour them for what he believed they had achieved, and it was felt that both needed this dignity to negotiate with the peers of France. It was hoped that the queen would produce an heir for Henry, although some grew uneasy after the first few years passed without a pregnancy. It was later said that Margaret had urged that Henry give up Maine, but that was not the case for she was herself a cipher in the bargaining and the decision was made long before she even met her husband.

Despite the agreed surrender of Maine there was considerable wrangling when the French came to collect, and there were calls for compensation and concessions. The commissioners appointed for the handover process did all they could to obstruct the final transfer and the English only left when Charles besieged Le Mans with an army.

While public opinion against the surrender was rising, some looked to Richard of York to champion their cause. York had himself lost favour with the council but as of the previous seven years was lieutenant in Normandy, now the front line in the French wars. His commission expired in September 1445 but he continued in this office, expecting to hear of its renewal and repeatedly complaining to the council over the arrears of funding that plagued his efforts. Suffolk saw him as potentially dangerous, and late in 1446 York was commanded to return to England in order to attend parliament. Once there he was given a new commission: ten years as lieutenant in Ireland. This was not a prestigious posting; Ireland was a traditional graveyard for overactive politicians. It was not quite exile, but to be removed from the most important of commands was very much a demotion.

York would rail at this ingratitude for years to come. To learn that Edmund Beaufort, soon Duke of Somerset, would succeed him in Normandy was the worst insult and a dire feud between the two began that day. There has been controversy both then and since over York's command in Normandy, and some believed him unsuitable at the time. Still, it must be said that York had laboured with poor resources and a general lack of support from the king's council and he had held the duchy intact during his command. To his dying day York believed his removal to have been politically motivated.

With Suffolk and those close to the king becoming increasingly unpopular it now fell to Humphrey, Duke of Gloucester to reappear in public life. Even after those years of obscurity in Wales the ageing 'Good Duke' showed little weakening of his resolve. He was still mindful of his wife's treatment and sought rehabilitation for both her and himself. The king had forbidden him entry to court, removed him from the Privy Council and denied him access to the royal person, but he was still next in line to the throne and had a strong personal following. It is often said that Humphrey's campaign was yet another attempt to gain leverage for himself, using the established ploy of standing up in support of the disaffected. There is every likelihood that this was part of his own political stratagem, but the issue posed serious questions to those who considered themselves chivalrous and his words found many a listener.[16]

For generations the knights of England were encouraged to view the war in France as their most fitting employment, to fight on until the final conquest. Peace without victory was a bitter pill, all the more so when hard-won territories were to be abandoned and their lordships relinquished. Without the benefit of hindsight, and without considering such dull matters as finance, Gloucester was voicing a widely held discontent and calling the government into question.

Suffolk decided to eliminate this problem too. He apparently started rumours that Gloucester was preparing a revolt in Wales and then called a parliament, taking care that the duke was summoned. The venue was first announced as Cambridge, but moved at the last minute to Bury St Edmunds, an area where Suffolk's influence was strong. Gloucester was led to think that his views would be heard. He might have still wished to press for a pardon for Eleanor.

On 18 February 1447 a delegation called on Gloucester at his lodgings in the town, headed by the Duke of Buckingham and including the Earl of Salisbury and Henry Beaufort (III), Somerset's eldest son and Earl of Dorset. Another present, the High Constable Viscount Beaumont, placed Gloucester under arrest. There were no formal charges, and before any further action took place Gloucester fell dramatically ill and died in custody. As in modern times, conspiracy theorists put forth their views and foul play on the part of Suffolk's faction was widely suspected. It is equally possible that Gloucester had a heart attack, but none of this is certain. He recovered his consciousness long enough to make his confession and passed away during the afternoon of 23 February. Whispers of the murder of the Good Duke began immediately.

It is not known if Cardinal Beaufort rejoiced on hearing of his old enemy's death. The cardinal himself had taken to bed for the last time, and his own hour would soon strike. He died on 11 April 1447 at his episcopal palace at Winchester in his seventy-second year. According to legend, when Death appeared in person on that day Beaufort was heard to offer all he owned for a few days more in this world. This is put down to his hallucinating in his final moments, but it was a typical parable for the time.

The cardinal's magnificent tomb stands in Winchester Cathedral, flanking that of the patron saint Swithin. The tomb is surrounded by an enclosure that doubles as a chantry, and Beaufort's painted effigy lies on top, his red robes much in evidence. His facial features might have been modelled on a younger self – there is no way of knowing, for the original was destroyed during the Commonwealth and later restored – yet the lavish and ostentatious style of the sepulchre is obvious. It is mirrored by that of his successor Bishop Waynflete, bearing the exact same design on the other side of the saint's tomb.

The career of Henry Beaufort (I), second and longest-living of John of Gaunt's legitimised children, spanned almost fifty years and four reigns. He had been a stout pillar of the Lancastrian regime since 1399, always the promoter of the dynasty and its wars of conquest in France, and particularly important as a banker and financier to the kings. He was not a particularly sympathetic character, often identified with the adverse consequences of the Anglo-Burgundian alliance, and like many a politician he had enemies within court and government and was hated throughout England, especially in the capital. He even incurred the anger of the kings he served at times. 'A man of great providence and sufficiency,' Polydore Vergil wrote of him later, 'who most of all supported the English affaires, being often in desitresse, with councel and treasure.'[17]

Whatever criticism can be levelled at him, Cardinal Beaufort was committed to his mission to serve the Lancastrian kings. His principal contribution was to secure the finance to prosecute the French wars, which was no mean feat given the disposition of the Commons. The nightmare scenario of the long regency from 1422 made demands on everybody, and Beaufort did all he could to sustain Henry V's endeavour. It was his sincere hope that Henry VI would take control of his kingdom as a grown man, and only the king's personal inadequacies undid this design in the long term.

It would be naïve to look for Christian values in most late medieval prelates. The Church was considered a viable career path, often for younger sons of nobles, and most bishops were simply feudal magnates in cassocks. All we know of Beaufort's own religious convictions show him as a conventional churchman who supported the war on heresy, then appearing in the form of Lollardy and Hussitism. Few men of the cloth found recognition as crusaders in that century.

His status as a cardinal caused no end of disruption to the English Church. Avid in their resistance to *praemunire*, the English prelates saw Beaufort's red hat as papal intrusion and sought to detach him from his Winchester see. Beaufort thwarted all attempts to remove him, and cardinals after him held English sees concurrently. Luckily for the English Church his connection with the papal Curia ended after his abandoned crusade and did not cause as much interference in England as expected.

Despite his loss of favour with Rome, his cardinalate enabled him to exercise his claim to an inflated role in England. One maddening aspect of the business was the way Beaufort styled himself 'Cardinal of England'. As a bishop he was technically subordinate to the two archbishops, but he carved out a position of seniority for himself and in cases like the double coronation this caused much annoyance over precedence. He was a man of personal ambition; to become a cardinal was his highest pinnacle, and he would never climb down.

Harriss, the cardinal's principal biographer, states that his actions demonstrated a self-righteous assuredness unusual for his day. Indeed, his confidence is very uncharacteristic in a time when the Church constantly exhorted its flock to think of their sins and be most contrite in their wish for redemption.[18] While Beaufort did make provision for charitable works, he was particularly anxious that his beneficiaries often prayed for his soul. His kings were glad of his services, even if he did not always act to plan, and his efforts and financial support were essential to their successes in France. It was a blessing for Cardinal Beaufort that having seen such an expansion in English territory, partially through his efforts, he did not live to see Normandy lost again.

What truce could last for twenty years? The French had not gained so much at Tours to throw away the possibility of driving the English out altogether. No longer the insecure young man in threadbare clothes on the day that Joan of Arc appeared at Chinon, Charles VII was both resourceful and in possession of large resources. He had built a new army, well equipped and well organised with state of the art cannon, and even created a corps of professional soldiers. A regular army was unusual for the times; it was the practice to engage soldiers for a single season's campaigning and there were few permanent garrisons. Now as ready as could be, all Charles needed was a pretext.

There is scope for debate as to what contribution Edmund Beaufort, Duke of Somerset made to the management and eventual loss of Normandy. According to one pro-York chronicler, '[by] negligence and untreuthe of him that was lieutenant therof for his abtyng the soudiers that were yn the garisones ther, and sende ham home unpayed of their wagesse wherby the strengthe of Normandye wasse loste'.[19] Interpretations of these events were very partisan, although some questions do emerge. The chronic problem Somerset faced was underfunding and arrears of pay from the Exchequer. Richard of York had suffered the same, although there was one mandate on record in 1440 to reimburse Edmund for amounts he paid at the siege of Harfleur whereas no such concessions for York are known.[20] However, the office of Lieutenant of Normandy was a nightmare that called for juggling the needs of the garrison with a near-empty treasury. Somerset might very easily have tried to economize by reducing soldiers. Now that the truce had been agreed, both council and parliament were even less generous over financing Normandy's defence, even though experience should have seen them prepare for the truce to break down. Somerset had a restless, discontented army and even he must have expected an attack.

On 22 August 1448, Adam Moleyns, Bishop of Chichester and Treasurer of Normandy, wrote a letter of complaint over Somerset's neglect of incidents on the borders with Valois and Breton territory. According to this account some of the Anglo-Norman troops were raiding the villages across the borders, and Moleyns blamed Somerset for this indiscipline. He believed that both Somerset and Suffolk were encouraging such activities. Further letters repeat the allegations.[21] If all this is true, one may wonder what Somerset was doing. Was he seeking to break the truce, even though it was risky while Lancastrian Normandy was so poorly defended? Perhaps he and Suffolk were using this as a means of drumming up support to finance a new campaign. They might also have wished to put pressure on the Bretons, who were drawing closer to Charles, but even this could harm the truce. Somerset might simply have been sloppy in his approach, or else allowed some raiding to allay restlessness among his subordinates without expecting serious consequences. Or perhaps he expected the truce to end anyway.

The efforts of the Duke of Bedford to win over the people of Normandy had not continued. While Bedford sought to involve the people as a whole, it was more often the English settlers who participated in the affairs of the duchy. The presence of lieutenants with French-sounding names such as Walere and Duchesne in Somerset's castle of Harcourt near Rouen suggests that he had Normans in his service, but there is little evidence otherwise.[22] After suffering more than a generation of warfare, plunder and brigandage the native population was at best half-hearted in its allegiance to Henry of England.

On 24 March 1449, François de Surienne, an Aragonese mercenary captain in the service of the English, laid siege to Fougères, a town with a formidable castle on the edge of Breton territory. This was no infringement of garrison discipline, for it transpired that Suffolk had encouraged the captain. De Surienne was a king's knight of long service, recently admitted to the Order of the Garter, but after he captured the castle the English disowned his actions and sent no supporting troops. He was so incensed that he sent the Garter back.[23]

Somerset hardly acted appropriately either. When the envoys from the King of France arrived to remind him that under the terms of the truce the English must immediately hand back all captured towns Somerset flatly refused, claiming that as the Duke of Brittany was a vassal of his king it was an unrelated matter. Charles then went to Duke Francis of Brittany and offered help regaining Fougères, on condition that he renounce his tenuous alliance with England. On 31 May, as talks with the English broke down, Charles declared the truce over and sent in his army.

A document exists among Sir John Fastolf's papers proposing that Somerset be summoned to answer a number of questions over his conduct. Some oblique references appear over what he did with certain monies, but the most significant queries concern the suggestion that he authorised de Surienne's attack on Fougères and told the captain not to surrender it for his life. It was also asked why he did not order that the town be given up when the

French king demanded it by the terms of the truce. Another charge concerned draining some fortresses of stores and artillery, leaving them indefensible. These were serious issues that the writer wished to raise, but no such inquest took place; Somerset did not return to England for some time.[24]

It is obvious that Somerset was party to this breach of the truce as much as Suffolk, but it is hard to understand what they sought to achieve. Few expected the truce to last, and now that Charles had possession of Maine the French had little need for peace. Perhaps the dukes hoped that they could take Fougères without disturbing the truce, hence their repudiation of de Surienne's actions. Some believed that the Breton treasury was held in the town, and it might have been a raid to pay restless troops. If they expected to resume fighting, however, bolstering the defences at Normandy was a more pressing concern. Issues of Anglo-Breton politics may have also been at the root of the matter, but in any case the move on Fougères at that point was weak on strategy and even common sense.

When 30,000 French troops entered Normandy in a three-pronged attack from the south, east and north, Somerset prepared to defend his charge. He expected his fortresses to hold and frustrate the enemy; lacking the troops to assemble a field army, he relied on a defensive strategy that he hoped would wear down the enemy. He might have had some misgivings about reduced numbers and finances, but he had at least prepared. There was no getting around the fact that his diminished force was spread thin across many castles, however.

He was soon dismayed at the attitude of the knights and commons of Normandy itself. Far too many towns and castles simply opened their gates to the invaders when they appeared, and others only put up token resistance. The English troops at Pont de l'Arche made a short-lived stand while those at Pont l'Evêque immediately fled. By the autumn of 1449 more than twenty towns and castles had been lost and Charles's troops were marching on Rouen itself. Some Norman captains even switched sides on the promise of payment.

Somerset could have done little else in the circumstances, but he called for reinforcements as the invasion was underway. The council had not been quick to offer funds since the truce began, but now they agreed to send a relieving force under Sir Thomas Kyriell, a Knight of the Garter and former Captain of Calais, although this took its time to come and would arrive too late to save Rouen.

On 16 October, the French king and the Bastard of Orleans brought their army to Rouen and besieged Somerset and his lieutenants. With only 12,000 men and poorly provisioned, he tried to defend the town with Shrewsbury's assistance, but it could not last and on 22 October he was obliged to open negotiations with the enemy. Charles vetoed any proposal that involved Shrewsbury's withdrawal. and Somerset was forced to leave him behind as a prisoner when he withdrew to Caen with his family. Shrewsbury would be released a year later in return for the surrender of Falaise.

Winter saw more disappointments for the English when the French took Harfleur, Honfleur and Fresnoy. Kyriell's force, only 2,500 strong when it finally arrived, landed at Cherbourg in March 1450. Ordered to relieve Bayeux, they stopped to besiege Valognes and tarried there almost a month; only after Somerset sent them extra troops did they go on to Bayeux. On 15 April the French intercepted this relief force at Formigny, 10 miles from Bayeux, where Kyriell was captured and nearly all his men were killed. By June Bayeux had fallen, as had Avranches and other towns, and the French cannon were wearing down the walls of Caen itself. When a cannonball broke down the wall of the room in the castle where Somerset lived with his wife and children, he decided that it was over for Normandy and retreated to Calais.

Richard of York was gaining support from those who blamed Somerset for the loss of Normandy. York himself railed from Dublin Castle that he himself could have kept the duchy but for the politicking that saw his commission given to Somerset. For both York and Somerset, however, the problem was the same: there wasn't sufficient funding to maintain the defence. The French wars had long been a bottomless pit into which large amounts of money were continually poured, true, and the English Council had seen the truce as an opportunity to cut expenditure. But a great deal was needed just to maintain the defence as it was, and a prudent policy should have seen Normandy prepared for the day the truce collapsed. The council seemed to think that the truce had ended the war. Perhaps Suffolk should have thought twice over intriguing in Breton politics.

The final invasion of Normandy happened on Somerset's watch when he faced a larger and better-equipped invader with his own poor resources and inadequate support. It is unlikely that York could have done much better, for while strategic decisions on Somerset's part could be questioned there were also doubts raised over York's suitability during his command. The main issues – Charles's formidable new army and the paltry support from the council – would have applied to both. The collapse was also indicative of the Lancastrian failure to win hearts and minds in Normandy. For all their claims, the English were still largely an army of occupation; the support of the Norman French was lukewarm at best.

The loss of Normandy broadened the division between York and Somerset, and this quarrel would have serious implications. At this juncture Somerset had little to worry about; York was still in Ireland, and although many in England thought highly of him he had little support among the nobles. The king still held Somerset in high regard despite his failure, and in April 1451 on his own petitioning Somerset was made Captain of Calais, where he expected Charles to strike next.

The widespread anger over the loss of Normandy was mostly directed at Suffolk and his followers at court. In 1449, when some of the first refugees reached Southampton, a mob lynched Bishop Moleyns as he landed. Despite the bishop's pleas and assertions that Suffolk was to blame, and that it had been the duke's idea to give up Maine, the mob hanged him.

The bishop's dying words nonetheless spread, and Suffolk was arrested. Although no formal charges could be made, on 7 February 1450 Parliament voted for Suffolk's impeachment, and he was declared guilty by attainder and condemned to death. Suffolk appealed directly to the king, however, and his death sentence was commuted to five years' banishment. This was typical of Henry VI, who could never reconcile justice with mercy and did little to ease the tide of anger. But Suffolk did not escape so easily. On 1 May, when he finally took ship, his vessel was intercepted in the Thames Estuary by the *St Nicholas of the Tower*, whose pro-York crew took him into custody. Determined that the traitor would not walk free, the sailors dealt with Suffolk themselves, beheading him with a rusty sword.

After 1450 there was little English territory left in France. There was Guyenne, the remainder of the massive Duchy of Aquitaine that the kings of England had held from the twelfth century, and there was also Calais, the fortified town and marcher region about it which the English maintained at colossal expense for its strategic and economic importance. The English expected French attempts on both soon enough. All but the most stubborn must have known that the Lancastrian dream was over, and there was no way of regaining the lands the English occupied before 1430. Even at this stage, however, Fastolf presented a strategy for the conquest of France. It is not known if the council even read the paper. His suggestions would have involved many men and expenditure beyond anything council was willing to contemplate at that time.[25]

It could be argued that after Arras the Lancastrian endeavour in France was on a road to inevitable defeat and that the English were simply seeking the best way to end the war without further losses. The French were unwilling to settle while they were winning, and it was Suffolk who reaped the blame for the predictable conclusion.

The behaviour of Edmund Beaufort during the events of 1449 leaves a blemish on his long track record of loyal and astute service to the cause of Lancaster. The blame for losing Normandy would follow him to the grave and beyond, feeding the popular belief that he had undone the successful labours of Richard of York. In reality, neither Somerset nor York could have done more than postpone the day when Charles's superior army came to collect.

8

FACTION AND FIGHTING

The fall of Suffolk left a vacuum in the centre of government and two contenders soon emerged. Richard of York was still popular, given his reputed successes in France, but the final decision lay with the king and despite recent reverses he and his household still favoured Edmund Beaufort, Duke of Somerset.

By his mid-forties Edmund had climbed a long ladder from landless younger son to duke, his means and responsibilities increasing all the time. His role as the real saviour of Calais in 1436 was not forgotten and as other generals of the French wars either died or retired Somerset came to the fore. Yet there was the final loss of Normandy, for which Somerset was widely blamed. After Suffolk and Moleyns were lynched many called for Somerset's blood too, but he prudently remained in Calais, although even there he was resented for harming morale as the symbol of defeat and loss. Despite this failure, in the next five years Edmund would take on the role of politician, servant of the king and focus of the resistance to Richard of York. In this cause he would triumph, suffer and perish.

The king was now a grown man. Although he showed no martial virtues and was slow on the uptake, he was at least behaving like a king. There were still reservations over his abilities, but royal government could at last function as expected with Henry having the final word on a matter, although it was maddening to see how easily he could be manipulated by those close to him. His own ideas were simplistic, and members of his household continued to influence his decisions.

In 1452 Henry ennobled his two half-brothers, Edmund and Jasper Tudor, the issue of his late mother's second marriage, creating them earls of Richmond and Pembroke respectively. In 1455, on his sanction, Edmund Tudor married Margaret, only child of John, late first Duke of Somerset.

The question of the succession remained unresolved. Henry was in his thirties but there was much concern that after five years married to Margaret of Anjou there was still no child. Was Henry taking the canonical exhortation to abjure fornication to an unreasonable extreme? Some believed so; he was considered simple-minded. There was even a rumour that his confessor, Bishop Aysgoth of Salisbury, was discouraging the king from any bedroom activities. Henry might have also been infertile, but there is no way of knowing.

In 1450 it was anyone's guess who would be the next king, but if Henry VI should die as suddenly as his father a serious crisis would surely follow. The king's uncles were all dead and had left no heirs, making Richard of York the only other legitimate descendant in the male line from Edward III, but many would not countenance him as king. In May 1451 Thomas Young of the duke's following presented a bill to the Commons to formally recognise Richard of York as heir presumptive, but a command in the name of the king immediately dissolved that parliament and sent Young to the Tower.

At the same time the question of the Beaufort succession not only persisted but came under renewed consideration. Did Edmund Beaufort himself believe he could be king? If so he still made no attempt to voice any opinion on this issue. Those who opposed

Richard of York's candidacy might have considered that Somerset could be king as a last resort, but it would have been dangerous to speak openly of this. York's supporters also wondered if the court intended to crown Somerset.

When the Commons impeached Suffolk in 1450, it was one of their charges that he planned to depose King Henry and crown his own son, John, the boy's marriage to Margaret Beaufort transmitting her claim to him. Margaret had been married as a child when Suffolk obtained her wardship but the union was later annulled. It is unlikely that this accusation had any foundation, but certainly some acknowledged that the Beaufort line offered a serious candidacy.

Which claims were valid, and how the precedence should be arranged, could not be fully addressed in such circumstances. It had become a wait-and-see situation and might have caused civil war in itself if Henry had died childless then. Politics were becoming heavily polarised and volatile, and it was difficult to reach any accord. There was discontent in many a quarter, and which soldiers returned from France were making worse.

'Jack Cade's rebellion', which first appeared in May 1450, is a misnomer, for there were uprisings in several counties of southern England, East Anglia and the Midlands, and Cade was only leader of the Kentish rebels. There was accordingly little coherence, although many of the rebels condemned the government for the loss of Normandy, called for retribution on the offending ministers and wished to see York as the king's principal counsellor. The real agenda of Jack Cade himself remains uncertain. Styling himself as Lord Mortimer, he claimed royal parentage and a relationship to Richard of York and at the same time laid his own claim to the throne. He was probably an Irish sailor, but the demands he made were illustrative of popular feeling.

On 3 July the rebels entered London and pillaged for three days. They captured and executed some household men including Lord

Saye and Sele and Bishop Aysgoth. Once they had made certain agreements with the king's officials most of the rebels drifted home, although Cade himself persisted; he was soon put to flight and later killed when apprehended. Smaller revolts persisted in Kent, where unrest continued for more than a year.

On 11 August 1450 the king recalled Somerset from Calais to appoint him Constable of England, essentially a military appointment requiring him to suppress further revolts and giving him access to serious military resources. But as soon as the duke returned to England there was uproar and calls were made for his impeachment and for some time he declined to leave the king's presence for fear of his safety.[1]

Even after the fall of Suffolk there was a tendency to accuse the king's household of misleading Henry with ill counsel, and many of Suffolk's associates remained as the focus for discontent. When Somerset returned to England he was often seen in the company of the same household men, which did him no favours in any popularity contest, and his enemies took to linking their accusations towards him with the other grievances.[2]

The parliament called that autumn elected York's chamberlain, Sir William Oldhall, as Speaker and showed its unmistakable support for Richard. In November that year the Duke of York himself appeared triumphantly in London, having left Ireland during his term of office there and expecting to take his place at the king's side, but was annoyed to find Somerset already so close to the throne. For a short time York enjoyed the ascendancy and even once took part in a public relations exercise where he rode with the king into the City of London.

The politics of the time had taken on a form that can easily be recognised. Somerset as the king's counsellor was now a figure of popular hatred, identified with every shortcoming and defeat that the country had known in recent years, while York was seen as champion for good government and order. Neither really deserved such reputations and neither had any illusions about the political climate, which was growing harsher and more volatile. The Commons presented a petition calling for the dismissal of over thirty people associated with the royal household, Somerset's name heading a list that included the Dowager Duchess of Suffolk, Bishop William Booth, Lord Dudley and several knights and gentry. The king agreed that they would remain at least a mile from his person on pain of forfeiture of possessions, but in practice most ignored it.[3]

Widespread hatred for Somerset probably caused one John Nellport, an esquire of the county of Dorset, to gather a host and attack Somerset's castle of Corfe, beat his servants there and carry away many of his possessions. Somerset had trouble recovering the goods when Nellport took sanctuary in a monastery, and he complained to Cardinal Kemp the chancellor.[4]

In December 1450 there was a violent attack on Somerset himself while at dinner in his lodgings at Blackfriars. The sources are vague on the events and who was involved but it resulted in Somerset being arrested on London Bridge and placed in the Tower, officially in protective custody. It was also said that it was York's men who caused the disturbance and that the Mayor and Commons of London gathered a force to save Somerset. It is alternately stated that York ordered the Earl of Devon to take Somerset into custody for his own safety and suppress the unrest, and he himself proceeded against those who had ransacked Somerset's lodgings.[5] It is hard to unravel what exactly happened, but it is likely that York was seeking to keep Somerset where he could not wield his influence. He might equally have been concerned for the safety of a fellow aristocrat faced with an unruly mob, but this was hard to believe in such partisan times. Somerset was his adversary in his ambitions and York certainly had not forgotten losing his command in Normandy. Edmund left the Tower two weeks later to keep Christmas in Blackfriars and did not return.

Although York did not strictly deserve a reputation for wise, capable counsel and sound military prowess, he was still the popular alternative to Suffolk and then Somerset. Just as Gloucester had been, York was the saviour of the people against the 'evil counsellors' of the court according to the word on the street, and the myth of his successful defence of Normandy reversed by Somerset's treason was still widely believed. York, trying hard to ease the smouldering unrest, intervened in a dispute between Lord Bonville and the Earl of Devon in the West Country, where he found in favour of Devon. This gave him further prestige as a righter of wrongs, but still the court gave him little cooperation and the court viewed all he did with suspicion. The king held the only vote that counted. Eventually a new council with Somerset and Cardinal Kemp as the principal figures was formed, with many of the old members also present. There was no attempt to include York in this, which would have been a prudent move.

In 1451 York's retainer Sir William Oldhall, the former Speaker, was accused of plotting to overthrow the king in favour of his master and was forced to escape into sanctuary. Others associated with the duke found themselves the object of suspicion if not accusations, and York himself affirmed his loyalty to the king and once again accused Somerset of treason.

Richard of York himself reappeared in England at this time. He had taken two years to assume his role in Dublin, which was not too unusual; some office holders in fact never appeared to perform their duties in person. In fairness it was shown that Richard had addressed his new role with a commitment, in particular establishing good relations with the Irish tribal chiefs and the Anglo-Irish nobles. As grandson of Roger Mortimer he held estates in Ireland and some important contacts. But he suffered the same trouble lamented by most holders of viceregal offices – payments from London failing to materialise – and he was soon £3,000 in arrears. At the outset York had appointed James Butler, 4th Earl of

Ormond as his deputy and although the duke was seldom absent this was a workable arrangement. But Ormond's death in 1452 gave the title to the younger James Butler, who was married to Somerset's daughter Eleanor and had been granted the earldom of Wiltshire three years before. The younger man was far from supportive of York.

In January 1452 Richard of York rose in revolt. It was a drastic move, and the most ill-conceived that he could have made at that juncture. Together with his own following he was joined by some of the rebels of 1450, but it was the nobles who held the real military strength in those days, many with private armies of knights and men-at-arms, and only the Earl of Devon and Lord Cobham rode to support him with their own meagre followings. It was a serious step to defy the king in arms, and even most of those who favoured York would not go this far. With a manifesto that included the removal of Somerset from all offices York progressed from his castle of Ludlow, crossed the Thames at Kingston and camped at Dartford in Kent while the king, Somerset and many of the other nobles brought a much larger force to Blackheath.

It did not take York long to realise that he had shot his bolt inadvisably when so few of the nobles rallied to him. His brother-in-law the Earl of Salisbury and his nephew the Earl of Warwick came to his camp at Dartford to parley on the king's behalf, successfully persuading York to abandon the revolt and throw himself on the king's mercy. When York eventually came to Blackheath to surrender he got off lightly; being relieved of the lieutenancy of Ireland and for a time imprisoned in the Tower before being released to house arrest at Ludlow. It was hard to persuade Henry not to be overly lenient, but Somerset had at least seen his rival politically destroyed by his own impetuous action. At this meeting York once again called for Somerset's removal from court, but the king refused to listen.

While Somerset was placed so well in the king's favour, there was ongoing concern over the many wardships granted. Where a landed aristocrat died leaving either an heiress or an underaged boy for an heir, the holder of their wardship, initially the king, had the use of the incomes of the estates and choice over the marriage of the ward, often securing it for one of his own children. It had become common to farm out such wardships according to royal favour, and Suffolk had been one major beneficiary. It was decided to recall all of these grants to the crown, and from 1449 this was attempted. The first Act of Resumption that Parliament passed that year was mostly ineffective when 186 exemptions rendered it inadequate. The executors of Cardinal Beaufort still had loans to collect and arrangements to pay them continued as before, which complicated the issue. The household men also kept many of theirs. A second Act was passed but again did not go far.

Finally in 1451 the new government, with the king's belated support, produced a new Act that had the desired effect with few exemptions. Of course many of these grants were restored to the same holder, but now the crown kept a tighter rein on them and many previous awards were now valid only for a term of years. Both York and Somerset suffered from the resumptions, but the result was much better for royal finances, where revenues could be better managed and for a time fewer resources were farmed out.

After the events of 1452 there was at last strong government in the land. Henry VI was taking an active part in affairs of state and many had less cause for anxiety. The announcement of the queen's pregnancy in 1453 made it seem that all was finally well again. The new council, having beaten off York's challenge, now gave the impression of responsible government. Cardinal Archbishop Kemp was still chancellor, and in 1452 he took the unusual step of translation from York to Canterbury. The mature Somerset and the septuagenarian archbishop were a strong team.

Somerset was at the height of his career in this short phase. He was well regarded at court and particularly close to the queen and rumours circulated as to how close. The long interval between the royal marriage and the birth of Margaret's only son, Edward of Lancaster, in 1454 raised suspicion about the boy's paternity and Somerset himself was believed to be the real father. There is no evidence to support this, but fifteenth-century rumour mills were as active as those today. It is true that Margaret thought highly of Edmund; at the very least she saw him as a valuable political ally, and after the loss of Suffolk he was the magnate closest to the queen. While it is entirely possible that Margaret could have taken Somerset as a lover, and even that the duke was father to her son after the king's failure to beget children, no hard evidence exists to confirm any of it and it must remain speculation. In the oncoming civil wars the Yorkists would take the allegation as read and were all too enthusiastic to publicise it.

The new council sought to preserve the remaining territories in France. It was certain that Charles would soon attack either the town and march of Calais or the region of Guyenne, if not both, but the English showed little enthusiasm to defend either. Richard Woodville, now Lord Rivers, was commissioned in 1450 to take reinforcements to Bordeaux, but no finance was obtained to transport them and the army never took ship.

Somerset and others expected the French to attack Calais first but instead Charles's army invaded and took most of Guyenne very quickly, meeting little resistance; Bordeaux and Bayonne had surrendered by August 1451. Richard of York again railed at Somerset for the poor handling of the war, but there was little he could have done given the general lack of support. In September 1452 the council finally sent an army to take back Guyenne, which succeeded for a short time. That old soldier John Talbot, Earl of Shrewsbury then led a campaign that regained most of the lost lands in Guyenne by October that year. The French were expecting the English to land in Normandy and left Guyenne poorly defended, and there was more popular support left for the English there than in Normandy.

The French army returned soon afterwards, in a three-pronged attack that had Shrewsbury engaging each force in turn. The Battle of Castillon on 17 July 1453 showed the English under Shrewsbury acquitting themselves well, the earl himself at seventy-five no less the great commander. But superior numbers, the French cannon at close range and the sudden appearance of the Bretons on the French side turned the battle. Shrewsbury was one of the many English dead, his army shattered. On 19 October, Bordeaux finally surrendered. This dismal battle brought disappointment to England; Guyenne had been the last remnant of three centuries of English dominion over the Duchy of Aquitaine.

Although he had little to do with the outcome, Somerset's enemies now accused him of contriving the loss of Guyenne as much as he supposedly had Normandy. Surprisingly for the time, however, the French did not then turn on Calais. For various reasons – its fortifications and surrounding marshland, its proximity to Burgundian territory, and the related politics and economics of the Wool Staple – the French were not so keen to complete the eviction of the English. Calais would remain an English town until the reign of Mary I.

No address was made to the growing trend towards aristocratic violence. The Devon–Bonville feud was but one of the conflicts that disrupted the countryside, most of them over issues of inheritance and land rights. The Middleham Nevilles, Somerset's close relatives, found themselves in armed confrontation with the Percy family. The Nevilles and the Percys had a long history of intermittent quarrelling, but as they usually shared the defence of the Scottish border region they often cooperated and at times intermarried. On 24 August 1453, a force of Percy retainers led by

Northumberland's son Thomas Percy, Lord Egremont ambushed a bridal party headed by Sir Thomas Neville, Salisbury's second son, at Heworth Moor near York. The prospect of certain estates forfeited by the Percys in 1405 passing to the Nevilles through inheritance was too much for the former to countenance, and a private civil war between the younger sons of both families and their followings resulted. There was also a related conflict where the Duke of Exeter locked horns with former royal servant Ralph, Lord Cromwell. The royal council had no real mechanism for restoring order in the regions far from London, and many of the magnates entrusted with keeping the peace in their areas were actually involved in these partisan activities. A tendency to solve disputes by force of arms was growing, but most of this aristocratic violence was inconclusive.

By 1453 there were ominous developments. One involved a linking of the conflicts, producing two factions in conflict rather than many, and another concerned Somerset's dispute over his inheritance. The early fifteenth century saw a large number of extinct peerages. Many a peer failed to produce a surviving male heir, and where heiresses brought large additions to existing catalogues of estates it was not difficult to build large holdings with many incomes. Many new peerages were created across the century, but apart from some granted for long-term royal service, many went to younger sons of existing peers, and few of these new creations lasted past the second generation. Edmund Beaufort himself was one such, created Earl and then Marquis of Dorset before inheriting his elder brother's titles and estates. The Middleham Nevilles gained three peerages for the younger sons and an earldom for their eldest, whose heir also became an earl through marriage.

The Beauforts were the focus of a network of family relationships. To forge dynastic connections was desirable, but their proximity to the Lancastrian monarchy and the influence they wielded also provided incentive for the noble families to establish family links with them. Somerset was well connected, to say the least; the last surviving Beaufort male of his generation, through his sisters' marriages he was brother-in-law to Thomas Courtney, Earl of Devon and to King James I of Scotland, and James II was his nephew. He was second cousin once removed to King Henry himself.

Due to the efforts of his late aunt Joan, Countess of Westmorland to promote her own children in the marriage market, Edmund's Neville first cousins were accordingly the Earl of Salisbury, Barons Fauconberg, Latimer and Abergavenny and the Bishop of Durham. His cousins by marriage into this branch were the dukes of Norfolk, Buckingham and York, the Earl of Northumberland and Lord Stanley, all important and powerful nobles. He himself had married into the Beauchamps, his deceased father-in-law being Richard Beauchamp, Earl of Warwick. His brothers-in-law were therefore Henry, Duke of Warwick, John Talbot, Earl of Shrewsbury, his Neville cousin Lord Latimer and the younger Richard Neville, eventual Earl of Warwick, who was also his nephew. He was uncle by marriage to Edmund Tudor, Earl of Richmond, now a rising figure in court circles. Through his second cousin Alice Chaucer's marriage to Suffolk he was related to the de la Pole family. He was later father-in-law to the earls of Wiltshire and Stafford through the marriage of his two eldest daughters. Given the marital connections of some of the families almost every important noble in the land was a relative of the Duke of Somerset.

But one cannot help noticing that this network of relationships also included Somerset's principal opponent Richard of York. The Earl of Devon was in there also, and at this stage was committed to supporting York, although after his death in 1458 his successor, another nephew of Somerset, was a strong Lancastrian. The Duke of Norfolk showed favour to York, while in the years to come Richard Neville, Earl of Salisbury, and also his son Warwick,

Fauconberg and others of the Middleham Nevilles would become York's most powerful allies against Somerset and his party. It is doubtful that there was much method in the creation of this web of legal and blood relationships, but the Beauforts were aware of the advantages. By the mid-1450s this network proved very fragile indeed.

It is generally accepted that the legend describing a confrontation between York and Somerset in a garden in the Temple where the two dukes plucked white and red roses as tokens of their defiance is not a real event. It has been a subject for Romantic painting but the story owes most to Shakespeare, whose knowledge of the events and personalities was at best vague. It was true that the two became alternative nuclei for discontented aristocrats, but this took time to turn from a personal quarrel to a building of factions.

In recent years some historians have called for a more suitable name for the dynastic civil wars of the later fifteenth century, as the 'Wars of the Roses' were so named from the myth that the two sides wore red and white roses as their badges. The term is still in use as a shorthand for the events for want of anything more appropriate. In fact, a popular tendency to talk of the singular *War* of the Roses is an annoying misnomer inspired by the title of an unrelated film. There were at least three separate wars, possibly six, and much fighting went on in between. Recently the term 'The Cousins' War' had come into use. This is no less inadequate a title, but it at least acknowledges that all the commanders on both sides were related. The blood that was spilled might not have been thicker than water in this case, but material needs lay at the root of many a conflict, and the unity of this family web would be shattered in the mid-1450s. When such matters intervened, the nobility of England proved to be a house divided unto itself.

In 1434 Somerset had married the daughter of one of the most prestigious earls in England. Richard Beauchamp, Earl of Warwick had three daughters by his first wife, Elizabeth, the Berkeley heiress, and Somerset married the second, Eleanor, herself already widow to the ninth Lord Roos. It is unlikely that Somerset had married for a share of the inheritance, gigantic though it was, for her brother Henry would expect to have it all. The advantage lay in the link with the Beauchamp family; no material inheritance was envisaged. Somerset's elder brother John had similarly married into the Beauchamps, albeit a cadet branch.

But Richard Beauchamp had married twice, also taking advantage of an available heiress, and soon after Elizabeth Berkeley died in 1423 he remarried to Isabel, heiress to the Despensers. This union complicated the inheritance by producing two more children, Henry and Anne (see Table VI).

The tomb of Richard Beauchamp in the Collegiate Church of St Mary in the City of Warwick is one of the most ostentatious examples of medieval sepulture. Aside from the metal effigy of the earl himself with all the trappings of his glory there are elaborate features about the tomb. It depicts Somerset himself as a 'weeper', one of the robed and cowled figures about the base of the tomb among others of close family. Like the others Somerset's face is covered and only his coat of arms identifies him.

When the old Earl of Warwick died in 1439, his only son Henry, still a minor, inherited the earldom and all his estates. He had lived in the royal household in the preceding years, with the king apparently thinking highly of him. Perhaps out of respect for the young earl's father, he was soon created first premier Earl of England and then Duke of Warwick. In 1446 the king even bestowed on the youth the unprecedented (and never repeated) honour of King of the Isle of Wight. Soon after this bizarre creation, however, Henry Beauchamp died. He had barely attained his majority.

Back in 1434, Richard Beauchamp, Earl of Warwick had married the two children of his second marriage to two of the children of Richard Neville, Earl of Salisbury. Almost certainly on his mother's urging, Salisbury sought marriage connections with the highest people; despite his Beaufort connections he still had difficulty, only closing the agreement with the payment of 4,700 marks. Richard and Cecily Neville married Anne and Henry Beauchamp, all as small children. The marriage of Cecily to the heir of the Warwick earldom was the most desirable part of the settlement; the six-year-old Richard, his father's namesake and heir, would be Earl of Salisbury himself in due course, and it was simply fitting for him to marry one of similar social standing. His bride, three years older, was not expected to bring a large inheritance.

But when Henry, Duke of Warwick died in 1446 the situation changed. The deceased duke and Cecily had a two-year-old daughter, also named Anne, who now became the sole Beauchamp heiress, but when she herself died three years later this brought an unexpected advantage for the Nevilles. Without little Anne as heiress the inheritance would have been shared between the four surviving daughters, but the law in this case precluded heiresses of half blood. This made the twenty-one-year-old Sir Richard Neville the new Earl of Warwick in right of his wife, although he was not allowed the dukedom and certainly not the Wight kingship. He was still Earl of Salisbury in waiting, but this Warwick earldom gave him means and power in his father's lifetime which enabled him to play his role in the events to come: history calls him Warwick the Kingmaker.

Young Richard Neville did not immediately gain all the estates he expected to inherit from the Beauchamps. Some of the various lordships and manors were heritable in tail male, which limited inheritance to the male line, and there were three dowagers who held a substantial portion between them while they lived.

The lordship of Abergavenny was a collection of estates which Edward Neville, another of Joan Beaufort's sons, had at least nominally acquired in part through its own heiress. Richard Beauchamp had denied Edward his half of the inheritance, as did Richard Neville once he gained the earldom. Somerset, like his brothers-in-law Shrewsbury and Latimer, felt strongly enough to contest the judgment, and for some years the dispute with his nephew the new Earl of Warwick dragged on.

In 1450 Richard Neville had also obtained the wardship of George Neville, the other co-heir, and thereby controlled the income of the entire Despenser inheritance. But on the passing of the Act of Resumption in 1451 this wardship returned to the crown and Somerset saw his chance. He soon requested the wardship of George Neville and consequently his half of the Despenser estates, which the king readily granted. But this included the entire Glamorgan marcher lordship, including Cardiff Castle, and many lucrative manors that Warwick decided he could not lose. By early 1453 Warwick was still occupying the estates, and now without royal licence.

Warwick appears as particularly greedy, but this is deceptive. While the earldom of Warwick was the richest lordship in England, it had lost incomes. Richard Neville could not inherit the Lisle barony as it had passed by entail to Berkeley heirs in 1439, meaning a loss of manors totalling about £550 a year in value. There had also been two periods of wardship on the Warwick estates in the ten years following Richard Beauchamp's death, and during the second the king had granted the farm of some of the estates to members of his household.[6] Such actions often devalued estates. The shortfall in the income of Warwick's estates has been estimated at over £1,000 a year.[7]

Motivated by his own financial difficulties, Somerset was seeking to obtain the entire Despenser inheritance despite having no right to half of it. But he had the king's favour and at a council meeting late in July 1453 it was agreed to send Warwick an order to hand over the entire Despenser lands. Warwick was not even invited to state his case. For all the close family links the Beauforts had with the Middleham Nevilles, this breach was serious. Family relationships did not prevent dire conflicts, certainly not where estates and inheritances were disputed, and both Somerset and Warwick riding roughshod over the laws of inheritance would have consequences for the country as well as the family.

During all this Somerset was considered a loyal counsellor and received assurances of the king's favour. Following the 1450 rebellions he headed several tribunals of oyer and terminer that tried such cases in various counties[8] and was later appointed justice in eyre for all England south of the Trent. He also gained the lordships of both Carisbrooke Castle and the Isle of Wight. These last gains might have irked Richard Neville, as they had previously been held by earls of Warwick.

But once Warwick defied both Somerset and the king, Somerset could persuade the king to take action on his behalf. Henry was preparing a progress through the north, as that region needed a show of royal authority, but Somerset contrived to have this royal progress diverted for his own purposes. Inexperienced as he then was in matters of state, Warwick prepared to defend Cardiff and his other disputed lands against the orders of the king. Somerset was sure that if the king himself appeared in Cardiff then Warwick would either back down or be seen as a rebel, and so he persuaded the king to come to Wales with him. Had he reached Cardiff, the ploy could have worked.

This first rupture in the family network did not in itself place Somerset and his Neville cousins on opposite sides of the coming political divide, but it had begun a process that would drive the Nevilles to the enemy camp. Somerset might have succeeded in gaining the disputed estates, but in August 1453 the king went mad. While in his hunting lodge at Clarendon on the way to Wales, Henry suddenly sank into a catatonic state. It was not long after hearing of the defeat at Castillon, and the shock of such tidings may have triggered the breakdown. He not only ceased to speak but sat still in his chair, staring off vacantly. Medical knowledge of the time had no effective remedy, and for months there was no change while his servants fed and tended him. Under Kemp's leadership the government carried on in the king's name and gave the appearance of business as usual, but as the weeks turned to months the court grew concerned.

It was hard to see what could be done in such circumstances: appointing a regent was discussed, but choices were controversial. Margaret of Anjou was the first suggested, but her pregnancy made this impracticable. By the precedent of 1422 the nearest adult Prince of the Blood would take the role, but this was Richard of York and there were inevitable objections. The queen and Somerset both attempted to block the appointment of York, but no other option met with agreement. Once Margaret had given birth to her son, Edward, on 13 October she offered little further opposition for some time.

By October 1453 York had returned to the council and was making his own influence felt. Then he made his move. On 23 November, having gained the assent of the council, he had Somerset arrested and placed in the Tower, and then ordered charges of treason to be prepared. Few now stood by Somerset. He had only dominated the council because the king thought so highly of him, and only his ally Kemp remained to support him. The Duke of Norfolk accused Somerset of treason, describing various actions by which Normandy and Guyenne were lost.[9] Warwick had his own quarrel and objected to the way that Somerset had manipulated the king over the recent dispute, and Salisbury was concerned over the violence done to his family and retainers by the Percys. When Kemp suddenly died on 22 March 1454 the council was forced into a decision. Five days later, Richard of York was appointed Protector of England. In Somerset's place he made himself Captain of Calais, the only front-line military command that remained.

When York appointed the Earl of Salisbury into the chancellor role vacated on Kemp's death, the choice was much remarked upon as Salisbury was the first layman to take it since Thomas Beaufort in 1412. In reality York's position was very weak and he was hard pressed to keep the Nevilles on his side. He placated Warwick by granting him the office of joint-chamberlain of the Exchequer, previously held by Richard Beauchamp and denied him in the past; in addition he granted to Warwick Boles and Warcotes, two manors in Norfolk, while the Glamorgan dispute was judged in Warwick's favour. Nevertheless York had little to be generous with, and had difficulty managing a council whose support was mostly lukewarm.

After Prince Edward's birth Richard of York could no longer claim to be next in line for the throne. Despite rumours already circulating over the boy's paternity he promptly recognised the prince as heir; to challenge the succession at this stage could have jeopardised his meagre support, for the others would only go so far to follow him. York had to content himself with Somerset languishing in the Tower, in relative comfort but with little opportunity to interfere. Although many were glad enough to have Richard of York at the head of the council table, there was a general unwillingness to bring charges for treason against Somerset. York then laboured to bring the Percys to heel and had Exeter confined in Pontefract Castle. All this was as expected, for the instability the conflicts caused had to end, but the Percy and Clifford families felt, with some justification, that his actions followed a partisan agenda.

In reality York only held executive power while the king was incapable of coherent response and there were no plans to review his commission. A year passed, and still none wanted to propose a long-term settlement. The implications, unprecedented and wide open to interpretation, could have been explosive and most preferred to leave the situation as it was. Hopes were first raised around Christmas 1454 when the king's carers reported from Windsor that he was showing some awareness at last, and in January, as if by miracle, King Henry recovered his senses.

York had no further mandate to head the government and the king, urged on by his courtiers, promptly relieved him of the protectorate. Salisbury found his position as chancellor untenable when he was ordered to obtain the release of Exeter; he soon resigned. The court was now dangerous for York, Salisbury and Warwick, and they withdrew with their friends.

It was not long before Somerset was notified of his release from the Tower. He might have already been out on bail, but even so his movements would have been curtailed and closely observed. Once he returned to court and to the ascendancy, his anger over the coup and his own imprisonment fuelled a desire to strike back, not only at York but also the Nevilles.

Perhaps it was Somerset who created the Yorkist faction. He sought revenge, not only on York but Warwick too, the latter over the Glamorgan business. Over Glamorgan and the problems they had with Percy and Clifford the Neville earls had supported York as Protector, but this was more of an understanding than an alliance. It was the menace of royal power wielded by Somerset that forced the Nevilles into a defensive union with York.

York's revolt of 1452 had come to nothing when almost none of the nobles rose with him. He might have been very popular as an individual, but armed rebellion against the king was too serious a step for most of his supporters. Even Salisbury and Warwick had then remained at the king's side. But in 1455 the Nevilles had no choice but to defend themselves, and the three magnates called out their followings and hastily assembled an army. They were joined by the Duke of Norfolk and Viscount Bourchier with their men. This was by no means a great surge of support among the nobles, but even these few portended a marked improvement on the previous revolt and translated into large numbers of armed men.

The king, still insisting on the last word and not exactly Somerset's puppet, appears to have first been advised that York and Somerset were opposing parties in a feud and that he should remain neutral. Henry therefore took the bold step of relieving Somerset of the office of constable and appointing the Duke of Buckingham in his place. He and his counsellors were probably wary of this personal quarrel hijacking affairs of state.

Yet the king soon showed himself far from even-handed. Perhaps Somerset had succeeded in changing his mind by May 1455 when it was announced that a parliament would be convened at Leicester. Most peers received the summonses as expected, but none went to York, Salisbury or Warwick, nor to any known to favour their cause. The king and his court saddled up and set out in a grand progress with their combined entourages for Leicester. York and the Nevilles were convinced that they would be condemned as traitors in the parliament. Somerset was not popular in London, and the court had strong followings in the Midlands; Queen Margaret herself held the castle and town of Leicester. This affair was perhaps another instance of Henry acting on the last piece of advice, this time from his queen. York and his supporters were understandably concerned over this possible indication of royal bias, and frustrated that they had no chance to make their own arguments. Their army hurried to intercept the royal procession through Hertfordshire.

From the first engagement of the so-called Wars of the Roses in 1455 the 'Yorkist' faction, the supporters of the Duke of York with the Neville earls most prominent, appears as a military force. The 'Lancastrian' side effectively consisted of those associating with Somerset and politically aligned with Queen Margaret. They are also known as the 'court' party, and since the return of Somerset they had effectively formed the government. Such terms are used here for identification.

In reality the two factions evolved and their objectives later concerned more than control of the government. While the court faction, the Beauforts in particular, held influence over the wavering king, their Yorkist opponents promoted the claims of Richard of York, not at this early stage as an alternative monarch but as counsellor to King Henry. Circumstances over the next six years caused this quarrel to mutate into a struggle for the throne.

It was only from this time that Somerset was seen in the company of Henry Percy, Earl of Northumberland and Thomas, Lord Clifford. Clearly united by a mutual opposition to the Nevilles, they would form the Lancastrian military leadership. There were many other magnates who sided with the king during this initial crisis, and the dukes of Buckingham and Exeter and the Earl of Wiltshire were also in the king's party. Even Salisbury's brother William Neville, Lord Fauconberg was reluctantly attending the king on that journey. Buckingham was in command, although Somerset was almost certainly advising him with the other magnates.

St Albans had grown on a spur of high ground north of the abbey founded by King Offa to commemorate Britain's protomartyr. It is the final resting place of Humphrey, Duke of Gloucester, in a crypt under the saint's tomb. Around a highway passing the abbey had grown a main street with a market, from which other streets branched. On 22 May 1455, the two armies met here. Richard of York had twice sent to the king professing his loyalty and a desire to negotiate. Henry did attempt talks, but York refused to lay down arms unless Somerset was handed over to him. With nobody willing to budge, the First Battle of St Albans soon broke out.

The Yorkists had the larger force and were ready for battle. The opposing court party was effectively a procession to parliament, which included the customary large following but for purposes of pomp and ceremony, not war. For Buckingham – and Somerset if he gave counsel to the former – the king's forces were better placed to fight a defence than to take the battle to the enemy in the field. They therefore planted the royal standard in the marketplace and prepared to face York's host.

Buckingham quickly realised that the town had poor fortifications, with a dilapidated town ditch at the foot of the hill to the east where the Yorkist army was gathering. But the streets that ran uphill towards the high street were narrow, and for all their superior numbers the Yorkists could only send a few at a time to fight as there was so little space. Hampered by bottlenecks, as the fighting began the Yorkists found it hard to make any progress up the hill.

Somerset had seen a lifetime of campaigning at home, in France and even on crusade in Bohemia, but Buckingham was officially in charge. As an old soldier near Somerset's age he might have at least consulted his colleague and other experienced commanders beforehand on strategy. Flight and an outright attack were both ruled out, but it seemed as if the defensive strategy alone might suffice in wearing down the enemy until they abandoned the offensive. This might have succeeded.

Battles were usually either won with superior strategies or with greater numbers, but sometimes luck could turn the battle one way or another, as could one enterprising action. When Sir Robert Ogle, a knight of Northumberland and Neville follower, noticed an undefended route through the allotments behind the main street he pointed it out to Warwick. Young Richard Neville had never been in France, nor had he served in any senior military role, and his father-in-law's title posed much to live up to. But Warwick, whose military successes would often result from his ability to seize the initiative, promptly led an attack up this track. Once his men had broken through some of the houses they breached the Lancastrian defence.

Emerging on Holywell Street, Warwick's men attacked the enemy defence lines from the rear. Somerset and the other Lancastrian commanders were so complacent that they had not even put on their armour. While the main Yorkist force was now finding its way into the market King Henry was wounded in the neck by an arrow. York had him taken to the abbey.

One legend has Warwick and Somerset meeting here in single combat, while another has Somerset taking shelter in the Castle Inn as the Yorkist soldiers surrounded him. Having once heard the prophecy that he would die beneath a castle, he had persuaded the king never to summon him to Windsor. Below the inn's sign of a castle, the unarmoured Edmund Beaufort, Duke of Somerset faced several Yorkist soldiers. He brought down four of his attackers before an axe blow finished him.[10]

Compared with what was to come, few were killed at the First Battle of St Albans. The Earl of Northumberland and Lord Clifford were the only other nobles to fall, which perhaps suggests that the Yorkists had intended to eliminate their personal enemies and were mostly concerned with finding them. York felt that the only way to prevent Somerset from controlling the government to his own exclusion was to kill him. It was no long-term solution; the three Lancastrians killed had sons who immediately succeeded to their peerages, each committed to avenge that day. Henry Beaufort, Earl of Dorset was sorely wounded in the battle but survived to become the next Duke of Somerset. Buckingham was also wounded.

At the request of the abbot, the bodies of the three Lancastrian nobles were gathered from where they lay in the street. Before escorting the king back to Westminster the victorious Yorkist lords had Somerset, Northumberland and Clifford interred under the chapel at the abbey and would later found a chantry that offered prayers for their souls, a gesture to heal the division among the nobles of England. This chantry was destroyed during the Reformation, and after the abbey became a cathedral the Lady Chapel occupied its place. As a final irony, while the bones of Edmund Beaufort lie unmarked with those of his allies, only a few yards away is the tomb of Humphrey, Duke of Gloucester, also underneath the floor but conspicuous in its dignity.

Edmund Beaufort was fifty when he was killed in the street that day. His record as a servant of the House of Lancaster, the preoccupation of the Beaufort family as a whole, has much to commend it. He was a soldier with many a military success to his credit and his failures were the failure of the English to give their soldiers adequate support. As a politician he did not succeed in maintaining the unity of the magnates, but that was not so easy to do in the circumstances. While many saw York as the deliverer of the realm, Somerset and the rest of the court party believed that he had ambitions to make himself king, and his later actions show that it is a reasonable assumption.

Somerset did not break the web of family relations by which unity of the nobles was maintained; it was already breached. Neville and Percy were first cousins, and Somerset's first cousin Salisbury was also Richard of York's brother-in-law. This network was far too fragile anyway; none were very supportive of their relatives when they stood to lose inheritances and incomes.

Edmund Beaufort was therefore killed on the first engagement of the Wars of the Roses. It is useless to speculate whether the Lancastrians would have been more successful with him in command when the civil wars began in earnest, but it is true that he had a wealth of experience and expertise that his faction sorely needed. Of those who had been commanders in the French wars only Buckingham remained to the Lancastrian faction, and his death in 1460 would cost his side grievously.

Somerset as a politician had shortcomings. On the continental stage he might have understood the need to defend Normandy better than most of the council, but this could only have postponed eventual defeat. His approach to government was too biased and only contributed to the political instability of the time. He could not have known that the quarrel with his nephew Warwick would be transformed into an attack on the Nevilles, forcing them to take up arms with York.

The death of Edmund, Duke of Somerset ended the second generation of Beaufort males. A third generation would continue their service to the House of Lancaster, but these were young men, inexperienced and not yet accomplished. But they did not have long; the Lancastrian monarchy was soon to face its most serious challenge. The king would need all the help he could get.

9

CIVIL WAR

When young Henry Beaufort was recovering from the wounds he sustained at St Albans he mulling over his dismal prospects. Having ridden into the town with the king in his father's entourage as Earl of Dorset he had taken the rough end of the fighting and was lucky to have survived. His father, the illustrious Duke of Somerset, had killed in the same fight so he now took his place as the third duke. But it was his tragedy that he was not his father.

Henry Beaufort (III), fifth Earl and third Duke of Somerset was born in or near 1436, the eldest of Edmund Beaufort's children. He was declared 'nearly of age' when his father died, meaning he was no older than twenty.[1] As Earl of Dorset he was named as present during the arrest of Duke Humphrey in 1447, but he could have only been there as a witness, a minor in receipt of an early political education.

It is possible that young Henry saw some active service in the final years of his father's lieutenancy of Normandy. He might have followed the duke about the ramparts of Calais in the early 1450s during preparations for the attack that never came, or even took part beforehand at Rouen and Caen in the last of the fighting. Even in their early teens boys did ride onto the field with armies; the thirteen-year-old Edward, Earl of March, eldest son of Richard of

York, was also present that day at St Albans but it is unlikely that a boy of his age would have been allowed into the front line to fight against grown men. It is unlikely that Henry had real fighting experience before St Albans, where he certainly was in the thick of it, and he had not held a senior command. But now he was Duke of Somerset, heir to his father's reputation as much as his title, and was expected to lead armies to victory.

Henry Beaufort was known for his gallant, debonair manner and had won acclaim for jousting, although to be a star of the tournament was not in itself ideal training for military leadership in the coming civil wars. He should have had more experience before he held such important commands; some of the young man's opponents had headed armies in France, yet within a few years he would be the most senior Lancastrian general.

Henry had three brothers: his eventual successor Edmund, John, and Thomas, who would die in 1463 while still a minor. None of them ever married, but Henry did have an illegitimate son, Charles Somerset, by his mistress Joan Hill. Charles's descendants would later become dukes of Beaufort, and although unrecognised at the time the male line of the Beauforts continues in the present day through them.

The Beauforts were no longer at the centre of government after the battle. Richard of York held the ascendancy with the Nevilles, the Bourchiers and the Duke of Norfolk as his supporters. King Henry was soon ill again, either from his injuries or another spell of dementia, and York duly appointed himself Protector a second time.

The late Duke of Somerset was declared the culprit for the political unrest, along with others. On 26 May 1455, four days after the battle, a petition was presented to Parliament that the late duke, together with associates Thomas Thorpe and William Joseph, had conspired to estrange the king from his conscientious and loyal kinsman the Duke of York and the Neville earls, to the detriment of the realm; this was the typical formula used to justify revolts against a king, blaming those who misinformed him. The full statement is much longer, with the second duke blamed for everything from the loss of Normandy and Guyenne to the unrest of more recent years.[2]

Thomas Thorp and William Joseph had drawn the attention of Somerset's enemies when he was influential at court. Thomas Thorp had connections with London and Essex, given his appointments on royal commissions.[3] He may have been a relative of John Thorp, a merchant of the Staple, and gained Somerset's patronage at Calais.[4] In these years he was second baron of the Exchequer, promoted to chancellor of the same body in 1455, and his son Robert was granted the keeping of the Newcastle customs.[5] There are fewer references to William Joseph, although he might be linked to Somerset's estates in the county of Somerset. He is described once as 'king's sergeant'.[6]

Both might have been resented for gaining office as Somerset's nominees, although it does not really seem that Somerset filled government posts with his own supporters considering only these two are known. As Yorkist influence waned after 1456 both regained office. Thomas Thorp was appointed Keeper of the Royal Wardrobe in the Tower in 1457 and given a commission to provide armaments while his son returned to his Newcastle post, and it was remarked that the original commission was annulled without reasonable cause. William Joseph appears in the historical record again to participate in a legal dispute in 1457.[7]

For eighteen months after St Albans Henry Duke of Somerset lived in the shadow of the triumphant Yorkists. As Protector once more Richard of York set to business with a council that at least acquiesced to him. Thomas Bourchier, the new Archbishop of Canterbury, filled the office of chancellor which Salisbury had vacated weeks earlier, while his brother Viscount Bourchier was now treasurer.

York's most remarkable appointment was that of his nephew the Earl of Warwick to the captaincy of Calais, a command he had held himself during the first protectorate. York certainly needed to keep the Nevilles on side if he was willing to hand them such a prestigious office. It was far from an easy appointment, especially for a young man of little experience. The Calais garrison had recently rebelled again after long months without pay and its men were seizing bales of wool from the merchants in payment. Warwick was kept out of Calais for some time and was hard put to pacify the troops but eventually succeeded in restoring orderly relations in the town and winning the support of the garrison.

A number of discontented nobles gathered in the court, angry at the ascendancy of the Yorkists but unable to do much about it, with young Somerset as one of its most illustrious names. There was Buckingham, who had himself recovered from wounds received at the battle, and also Henry Percy, the new third Earl of Northumberland, and John, ninth Lord Clifford, the last two of whom shared with Somerset an urge to avenge their fathers' deaths at St Albans. The Duke of Exeter was another member of their party.

Meanwhile, there was a new player in the conflict who took an interest in these disaffected nobles. Queen Margaret of Anjou had grown extremely concerned over the activities of York and his supporters since the birth of her son, and suspected that Richard was preparing to usurp the infant's throne. Margaret therefore took to intriguing with the aforementioned nobles and provided a focus for the Lancastrian party as it developed its distinctive identity.

There were still questions in the minds of many over the paternity of the infant Edward of Lancaster. Some commented upon the suspiciously long period between the royal wedding and the happy event. The rumours continued to name Edmund, late Duke of Somerset, and his close association with the queen was often mentioned, although his was not the only name that came up; a similar rumour that the prince was a changeling also circulated.

Of course those who favoured the Yorkist claim to the succession found it easy to believe that King Henry was not this child's real father, and as no certain means of verifying paternity existed in those days nothing can be proven either way. When the renewed civil wars raised the stakes the Yorkists would invoke this issue to justify their usurpation, but at this time Richard of York was hardly using his restored ascendancy to gain the throne. As in the first protectorate, York's position was too weak, his committed supporters thin on the ground, and to go that route could easily turn his fragile support against him. In fairness to York, he was conducting his role as Protector to the letter. He turned down a proposition from James II of Scotland to support his claim to the throne, and although conscious of his claim to the succession he concerned himself with protecting the kingdom from its enemies and disruptors. The Scottish king's proposal was far from sincere anyway; James was also offering Charles of France an alliance where the two would seize Berwick and Calais at the same time.

Margaret was nevertheless convinced of the Protector's intentions to deny her son the succession. She and young Edward remained in the Midlands, usually at Leicester and Kenilworth, while the Yorkists tactfully held onto the king to ensure that he remained in London. Seeking allies, Margaret began an association with young Somerset and also with Buckingham, Northumberland and Clifford.

The second protectorate was suddenly over when the king appeared in Parliament on 25 February 1456 and declared himself able to rule on his own again, although he did emphasise that York would be his main counsellor. One could easily suspect that he was being manipulated, and the hand of his queen was soon obvious. Although York had been recognised, his supporters were removed one by one from their government offices. Laurence Booth, Margaret's chancellor and confessor, replaced Thomas Lisieux as Keeper of the Privy Seal and Margaret contrived in 1457 to have Booth consecrated Bishop of Durham on the death of Robert Neville.

Soon afterwards Viscount Bourchier was relieved of the office of treasurer and his place taken by John Talbot, second Earl of Shrewsbury, who was closely connected with the royal household. Not long afterwards the chancellor, Archbishop Bourchier, was also replaced, this time by Bishop Waynflete of Winchester, the king's own confessor, which caused a short breach between the court party and the Duke of Buckingham, who was half-brother to the Bourchiers. Richard of York's hold on government was being gradually eroded. In 1458 the Earl of Devon died and was succeeded by Thomas Courtenay, son of John Beaufort (I)'s younger daughter Margaret. Margaret made sure that the new earl, a committed Lancastrian, would marry her cousin Marie of Maine. At the same time she arranged a marriage for Buckingham's second son to Edmund Tudor's widow Margaret Beaufort.

Of all the Yorkists, Margaret found Warwick the most difficult to dislodge. The young earl had made a success of his command at Calais and had both the garrison and the merchants supporting him. Perhaps with this in mind she made Somerset Constable of Dover Castle and Warden of the Cinque Ports, possibly to offset Warwick's leverage.[8]

In May 1458 funding for Calais under Warwick's command suddenly ended. In October the same year Warwick himself was summoned to Westminster to answer charges of piracy in the Channel. During the hearing a brawl began between the king's men and Warwick's Calais soldiers, and Warwick was forced to break off his testimony to fight his way out of the palace. As the only Yorkist who held a position of power, he was still a target for the queen.

There was deep concern in both the court and the country over the political divide. A Great Council convened in November 1457 called for the mending of the political quarrel that by now showed every sign of turning once more to violence. Nothing came of this meeting, but at a new gathering in London in March 1458 an agreement emerged that was vague in content but commendable in spirit. On Lady Day, 25 March 1458, the celebrated Love Day pageant was staged. The king walked in procession to St Paul's and in his train came first Richard of York together with Queen Margaret and then Somerset paired with Salisbury, followed by other nobles of each faction together. The Yorkists agreed to endow a chantry for the Lancastrian lords killed at St Albans and to make compensation to their families. Lady Day was the first day of the year at the time, making this very much a fresh start.

This outward show of reconciliation was for both sides only a brief lull in preparation for more fighting. Margaret ordered the recruitment of archers in Cheshire while Salisbury called together the gentry of north Yorkshire. Warwick, meanwhile, mustered troops from the Calais garrison for use in the Yorkist cause.

In June 1459 Margaret urged that a parliament be called at Coventry. With echoes of 1455, York, Salisbury and Warwick were not summoned. It was once again far too obvious a prelude to attainting them and York therefore prepared to fight again. Salisbury called up his following and on York's summons led it across the Midlands to an intended rally at York's castle of Ludlow. Margaret was already preparing and she instructed Somerset to patrol the Midlands in case. Buckingham, then the senior commander of her faction, was commissioned to raise an army in the king's name.

On 23 September 1459, at Blore Heath near Market Drayton, Salisbury's men met a Lancastrian force and engaged. Very quickly some two thousand Lancastrians were killed, including its commander Lord Audley, whose heir was captured. Audley had planned to prevent Salisbury from joining with the larger Yorkist forces until armies led by Buckingham and Somerset arrived. When the enlarged Lancastrian host encountered the enemy at Ludford Bridge on 12 October both York and Warwick had joined the Yorkist force, the latter bringing a large army from Calais. The Yorkists had also built a hefty earthwork that counted to their advantage. As in 1455, messages from both sides urging loyalty and requesting dialogue came to nothing. The Lancastrians soon attacked.

The appearance of the Andrew Trollope at this point had an important bearing on Somerset's command of the Lancastrian forces. Trollope was an old soldier of the French wars; although as an esquire his lowly status gave him few roles of importance, he had a better sense of strategy than most. In 1459 he was Master Porter of Calais and commanded a contingent of the red-jacketed soldiers that Warwick brought from the town garrison.

Little is known of Trollope before the battle. He was probably born around 1400 or earlier, and his grown-up son David Trollope was also fighting. He is said to have been born into a County Durham family of dyers before becoming a career soldier. He was mentioned for his part in the occupation of the island of Tombelaine off Normandy in 1423. He had fought in the following of Sir John Fastolf and later that of Edmund, second Duke of Somerset in his final defence of Normandy; it was Trollope who surrendered Fresnay to the French in 1450. When Somerset decamped to Calais that year he took Trollope with him and gave him a place in the garrison. Trollope remained when the captaincy changed but was more closely associated with the Beauforts than with Richard of York and Warwick. He was married to a sister of Osbert Mundeford, one of Somerset's lieutenants in Normandy.

Trollope could well have faced a crisis of loyalties at Ludford Bridge when he found himself about to face the king in rebellion.

He had long been Warwick's diligent lieutenant – perhaps more so than his fellow officer Richard Woodville, Lord Rivers – but he had simply been following the Captain of Calais, who was the king's representative in the defence of the town. Surely Warwick could not expect Trollope to follow him into high treason against his king.

At the same time Trollope's long and close association with the Beauforts may have swayed his judgment. Although no evidence exists, it is possible that Somerset contacted Trollope in secret beforehand with the intention of luring him over. It was common in this conflict to cultivate possible traitors on the other side; Warwick would later gain his break at Northampton by exactly the same method, and Trollope would by no means be the last to turn his coat at an opportune time in those civil wars. However, Warwick was essentially Trollope's patron, and to defy him could see the old soldier lose all that he had.

Taking all of this into consideration, at a crucial moment Trollope took his troops over to the Lancastrian side. This left a gaping hole in the Yorkist line, and their well-organised defence collapsed. Richard of York abandoned his army and fled to Ireland, taking with him his second son, Edmund, Earl of Rutland. Warwick, Salisbury, Fauconberg and York's eldest, the Earl of March, escaped to the West Country before taking ship to the Channel Islands and then Calais.

Once the Yorkist revolt had disintegrated, Margaret prepared to have the Duke of York and all who had sided with him attainted. As a preliminary they were dismissed from all their royal offices. At Margaret's urging Somerset was appointed the new Captain of Calais and ordered to hasten to secure control. Given the defection of Trollope and most of those at Ludford Bridge, Somerset had every reason to believe that the soldiers there would accept him as their commander.

It seemed fitting for young Somerset to take on this role, given that both his father and grandfather had held it. With Lord Roos, the new Lord Audley and Trollope in his following, Somerset took ship and arrived in Calais harbour in November. He beat on the city gate and demanded entry in his official capacity, but the guards informed him that they needed the assent of the Captain of Calais before the gates could be opened. Warwick and the other Yorkist fugitives had already installed themselves in the town, and despite Trollope's defection most of the garrison remained loyal to Warwick.

The March of Calais was dotted with castles, although some had been gutted during the 1436 attack. With the help of Trollope, who had numerous contacts in the march, Somerset took possession of the key fortress of Guines, from which he conducted guerrilla activities against the Yorkists ensconced in the town. But Somerset's small force was little more than a nuisance against the formidable defences at Calais. An assault on Warwick's men at Newham Bridge on the road south from Calais was soundly beaten back.

While the Yorkist lords could feel fairly safe within the walls of Calais, their cause was not gaining ground. Their leader had run out on them and the attainders passed by the October parliament had caused their lands and possessions to be placed in receivership and their families to be dispossessed. More of the Calais soldiers then defected to the Lancastrians at Guines.

As 1459 turned into 1460, both sides considered their next moves. In March Warwick took ship to hold a conference with Richard of York in Dublin Castle. Certain agreements were made on aims and strategy, although it appears both came away with different understandings over the ultimate objective; York seemed to mistakenly believe that Warwick would support his becoming king. In any case, the Yorkists now grew in confidence as many headed to Calais to join them. Warwick led raids across the Channel starting in January, capturing Lords Rivers and Audley, the latter joining the Yorkists as a result.

Meanwhile, Somerset wrote to the court protesting that he needed more troops and resources to dislodge the Yorkists in Calais. Since the fiasco at Newham Bridge the Lancastrian leadership had not given him much support; the old problem of underfunded soldiers in Calais was emerging once more. Somerset's plans to take Calais itself were over-ambitious, for only a long and sustained siege with a large army and siege weapons could accomplish this, and Somerset had a small force and no ships with which to blockade the harbour. The court still agreed to send him funding, however, and prepared by collecting boats in the Channel ports for large troop landings.

This did little good when the Yorkists struck at Sandwich on 21 May, just as the troops were preparing to sail. This time Fauconberg remained behind to hold the town so that the Yorkists could bring the fight back to English soil; there were many Yorkist supporters about the Cinque Ports. If Somerset was aware that Warwick, Salisbury, March and others were sailing for England in June he could not stop it. Over the following weeks his enemy marched into London and gained its instant submission, and then into the Midlands where, on 10 July, the Yorkists scored a spectacular victory at Northampton. Buckingham, Egremont and other Lancastrian lords were killed and Warwick set out for London with King Henry in his custody.

Somerset could do little but continue his skirmishes in the Calais march until September, when Warwick returned to Calais and sought to end this petty annoyance. Meeting the earl at Saint-Pierre-les Cailleux, Somerset finally agreed to surrender Guines in return for safe passage with his pitiful following. He also promised not to fight against Warwick again. He first crossed to French territory for safety and then took ship for his castle at Corfe, where he awaited further news.[9]

Although neither side could claim to be in control of the country, the Yorkists were now the best-placed. They had London and the south-east, whereas Margaret was still strong in the Midlands and the north. Since Northampton the Yorkists had the king under a tactful house arrest at Lambeth Palace, which gave them credence for acting as his government. Bishop George Neville of Exeter, Warwick's younger brother, was now chancellor and was issuing writs in the king's name. The attainders were ignored and the Yorkists were clearly at an advantage.

But when Richard of York finally stirred from Ireland in September he was disappointed. In the Palace of Westminster he met his assembled supporters, but he quickly discovered that none of them were prepared to hail him as king. After their talks in Dublin, York apparently believed that he had Warwick's approval to take the throne for himself. But this was too dangerous a step for the magnates when it meant deposing an anointed king. The best that York could achieve at this time was a revision of the succession. The Yorkists had control over King Henry, who would remain king while he lived, so they drew up the Act of Accord by which it was declared that Edward of Lancaster was not the king's son, thus excluding him. This made York next in line for the throne.

But even this was a dramatic assertion. There was no evidence that the queen had conceived Edward by an extramarital affair; it was mere gossip mongering, accepting without verification that Margaret was an adulterer and her son a bastard. Richard of York was ten years older than the king and his hopes of inheriting the throne were limited, but it was almost a miracle that so much was accepted by his confederates; to go further would risk losing vital support.

Towards the end of the year the fighting began again, centring on Yorkshire. Somerset was summoned by Margaret to Hull, where he met with the earls of Pembroke, Devon, Wiltshire and Northumberland and a number of lesser nobles including the northern lords Clifford, Greystoke and Latimer. When Richard of York heard that this new Lancastrian army was harassing his

Yorkshire tenants and forcing others into military service against him, he decided to confront them. After despatching the Earl of March to Ludlow on a recruiting drive and charging Warwick with the keeping of the king and London, York brought his army north with his second son Rutland and Salisbury.

Henry Beaufort and his second cousin Richard Neville had the same problem: they inherited the titles, roles and to an extent the reputations of heroes of the French wars, but neither had much opportunity beforehand to gain the experience needed to fill their robes. The mention of 'Warwick' and 'Somerset' conjured images in the minds of mid-fifteenth-century Englishmen, valiant leaders of men, stout pillars of service to the king and able commanders. Both Edmund Beaufort and Richard Beauchamp had made their mark through a lifetime of personal achievement, and much was expected of the two young men who now bore their titles.

Warwick had first won honour at St Albans by acting on the advice of Sir Robert Ogle. As Captain of Calais in the past few years his leadership skills were honed, as was his seamanship. Henry Beaufort, succeeding to his dukedom shortly before his minority ended, had none of these opportunities. His first command in the Calais marches had not produced any spectacular result, although not due to any failing on his part. To have Andrew Trollope as an advisor counted better in his favour, but Somerset was still not yet equal to his role.

But Somerset was the most senior nobleman in the realm. The Duke of Buckingham was now dead and the other Lancastrian magnates were at best earls. The Duke of Exeter was of their party but was probably considered too unstable for command. The most experienced soldier was probably the third Earl of Northumberland, who had also inherited his title at St Albans but was now in his forties and as Lord Poynings had been Warden of the East March. In all commonsense Somerset would not have been appointed to command the Lancastrian army simply because he was a duke, but he was nominal commander and would then be expected to confer with Northumberland and the other earls, which is not always conducive to strong leadership. The part of Andrew Trollope as advisor is remarked upon throughout this campaign.

The events of what can be called the Wakefield campaign in the closing weeks of 1460 have recently been subject to revision.[10] The tangle of myths that grew over the battle and related events is partially the result of the second-hand stories that the chroniclers, most based in London, reported without verification. Here we are concerned with the activities of Somerset and his retainer Trollope, over which the chronicler Waurin says the most, but Waurin was not present either, and his information, mostly uncorroborated, is as suspect as the rest.

When Somerset received the summons from Margaret in December he and Devon led a contingent from the West Country to the rallying point, which may have been Hull or Pontefract; historians disagree. At or near Worksop they unexpectedly encountered the Yorkist vanguard. It was not a significant exchange, and the enemy was not as severely harmed as some believe, but it alerted the Lancastrians that the Yorkists were close by. Some thought Richard of York should not have gone so far north; better to await further recruits and supplies at Nottingham. But he struck out for his own stronghold of Sandal Castle near Wakefield, arriving shortly before Christmas.

As the Lancastrian force approached, both sides decided to suspend military activity for the duration of Christmas festivities. Despite some criticism of Richard of York's lack of preparedness at this juncture it must be remembered that it was commonly expected that at least an unofficial truce would come about at such a time; Christian knights would not kill on the Lord's Nativity and normally kept truce during the twelve-day feast. Clearly York did not reckon that the other side was making its own preparations during this period. It is even recorded that Somerset called at the castle under safe conduct and assured York of a truce to remain in force until Epiphany.[11]

Sandal was not a large castle and must have been cramped for a large army – the soldiers probably bivouacked in its grounds or just beyond – but it was well-placed for defence, which Margaret doubtless understood as she consulted with Somerset and likely Northumberland and Clifford too. They ruled out taking the castle by storm or siege, but luring the Yorkists into the open would not be easy either.

Once again it appears, according to Waurin, that Andrew Trollope contributed much towards resolving the Lancastrians' problems. He says that Trollope, '*un tres soubtil homme de guerre*', suggested the subterfuge that was used.[12] First, in several verbal exchanges the Lancastrians derided York for skulking behind castle walls for fear of a woman. On or near Christmas Day Lord John Neville, the Earl of Westmorland's brother and Warwick's cousin, visited the Duke of York during the truce and requested a commission to raise troops. Once York in his role as Protector granted the request, Neville showed that he had acted 'under false colour' and brought his troops, probably less than the 8,000 often cited, to the service of the Lancastrian cause.[13]

The fighting resumed very soon after Christmas. In the final week of December there were attacks on the foraging parties the Yorkists sent from the castle to address their dwindling supplies. Over this period at Trollope's suggestion some 400 of his men were falsely recruited into the Yorkist forces. Trollope also spread a rumour that Yorkist reinforcements were soon to arrive – a fiction engineered to raise York's confidence.

When York's men did engage the main Lancastrian force, he was over-confident. There is another story that in addition Trollope himself appeared before the battle with a new contingent claiming to be Yorkists from Lancashire. This is suspect, for he would have run a serious risk of jeopardising the strategy if he were recognised.

Warwick was not present, but York himself could easily have known the old soldier.[14]

Although the Yorkists drew blood on the opening engagement, the Lancastrians had the advantage and prevented their enemy from manoeuvring. A number did succeed in breaking out but the cost in lives and leaders made a depressing account when it reached Warwick and March in their respective positions. Richard of York was himself killed, apparently late in the battle after a last stand with his inner circle. His second son, Edmund, Earl of Rutland, was supposedly stabbed by Lord Clifford as he retreated across Wakefield Bridge. Salisbury surrendered and was taken to the Lancastrian stronghold of Pontefract, where he was killed the following day. The death toll included many of Salisbury's seasoned followers, including his second son, Sir Thomas Neville, along with Sir Thomas Harrington and Sir James Pickering. In all, the Yorkist army suffered its most severe blow on that day.

But although Somerset was at least nominal commander of the Lancastrian forces, none of the sources attribute the success to any personal act of his. He would have been hard pressed to pit himself against Richard of York and the Earl of Salisbury, both of whom had over thirty years' experience on many a campaign. As the Lancastrian stratagem was a resounding success, at least Somerset could not be blamed for another failure; indeed, all the available references point to Somerset simply facilitating Andrew Trollope, whose obvious skills and long experience made all the difference.

Lancastrian euphoria over the success at Wakefield was soon dulled when news came of Mortimer's Cross, where York's heir the Earl of March defeated the earls of Pembroke and Wiltshire on 2 February 1461. While March and Warwick were still at large with their armies, the civil war was by no means over. Margaret and the Lancastrian lords decided to march south.

With the deaths of York and Salisbury, a generation of leaders had come to an end. The Lancastrians had already lost the commanders who had served in the French wars, but after Wakefield both Yorkist magnates were replaced by their sons as well: Edward, Earl of March and Richard Neville, Earl of Warwick. Both had recently won significant battles while in command, Warwick at Northampton and March at Mortimer's Cross, which somewhat evened the odds. Both sides had the benefit of advice from middle-ranking career soldiers with a flair for strategy, with Lord Fauconberg and Sir Thomas Kyriell performing Trollope's role on the Yorkist side.

Warwick had ordered his troops to intercept them at St Albans, rather than waiting to defend London. It is generally felt that Warwick was expecting to reprise the 1455 victory. This time it was the Yorkists who prepared to defend the town against their enemy. Again it was Andrew Trollope who took the initiative, and his troops took their opponents by surprise when they entered the town on 17 February by an unmanned northern gate.

Soon the Lancastrians had control of the town and forced the Yorkist army onto Barnard's Heath. The Yorkist forces were divided and Warwick's brother Sir John Neville, now Lord Montague, was hard pressed while Warwick himself led a charge to rescue him, even though it was too late. Worse still, Sir Henry Lovelace, who led a contingent of Kentishmen in the Yorkist army, changed sides at this juncture, which destroyed the Yorkist resolve and caused their line to fall apart. Despite Warwick's attempt to rally his troops nothing more could be done, and the Yorkist leaders were forced to flee.

In their flight, the Yorkists left King Henry behind. Two Yorkists, Lord Bonville and Sir Thomas Kyriell, remained behind to ensure the king's safety before handing him over to the Lancastrians with an understanding of safe conduct, but Somerset decided to arrest the two men. When they protested, his associates advised him that no safe conduct agreements applied to traitors. Somerset was reluctant to act as the enemy had his own brothers Edmund and John in custody and such an act could bring reprisals. According to legend, Somerset asked the seven-year-old Edward of Lancaster what to do and the boy, already known for his bloodthirsty disposition, declared, 'I think their heads should be struck off, uncle.' Almost amused, Somerset ordered this to be carried out. In reality, Margaret decided on the executions and allowed her son to announce them.

The Second Battle of St Albans was hailed as a victory for Somerset, although apart from the sordid legend above the accounts attribute little to his leadership. Once again Trollope was praised; he was injured by a caltrop and lamented that he had only killed fifteen Yorkists, but he was knighted after the battle. The main success of the day for Somerset and the Lancastrians was to have regained custody of the king and reaffirmed their claim as the rightful government of England. The victory could be described as Warwick and the Yorkists losing the day with a poor strategy and Trollope astutely exploiting it.

While Warwick had escaped to the west in order to join with the Earl of March's forces Margaret sought the submission of London. The south-east and London had not given her much support but its mayor and aldermen were pragmatic enough to enter talks while the Yorkists, to whom they had submitted the previous year, were expected to lose. As a goodwill gesture the London leaders paid for provisions for the Lancastrian army as they were in fact fearful of pillaging northerners. But as these supplies were leaving the city via Bishopsgate a mob appeared and attacked the wagon train, plundering the goods. On hearing of this, Margaret decided to withdraw to the north. The retreat left a vacuum, which the various Yorkist lords filled as they arrived in the city from 26 February to hold a conference at Baynard's Castle. Losing the king to the other side was a blow to Yorkist credibility, and chances of regaining control over him were slim. Stakes had been raised and a more radical action was now in order. The earls of Warwick and March had debated this at length when they met soon after the battle.

The Yorkists were now thinking the unthinkable. Six months before they would not consider deposing a legitimate king and replacing him with Richard of York, but they now knew that desperate measures were needed. Armed with the Act of Accord of the previous meeting, and inventing a 'tradition' that the Londoners had a voice in the choice of their ruler, the Yorkists called a meeting at Smithfield on 1 March where Bishop George Neville, Warwick's brother and Chancellor of England, read a chronicle of the 'crimes' of Henry VI to the multitude and presented the Earl of March as an alternative king. The horde predictably endorsed March, and this was considered grounds enough to proclaim him as King Edward IV.

England now had two kings, although the writ of each king ran in different regions. The debate persisted over whether an anointed king could be deposed, but everyone knew that this matter would only be solved by bloodshed. No sooner was Edward IV acclaimed as king than he made preparation with his confederates to confront the Lancastrians, who were then using the city of York as their capital. At almost nineteen, able and astute beyond his years and blessed with both good looks and a charming manner, Edward was far more convincing a king.

It was Somerset who chose to make a stand at Towton, possibly still advised by Northumberland and Trollope. It was the best choice of ground he could have made, on the highest point between the city of York and the advancing Yorkists, giving the defenders the advantage. Somerset should have taken note of the Cock Beck, a narrow stream to the west of the field, but perhaps he was not considering the prospect of retreating in that direction; it would have made it difficult for his army to manoeuvre. Thus under the joint command of Somerset and Northumberland the Lancastrians held the high ground. Almost certainly on Trollope's suggestion, as it resembles his favoured strategy of preparing surprises, a small ambush party was concealed in Castle Hill Wood, to the west in a bend of the Cock.

In all fairness to Somerset, Towton could easily have ended with a Lancastrian victory. In the largest and bloodiest battle ever fought in the British Isles, both sides fought doggedly and casualties were high from the start. The Lancastrians had the disadvantage of snow and sleet blowing in their faces, but as the day wore on none could say for certain who was winning. At the first onslaught it even looked like Somerset would win a spectacular victory. Leading some 7,000 troops, with Trollope commanding a Welsh contingent of similar numbers on his left flank, he drove the Yorkist knights from the field. The Earl of Northumberland on his other side did not make the same progress, and the initial thrust was followed by an exchange with the Yorkist left flank. In a lull in the fighting King Edward rallied his following with a pep-talk, and the Yorkists found a new lease of life.[15]

But even then Somerset was gaining ground, and once the ambush party appeared it came close to breaking the Yorkist line. The late arrival of the Duke of Norfolk then turned the tables once more, and the Lancastrians were forced back towards the Cock. Their backs to the stream, there was a general panic as some Lancastrian soldiers tried to ford it, and others were seeking to clamber over them, crushing those below.

By the time Somerset withdrew to York, the death toll ran into thousands, the vast majority on the Lancastrian side. The list of the dead when it was made began with the Earl of Northumberland and went on to name Lord John Neville, Lords Dacre and Welles and a roll call of knights and gentry including Sir John Heron of Forde, Sir Robert Tailboys and Sir Andrew Trollope along with his son. Lord Clifford had been killed in an engagement at Ferrybridge the night before. The Yorkist dead, including Lord Fitzwalter and Sir Thomas Parr, were few in comparison. Some forty-two captured knights were beheaded on Edward's orders, as was Somerset's uncle the Earl of Wiltshire. But Lord Fitzhugh, Lord Rivers and his son Anthony Woodville were among those pardoned, and some such as Henry Percy, Northumberland's heir, were kept as prisoners. Estimates of the dead run to 9,000 Lancastrians and 800 Yorkists.

Towton decided who was king of England. With some of the remaining Lancastrian lords Somerset rejoined Margaret, King Henry and their son at York and, seeing that making a stand in the city would be unwise, they prudently fled north. What little of their army survived was scattered. After Towton many towns and individuals previously loyal to King Henry now submitted to Edward, for they knew there was little point in further resistance. Somerset and the Lancastrians still fought in the far north for the next three years, but winning back a kingdom was much harder than fighting to keep it.

If Edmund Beaufort had been Duke of Somerset in 1461 would the outcome of Towton have been different? Henry Beaufort was not his father but was expected to act like him. He had to learn how to command armies and was not a complete failure at this. Yet the chronicles do not name him specifically as doing noted service, and others are known to have contributed to the victories at Wakefield and St Albans. Somerset chose Towton as the best place to defend, and could have done little more; his choice was good as any. There was no recorded disagreement with his strategy. Whatever stopped Northumberland from advancing with the rest of the Lancastrian force changed the entire course of events; if he had managed it, Somerset would have been lauded as having saved England for Henry VI.

After Wakefield and Towton many senior commanders on both sides were dead and their sons were mostly short in experience. It is certain that advisors of lower social rank but rich in expertise from previous wars aided both sides. When Sir Andrew Trollope lay with the dead on Towton field his cause suffered from the loss.

There had been far too much left to chance in the whole affair. Both sides had won and lost plenty when they met that Palm Sunday in 1461, and who would win that day was anyone's guess. It was a harsh encounter, but the Yorkists gained the advantage with a little luck. Somerset had done the best he could, but events turned against him. This third Duke of Somerset would remain loyal to the House of Lancaster, even as it lost the throne, and for three more years he laboured to regain the kingdom for Henry. All the while, such a prospect grew increasingly slim.

10

SOMERSET AND EDWARD IV

For all the service the Beauforts had rendered to the crown from 1399 onwards, once the House of York gained the throne there was no place for them. In a manner that would have made his father and grandfather proud, Henry Beaufort remained loyal to Henry VI and his family even in their straitened and hopeless circumstances. He had the opportunity of regaining his wealth and power in the new regime, but rejected it all.

Edward IV entered the city of York itself a few days after the Battle of Towton. He then led his army northward in order to prevent what remained of the enemy from securing the far north against him, and for a time this was fairly straightforward. In Durham Bishop Booth offered no resistance and after a short imprisonment was all too ready to serve the new king. The city of Newcastle submitted without question. Further north, in the border region of Northumberland, there would be a drawn-out war of resistance that plagued the new regime for the next three years. But apart from Wales and Northumberland there was little further fighting. The country as a whole seemed to have assented to the accession of Edward IV, if only out of recognition that the Lancastrians could not resist him any further. The new king turned west to suppress some resistance in Lancashire and eventually returned to London. He left the pacification of the north to Warwick, who was assisted by his brother John Neville, Lord Montague and others of the Neville affinity. They succeeded, but it took far longer than expected.

On 26 May 1461, Margaret and her party reached the Scottish court. They found it in a state of uncertainty; James II had been killed by an exploding cannon while his army was retaking Roxburgh the previous year. The new king, James III, was a child, his mother Mary of Guelders acting as regent and under pressure to recognise Edward IV. But the court was much divided and Bishop Kennedy, its most influential member, urged Mary to give support to the fugitive Lancastrians. Margaret was generous in her promises over what she mostly did not possess, and the Scots took the bait. It was not difficult to hand over Berwick, recently held by the dead Earl of Northumberland, but she also pledged Carlisle to Scotland and promised English titles and lordships to some Scottish nobles. In June 1461, Montague was hard pressed to drive back a combined Scottish and Lancastrian army from Carlisle and a short time later a Lancastrian force raided County Durham.

This new phase in the dynastic conflict saw Somerset adjusting to new conditions. The small Lancastrian court in exile sought foreign aid and cultivated its sympathisers in England, particularly those in Northumberland. Somerset was in fact an uncle of King James, although there is no sign of this gaining any favour for the cause. Edward IV was seeking to counter Margaret with a two-pronged Scottish policy where through diplomacy he sought to persuade Queen Mary to abandon the alliance with Margaret. At the same time he intrigued with rebellious Scottish nobles.

In July 1461 Somerset went as part of an embassy to King Charles VII of France, hoping for money and troops to aid the Lancastrian war effort. By the time he arrived Charles had died and the new king Louis XI, who then favoured the Yorkists, soon had the envoys imprisoned at Arques, their letters of safe conduct from Charles no longer valid.[1] Louis released them soon after and Somerset returned to Scotland, taking ship at Bruges. The French would later send military aid to Margaret, but not very much and Louis later rethought his stance towards Edward.

In the south of England Edward IV was succeeding in restoring stability. As a dashing, handsome and charming young man he was personally popular; it was not difficult to present a more positive image than Henry VI, whose eccentric manner had been cause for concern and whose lack of decisive government had caused so much discontent. Edward's court was known for its lively, colourful style, with many young people near the king's age engaging in revelry almost every night. His two surviving brothers, George and Richard, were respectively created dukes of Clarence and Gloucester.

Edward IV was a Beaufort in the female line. His grandmother was Joan Beaufort (I), daughter of John of Gaunt and Katherine Swynford, whose own youngest daughter, Cecily, had married Richard of York. From 1461 every monarch of England and then Great Britain was a descendant of Gaunt and Katherine, and counted the Beauforts among their ancestors.

The new king needed to make a statement that civil war was over, and this required a delicate balance between action against those who still opposed him and a general acceptance and reconciliation. When the first parliament of the new reign met on 4 November 1461 at Westminster one main concern was condemnation of the former monarchy. A long and graphic invective was reserved for the deposed King Henry, declared guilty with many of his party on up to ten counts. Interpreted as treason, these charges included conspiracy to murder Richard of York (the Battle of Wakefield), fighting at St Albans and Towton on the Lancastrian side and conspiracy with the Scots against England, especially in giving them Berwick and aiding their attempt to gain Carlisle. Those named as having taken part in these actions were attainted. In nearly all of these accusations the Duke of Somerset either headed the list or took second place to the Duke of Exeter. Only on two counts relating to the attempted seizure of Carlisle was Somerset not named, as he was on his mission to France when this happened.[2]

Given the numbers who fought for the Lancastrian cause only a fraction were in fact attainted. Most of the Lancastrian nobles appear, as do several knights and even yeomen, all declared traitors. Many, such as the Earl of Northumberland, Lords Clifford, Neville, Welles, Dacre and Sir Andrew Trollope (listed as an esquire), were attainted posthumously and others, Somerset included, were still at large.[3] Most of those who had fought on the other side were not penalised in this way.

Once the attainders were passed, Edward took the greatest of pains to win over the balance of the Lancastrian force. This was a controversial policy at the time, but basically a sound one. Civil war had bitterly divided regions, communities and even many a family, and such animosities would hardly aid the restoration of order. To have attainted or even removed from office everyone who had supported the other side would have disrupted the administration of the provinces where some families traditionally held positions as justice or sheriff. There were bonds of commitment between the nobles, gentry and common people of each region, for many served those of higher rank and often depended on them for sustenance and support; such loyalties could not be easily redirected. The entire social fabric was at risk of being torn apart and Edward knew that continuity was needed. He was also mindful that he was widely considered a usurper and hoped to counter this by offering opportunities in the new regime in return for compliance. Above all he knew that the Lancastrian cause was far from dead, and he still hoped to draw away some of its potential supporters.

During the civil war Lords Audley and Greystoke had been induced over to the Yorkist side. The young Duke of Suffolk and the Earl of Shrewsbury were now often seen at Edward's court while both their fathers had been prominent Lancastrians. Bishop Laurence Booth was now Edward's confessor and gave his support in the north; to gain his cooperation was preferable to any attempt to dislodge him from Durham. It was considered a better policy to gain acceptance from most of Edward's former enemies and to draw a line under the civil wars, at least where this was possible.

One certain success in this reconciliation programme was Richard Woodville, Lord Rivers, who with his son Anthony was captured at Towton, pardoned and then reintegrated into public affairs. The Woodvilles had been the staunchest Lancastrians ever since the elder was an esquire in Bedford's household, when he denied Duke Humphrey entry to the Tower in 1425, but once he pledged loyalty to the new king the Woodvilles would remain faithful to the Yorkist monarchy ever after, although Edward's marriage in 1464 to Rivers' daughter had much to do with it. Rivers was heard to comment that the cause of Lancaster was at an end when he threw in his lot with Edward.

But this policy had some noted failures too. John de Vere, twelfth Earl of Oxford, who famously rode out to fight for Henry in 1455 and arrived a day too late at St Albans, and who in 1460 pleaded infirmity as reason not to participate in the fighting, was also received into Edward's grace but later condemned for planning treason. His eldest son, Aubrey, was close to Margaret. Edward received the submission of the two in 1461, but in February 1462 both were arrested on allegations of a plot against the king and subsequently executed. Even then Edward agreed that the younger son, also called John, could succeed as earl without the expected attainder. For some time this thirteenth earl appeared to support the regime, but he later declared again for Lancaster.

Some believed that Edward was far too liberal with his forgiveness, and that many he forgave were either plotting or awaiting an opportunity to turn against him again. He might have been over-confident of his own ability to charm. It was only when his efforts to lure Somerset to his side backfired that he understood how fragile his reconciliation policy could be.

Late in 1462, Edward was again in the north after Margaret had invaded Northumberland with Scottish and French support. While Edward remained at Durham stricken with measles his army laid siege to Bamburgh and Dunstanburgh, two of the important castles in the region. Somerset, in command on seizing Bamburgh, waited for a delayed relieving army but finally surrendered on Christmas Eve when it failed to arrive. Sir Ralph Percy, brother of the late Earl of Northumberland and seneschal of the other castle, also surrendered. But when brought to Edward at Durham they were both received into the king's obedience. Percy was even made seneschal of both Bamburgh and Dunstanburgh and commissioned to receive repentant rebels into his service according to his discretion. This was an honour usually reserved for a royal servant whose loyalty was certain.

Somerset had even better treatment. The last survivor of the Lancastrian commanders and determined enemy of the House of York was received like a long-lost friend, even though it is unlikely, given their fathers' feud, that they knew each other very well beforehand. Edward took Somerset back to London with his court and on 10 March 1463 had the attainder reversed. He was soon confirmed as Duke of Somerset and regained his estates and incomes.

This was the most dramatic of reconciliations, or so it seemed. For almost a year Somerset lived in the Yorkist court, where the king made such a show of favouring him as if they had been the best of friends throughout their lives. Somerset was near in age to the king, and enjoyed the revelry and court activities as much as he did. They even slept in the same bed at times; this did not necessarily have any sexual connotation but was a practice traditionally reserved for the closest of friends.

But the Yorkist court despised him. They cringed as Somerset sat next to the king at tournaments he had called so that his new friend could take some relaxation after his labours. Those who had been loyal Yorkists all along remembered Somerset fighting against them and found their king's new attitude hard to accept. Others formerly of the other side were also attending court and were at least partially accepted there, but Edward's obvious doting on Somerset was over the top. Warwick in particular made known his ill-feeling towards reconciled Lancastrians. He had old issues with Rivers, but Somerset was surely the bitterest of his enemies.

The king was using Somerset as a propaganda tool. Although pro-Lancastrian feeling was still smouldering throughout the country there was a growing acceptance that the return of the old regime was unlikely, and to find accommodation with the Yorkist monarchy was the best course. If the last remaining Lancastrian commander had become a prominent Yorkist the defeated side would lose further credibility. Somerset probably found it difficult to physically leave the court, as if he were a prisoner.

Edward eventually took note of this ill-feeling after a riot broke out against Somerset at Northampton when the royal party arrived there with the duke in attendance. After this, at Somerset's request the king gave him a command in north Wales; he thought it would at least keep him out of danger at the court, but soon realised that he had been too trusting. In December 1463 Somerset rode off to his new office with a following but suddenly turned north again and rejoined the Lancastrian army, dropping his pretence of reciprocating Edward's friendship as soon as he left his company.

The duke first stopped at Newcastle where the king had sent some of Somerset's retainers and took command of the castle there, disrupting the supply chain for the Yorkists in Northumberland. Outraged, Edward sent an order to arrest him. Woken up in the middle of the night when the Yorkists came for him, Somerset escaped without his shoes and eventually reached Alnwick where he rallied those still loyal to King Henry.

Contrary to this 'act of supreme folly', as one historian dubbed Edward's policy towards Somerset,[4] some have written as to how effective the reconciliation would have been had it worked, but the king had made a supreme effort for little gain. Edward was now more skilled at statecraft and may have at least suspected that Somerset's manner at court was too good to be true, and really should have kept the young duke on a tighter rein, or at least had him watched. Somerset nevertheless had a year to convince Edward of his new alignment, and must have been determined to appear sincere.

Could Somerset have settled into life as a Yorkist courtier? From a pragmatic viewpoint this was the logical course that many had already taken. It guaranteed a life of safety, comfort, wealth, power and royal favour, and if the Beauforts had become as avid supporters of the House of York as they had been of Lancaster they would have at least kept their estates and titles. The Lancastrian faction could not have sunk much lower in its fortunes, and as time was passing the Yorkists felt their hold on the country becoming more secure.

But Somerset was no sycophant. That he consciously abandoned his new status for an uncertain rebellion which was then losing impetus shows how committed he was to Lancaster; he voluntarily gave up a life of wealth and pleasure for his belief in the legitimacy of Henry VI. His submission to Edward was in fact pragmatic, preferable to being beheaded, but he returned to his original colours as soon as he could. In doing so he brought a new lease of life to the Lancastrian cause and thwarted Edward's attempts to show that it was withering. Sir Ralph Percy had already returned to the Lancastrian fold and the Neville adherent Sir Ralph Grey had also changed sides. The Beauforts had always served the Lancastrian kings and Somerset made his fundamental loyalty clear by his act.

Margaret and her confederates had no lasting gains, even when Somerset returned and Northumberland was an intermittent battleground. Percy and Grey were both pardoned once again and both later turned their coats once more. But lack of real progress was affecting morale. Margaret did succeed in securing French aid in Northumberland for a time, and in July 1463 a French, Scottish and Lancastrian army besieged Norham Castle in vain until Warwick and Montague relieved it. The Scots were now cooling towards the Lancastrians.

Shortly after this Margaret took her son and some of her household by ship to Sluys. She claimed to have gone to raise further funds and troops from France, but she did not return. Upon reaching Philip the Good's court she received a warm welcome, but she soon found the Burgundians were not moved to act in her cause. A truce between England and France in October ended her hopes for further aid from Louis, and she remained in France.

Margaret probably knew that the Scots were reconsidering their support for her cause and suspected that Scotland would soon not be safe for her. If this is the case, she abandoned Somerset and some of her other supporters to a hopeless fight. It is true that she also left her husband behind, but then her prime concern was always her son, and to take Henry too would make it seem more likely that she was fleeing. She and Henry never saw each other again. Somerset, left in Scotland with the Lancastrian remnant, had reason to be concerned. Not only was his cause losing support in the Scottish court but the queen herself, Mary of Guelders, apparently adopted a violent hatred of him personally. According to William Worcester she and the duke had an affair, and her reputation was somewhat in question. On hearing that Somerset had given Louis XI an account of their sexual activities, she now held Somerset 'in the greatest hatred' and sought to have him murdered.[5] Despite this, Somerset fought on as the options narrowed. The death of Mary of Guelders in 1463 resolved the ambivalence in Scottish policy, and Warwick was finally able to gain first a truce in December that year and then further peace talks. They eventually agreed to sign a treaty whereby the Scots abandoned their alliance with Margaret and undertook to give the Lancastrian leadership no further shelter or support.

As a faithful subject of Henry VI, Somerset reacted to the troubling news by embarking on a desperate campaign, although most others had effectively given up in Northumberland. With lords Roos and Hungerford, Sir Ralph Percy, Sir Ralph Grey, Henry Bellingham and other dissident elements he seized Norham Castle and various towns in the county in the spring of 1464. This succeeded in jeopardising the pending peace settlement, and talks were postponed.

In April 1464, Somerset's small force sought to ambush Montague's party as it went north to meet the Scottish ambassadors and bring them to the final peace talks. An intelligence war decided the outcome when Montague's scouts told him of the planned ambush and he took a different route while sending for reinforcements; soon the Yorkist force far outnumbered Somerset's men. When the armies engaged at Hedgeley Moor, north of Alnwick, on 26 April the Lancastrian left flank broke and scattered. The remainder fought on, worn down and losing men by desertion. When Sir Ralph Percy was slain the bulk of the force fled, and Somerset was forced to withdraw with Hungerford and Roos.

At the same time King Edward moved north with a large army. Somerset raised new troops and brought them, with the surviving Lancastrian leaders and Henry VI himself, to occupy the upper Tyne Valley. The Scottish envoys were now in York and the treaty that would drive the Lancastrians from their base in Scotland was all but signed. Perhaps Somerset knew that this was his last throw of the dice. The chances of the Scots changing their mind about him were slim, but if he could claim a substantial victory before the Yorkist artillery arrived they might reconsider. But his best was not good enough; Somerset once again had poor resources at his disposal and by now lacked Scottish and French reinforcements. On 15 May the Lancastrian forces were unprepared when Montague came upon them at Hexham and put them to flight. Somerset was captured.

This was the end for Henry Beaufort, Duke of Somerset and obviously acting on Edward's instruction, Montague had him beheaded the same day. For all the efforts Henry Beaufort had been obliged to make over the previous nine years, his life ended in failure. Roos and Hungerford were both caught the day after the battle and also summarily executed. In the parliament called later that year Edward had Somerset's pardon posthumously revoked, and with a new attainder the dukedom of Somerset was declared extinct. Soon the Yorkist army regained possession of the upper Tyne region and then laid siege to Bamburgh Castle, where Sir Ralph Grey maintained the last defiance. Once Bamburgh capitulated and Grey was executed, the Lancastrian resistance was effectively finished.

Somerset had brought Henry VI on this last campaign, possibly to raise morale but more likely because he feared that the Scots would seize him once the treaty was signed. The deposed king was taken into hiding after the Hexham defeat and spent over a year being moved from place to place by his supporters until he was finally captured in Lancashire and escorted to imprisonment in the Tower of London. At Harlech in Wales, Sir Richard Tunstall, formerly Henry's chamberlain and a member of the Percy affinity, continued to hold the castle in anticipation of a Lancastrian landing, but by now the young King Edward knew that his rule was secure and the northern interlude was over. He probably believed that the threat from Margaret had ended too.

The tragedy of Henry Beaufort lay in his obligations as Duke of Somerset, head of the Beaufort family and a leading

Lancastrian magnate, with all this role demanded. He was not incompetent, and in fact had good advisors, but luck was not on his side much of the time and his final campaigns were hampered by poor resources. It would have been better if he had gone into exile with Margaret rather than throw himself and all that remained against the enemy in a doomed act of desperation.

It is sad to think that he could have kept his estates and titles and remained in the favour of the new regime but threw it all away only to die on a stricken field by the executioner's sword. Edward IV was willing to give him so much, but at the price of his integrity. Despite a patchy military career, Somerset's commitment to Henry VI and to Margaret cannot be denied.

In fairness to Somerset, even if he had accepted life as a tamed Lancastrian in Edward's court he would have never have felt truly secure. There were simply too many powerful elements there who resented his presence deeply. Too many would have been waiting for him to put a foot wrong, and false accusations could be made whenever the king was in a mood to hear them; indeed, it is altogether possible that the twelfth Earl of Oxford and his son had met their deaths in this way.

It was too often the consequence during this period of civil war that fighting on the losing side meant attainder. The forfeiture of all material wealth would spell disaster, not only to the noble but to their families and descendants, and many widows and orphans were reduced to living on the charity of others. It appears that Somerset's family did not suffer so much, however, and his mother and his unmarried sisters were provided for, although the daughters found their marriage options scaled down with their reduced status.

With all of Somerset's possessions in the hands of the king, there were rewards to be won. In 1467 the king granted his moveable goods to Lord Wenlok, Warwick's lieutenant, as well as those of

Sir Andrew Trollope. He also gave some of Somerset's outlying estates to royal servants, while Clarence gained Corfe Castle.[6] In 1468 he granted one Thomas Bledlow various household treasures that had belonged to the duke, almost certainly from his London home. The items listed included much gold and silver gilt plate, three tables of gold garnished with rubies and other jewels, and the figures of a 'plowman' and a 'mylkwyf' in gold encrusted with precious stones.[7] The king also had possession of lands held in dower by Eleanor Beauchamp, Dowager Duchess of Somerset and mother of the third duke, who had remarried since 1455. He seems to have allowed her to keep the estates. He eventually granted some to Gloucester, but only after her death in 1468.[8]

The younger daughters of Edmund Beaufort (I), too young to marry before the destruction of the noble house, did at least find husbands, although beneath them in status. One daughter, Joan, married Christopher St Lawrence, Baron Howth, a Yorkist from Dublin and then an official of the English Exchequer who later became Lord Chancellor. This was a prestigious union in the circumstances.[9] Her sister Elizabeth married Sir Richard FitzLewis and died some time before 1472. Another sister, Anne, married Sir John Paston, prominent in the gentry of Norfolk and a confirmed Yorkist.[10] There is also mention of yet another sister, Mary, but nothing as to her fate. It could be said that the remaining Beaufort daughters survived the fall of their house, and though they lost status they were at least comfortable. Some of them – Margaret, Eleanor and Joan – were later widowed and remarried, all into the gentry.

Within months of the final victory in the north Edward IV had new cause for concern. Richard Neville, who had added his father's earldom of Salisbury to that of Warwick, acquired a long list of estates and offices for his service towards the Yorkist success. Not only confirmed as Captain of Calais and Warden of the West

March, he was now Chamberlain of England, Admiral of England, Ireland and Aquitaine, Warden of the Cinque Ports, Constable of the Duchy of Lancaster and held several other lucrative posts having also gained many estates, including those of the dispossessed Lord Clifford. He had amassed far more than anyone but the new king.

Of his brothers, John Neville, Lord Montague was finally rewarded in 1464 with the earldom of Northumberland for his actions at Hexham. The youngest, George Neville, then Bishop of Exeter, had been Chancellor of England from 1461 and also became Archbishop of York in 1464. During the uncertainty of the intermittent war in the north Edward relied strongly on the Nevilles and their retinue to defend his land. It is noticeable that he was not as well-disposed towards them after the Lancastrians had been crushed.

The first signs of tension between Edward and Warwick appeared in September 1464 when the king married Elizabeth Woodville in secret without even consulting his foremost courtier. Kings would normally marry for reasons of state, and Warwick had already been negotiating a match between Edward and a niece of King Louis of France. Elizabeth Woodville was the widow of a Lancastrian knight and the daughter of Richard Woodville, Lord Rivers, whom Edward soon raised to the dignity of Earl Rivers, no doubt to Warwick's chagrin given the bad blood between them since Calais. The promotion of the new queen's greedy and ambitious relatives, and their obvious influence on a foreign policy that favoured Burgundy (Elizabeth's mother, Jacquetta, was of the House of Luxembourg and Bedford's widow), frustrated Warwick. Over the next five years, relations deteriorated.

It was widely accepted by this time that the cause of Lancaster was at an end and that the Beaufort dynasty was a thing of the past. Events in 1470 would prove the folly of this belief when the York–Neville alliance broke in two. There were still male Beauforts living, and when the time came they returned to the limelight. The House of Beaufort would rise again.

11

THE LAST BEAUFORT DUKE OF SOMERSET

Although the execution of the third Duke of Somerset in 1464 disposed of the last of the Lancastrian generals, this did not the end the struggle of the two houses for the throne. No prophecy ever hinted that Henry VI would one day be king again, nor that a Beaufort would stand once again among his main counsellors as Duke of Somerset. In less than seven years after Hexham all this came to pass.

Margaret of Anjou had left for France with her son in 1463. While she remained there she could provide a focus for discontent, but she could not do much in those years without an army of any size or powerful supporters. Once King Henry was captured in Lancashire in 1465 he was taken to London and paraded through the streets in a humiliating manner before Edward had him locked in the Tower, by some accounts no longer in possession of his right mind. Henry was more use to the Yorkists alive and their prisoner; his death would have allowed the Lancastrians to proclaim Edward of Lancaster their king in his place.

Henry Beaufort had two younger brothers still living, Edmund (II) and John (III), of which the former would have succeeded him had the second attainder not ended the dukedom. Of course the persistent Lancastrians still considered Edmund as fourth duke, but he had no estates or other incomes. He lived in exile in the typical manner of a pretender, awaiting the chance to come into his own.

Edmund (II) Beaufort was born in 1439 and on reaching adolescence fought in the civil wars alongside his father and brother, but as a younger son he had few opportunities to make his mark. John (III) was born about 1440 and was never known for any distinguished actions but simply followed Edmund throughout the events. Like their elder brother Henry, both remained unmarried. In 1460 Sir Edmund Beaufort was holding Carisbrooke Castle on the Isle of Wight as his elder brother's deputy against a Yorkist siege. When he was forced to capitulate, Sir Geoffrey Gate, Warwick's lieutenant from Calais, sent him and his brother John to Guines as his prisoners. Both were still prisoners in February 1461 when the third duke was in a quandary over the killing of Bonville and Kyriell after the Second Battle of St Albans, for it would have endangered his own brothers' lives had the Yorkists decided on reprisals. The two Beauforts survived, and might have escaped, or at least were at liberty when they made their way to the Burgundian court after these events.

Both Duke Philip and King Louis were hedging their bets over the Yorkist monarchy, and Philip decided the Beauforts were useful enough to maintain for the present. Edmund's ducal title was recognised in Philip's court and for a time he probably held a military command in Burgundy. It was by no means unusual for medieval rulers to harbour dissidents and exiles from other countries for their possible use either as pretenders or bargaining chips at some later date. For a time the two Beauforts lived as Philip's pensioners, although as he reached an accord with the Yorkists their presence in his court drew comment in England. The Duke of Exeter also lived under Philip's favour at this time.

Louis XI had made serious enemies early in his reign, and by 1464 a coalition of greater French nobles, including Philip the

Good, had risen in revolt. The War of the Public Weal as it was known saw Philip's son Charles, Count of Charolais engaged in military activity, his father now too infirm to take to the field. What part the Beaufort brothers played is not known but it is likely that they were awarded military roles appropriate to their assumed rank and therefore gained some experience; exiles maintained by a ruler were often expected to be of use to him, even in martial contexts. By late 1465 Louis had made peace and given enough concessions to his enemies to end the fight unscathed.

Charles the Bold, Count of Charolais and then Duke of Burgundy on the death of Philip the Good in 1467, had plans of his own. He drew closer to Yorkist England with his marriage to Margaret of York, sister to Edward IV, although this did not mean any real commitment, and Edmund Beaufort still petitioned for his support for Margaret of Anjou. Charles had issues with Louis of France but at the same time was cautious of committing himself.

When Margaret of Anjou returned to France she took up residence with her son at Saint-Mihiel in the Duchy of Bar in eastern France, one of her father's lordships, where she lived in comparative comfort on the generosity of her cousin King Louis; like Philip, the French king knew the value of pretenders. Hers was typical of many a court-in-exile, where dispossessed Lancastrians lived under the impression that they would return some day and regain England, and where their court culture had them retain their titles and precedence, even though they had lost everything else.

Louis XI while Dauphin had shown open support for the Yorkists during the civil war, but on succeeding to the throne months after Towton had to contend with a strong king in England, and although still well disposed towards Edward he had a new agenda. He had given Margaret military aid in Northumberland in exchange for Calais once the Lancastrians regained England; it was too good an opportunity to miss. The French expedition to Northumberland under Pierre de Brezé did not accomplish much, however, and Louis agreed to a truce in October 1463, knowing that Margaret would not be in a position to give him Calais. He then cultivated good relations with Warwick, offering flattery and secretly sending him gifts; he saw how powerful the earl was in England.

Margaret and her son Edward of Lancaster, now in his mid-teens, presided over the likes of the dispossessed Duke of Exeter, Thomas Courtenay, titular Earl of Devon, Jasper Tudor, still styled Earl of Pembroke, the Butler heir to the Ormond earldom and others including her chief counsellors Sir John Fortescue and John Morton, all wanted rebels in England. At some time before 15 December 1464, Edmund Beaufort, now Duke of Somerset, and his brother John joined Margaret's small court, their presence mentioned in a letter from Fortescue on that date.[1]

The Beauforts were treated with the honour expected of their rank and knew the queen's generosity, but they had little wealth of their own. This was the life of many an *emigré* over the centuries, and most of them would spend the rest of their lives in some foreign retreat waiting for a day that never came. Margaret was still in contact with some supporters in England, but she had no resources to mount an invasion. Even so, Margaret refused to believe that it was all over.

The Beauforts and Exeter also kept their association with the Burgundian court for a while afterwards. Perhaps they continued to attend his court on occasion, to keep the channel of contact open while both Louis and Philip watched for developments. Philip's successor Charles of course opted to favour Yorkist England, but Somerset was still attending the Burgundian court; John Paston was in Bruges when Charles married Margaret of York in 1468 and remarked that Somerset had only departed the day before her arrival; obviously a diplomatic absence.[2]

The events to follow could not have been foreseen so easily, dramatic as they were. In the summer of 1470 the two most unlikely converts to the cause of Lancaster came to join Margaret's shadow court. One was George, Duke of Clarence, brother of King Edward himself; the other was Richard Neville, Earl of Warwick.

The events of the previous two years had placed these two in open revolt and then in flight. Since the Woodville marriage of 1464 Warwick and King Edward had not known the best relations and Warwick had felt himself marginalised in affairs of state. Edward's reconciliation with the Woodvilles was one bone of contention related to others. Warwick had seen Richard Woodville, who had constantly schemed and spied on him at Calais, not only raised to equal rank as an earl but basking in royal favour when the king married his daughter. The pro-Burgundian foreign policy was also annoying; Warwick hated Burgundy from his days at Calais and was himself intriguing with (and being manipulated by) King Louis.

Edward had less reason to depend on Warwick and his family after the north was pacified and might have come to the conclusion that he had given them too much power. The king had kept on good terms with John Neville, first Lord Montague and from 1464 Earl of Northumberland, and the two had long been personal friends, but relations between the king and the other brothers had soured. In 1467 Edward had suddenly dismissed Archbishop George Neville from his office as chancellor, even turning up personally at his house to demand the Great Seal. While the king continued to reward Warwick, the earl nonetheless harboured discontent.

George, Duke of Clarence had barely reached manhood and harboured ambitions of his own, which his brother the king mostly denied him. Edward vetoed various marriages to heiresses that would have given Clarence wealth and power, and in particular was opposed to a union with Isabel, Warwick's elder daughter and co-heiress. Warwick accordingly had little difficulty cultivating Clarence's caprices, and when the forbidden marriage of the young duke and Isabel Neville was solemnised at Calais on 11 July 1469 this heralded open revolt against Edward.

Warwick defeated the Yorkist army at Edgcote in Northamptonshire on 26 July, capturing Edward the following day. He executed Earl Rivers and other prominent Yorkists, and attempted to govern with the king in custody. But this arrangement did not last and Edward freed himself when other Yorkist nobles entered his company. Warwick contented himself with believing that the king was chastened by this show of force.

But Edward soon embarked on building a new power base. He set about augmenting the role of his youngest brother, Richard, Duke of Gloucester, and also relied on the loyalty of his brother-in-law Anthony Woodville, now the second Earl Rivers, and his friend William, Lord Hastings. A more drastic move was to release Northumberland's heir young Henry Percy from the Tower and restore him to his father's earldom, which involved relieving John Neville of the same dignity. Although compensated with the new creation of Marquis Montague, John made no secret of his discontent.

Warwick again rose in revolt the following year, this time with a tale that Edward was a bastard and Clarence the rightful king. After a rebellion instigated by Warwick met defeat at 'Losecoat Field' on 12 March 1470, both Warwick and Clarence were forced to flee. After a time sailing a pirate flotilla in the Channel the two found their way to Paris where Louis, seeing an opportunity, directed them to talks with Margaret. They were now landless exiles and needed more resources if they were to recoup their fortunes. Margaret knew how much use they could both be to her, and was willing to listen. But she would not let go of previous insults, in particular something that Warwick had apparently once said to her. She kept him on his knees for at least fifteen minutes begging her pardon, and then showed herself the soul of forgiveness. Her pleasantries were far from sincere and she certainly planned to dispose of him after he had helped achieve her aims.

Warwick and Margaret even married their children to each other. It did not seem a happy union for Anne Neville, who had accompanied her father into exile, when she was matched with the seventeen-year-old Edward of Lancaster, by all accounts a thoroughly unpleasant young man still obsessed with bloodletting and revenge. Luckily for her, Margaret had told her son not to consummate the marriage so that it could be annulled more easily afterwards.

Thus Edmund Beaufort, titular Duke of Somerset, found himself in council with Queen Margaret, her son Edward, the Duke of Exeter, the earls of Devon and Pembroke, and now Clarence and Warwick. The Earl of Oxford had recently come to join the court as well. With a more prestigious line-up before him, and growing concerned over King Edward's pro-Burgundian attitude, Louis was now willing to give troops, funding and naval support to the Lancastrians. The council decided on a grandiose campaign to win England back and make Henry VI king again.

Somerset remained behind with most of the Lancastrian lords when the army sailed in September; with the force were Warwick, Clarence and Jasper Tudor, Earl of Pembroke. The campaign was effectively a reprise of Warwick and Clarence's revolt, now reinforced with troops and resources. Margaret was obviously sending Warwick to accomplish her own desire, or to his death as the case may be, and his failure would do her little harm. He could not have been very trusting of Margaret given their history. He might have had an agenda of his own in all this, but he had little choice but to follow the plans with Margaret for the present. Perhaps Pembroke was with him simply to watch for possible treachery.

The campaign itself was both successful and almost bloodless. Warwick's cousin Lord Fitzhugh raised revolt in the north and Edward brought a fairly small force to put it down. On 7 September 1470, Warwick's army landed in the West Country and was soon joined by the Earl of Shrewsbury and Lord Stanley, along with many other elements who either had grievances against the Yorkist monarchy or reservations over its legitimacy, or else simply saw this as an opportunity to gain wealth and influence.

Edward was manoeuvred into East Anglia where poor communications through the marshlands made it difficult for the Yorkists to escape and where they lacked sufficient troops to fight a pitched battle with the invaders. Soon his hopes of reinforcements from Northumberland and Montague were dashed when he learned that the former had not stirred from his castle at Bamburgh and that the latter had defected to the Lancastrians. Edward survived by paying off his soldiers and taking ship from Ipswich together with Gloucester, Rivers, Hastings and their close followings. By doing so he escaped, but he had left Warwick free to secure London and to restore Henry VI to the throne.

The 'Readeption', as Warwick named the event where the Lancastrian king took his place as ruler once more, was a time of inconsistencies and improvisations. Our knowledge of events in the six months following Edward's flight is sketchy, after the returned Yorkists destroyed many of the records. It is unlikely that Henry really presided over the business of government; some sources even talk of him sitting on the throne in imitation of a sack of flour. Others give him lucid pronouncements, however. Five years in the Tower, in which time he apparently believed all along that he was still king, had taken its toll, but some actions suggest he had not sunk into a state of complete dementia. As the Edward's wife Elizabeth Woodville was now in sanctuary in Westminster Abbey and about to give birth, Henry appointed a butcher to attend to the needs of her household. If there is any truth to the story of Henry receiving the fourteen-year-old Henry Tudor and predicting that the boy would one day be king, the king had kept some of his wits.

Philippe de Commynes, then in the Duke of Burgundy's service, claims that Somerset and Exeter were present at Brussels when Charles was speaking with Edward over his requests for military aid and the two urged Charles to side with the Lancastrian English regime, although ultimately without success.[3]

Somerset, together with the Duke of Exeter and the earls of Oxford and Devon, only came back to England in February 1471 and were not involved in the fighting. If Warwick had failed they would not have risked themselves. Young Somerset probably felt out of his depth when he attended council, where it was far from certain who was in charge. Warwick was almost certainly the most influential, and Somerset resented him; they were second cousins, but the bad blood between their fathers had long broken family ties. Somerset would have identified himself with Exeter, Oxford, Devon and Pembroke, those who had always been Lancastrians, and may have resented sitting at the same council as the 'new Lancastrian' faction of Warwick, Clarence, Montague and Archbishop Neville, who had only come over during the past year. Others, such as Cardinal Bourchier and Lord Stanley, showed little enthusiasm for the new regime but participated nonetheless.

Warwick pressed continually for Margaret and her son to return to England. He was aware that continuity had to be restored, but like his allies he must have known that Margaret would not tolerate his presence once her dynasty was secure. He made arrangements to bring them, but Margaret was slow to leave Saint-Mihiel.

It is not known whether Edmund Beaufort was officially recognised as Duke of Somerset in Readeption England. The new regime apparently ignored the Yorkist attainders as invalid, but there is no sign of Edmund receiving the estates his brother had held. We do not know much of the business of the restored Lancastrian government, but too many revisions in land ownership in those six months could have provoked instability. John Beaufort was created Marquis of Dorset during the Readeption, but this was again nominal and no lands were specified.[4]

Opinion was much divided on the Readeption. Some likely saw it as the return of a rightful king to his throne, conditioned as they were to reject usurpers, but once Henry IV took the throne in 1399 the precedent had been established that a capable man could depose a less able king. Henry VI had not been too successful a king in his long reign, but he was much loved and seen as a saint-in-waiting, as he was so treated after his death. Edward IV had enjoyed a moderately-successful nine years before his flight, and had at least restored stability and peace to the realm. He was also physically attractive, pleasant and the embodiment of martial virtues. Had the monarchy been elective, he would have been the more likely candidate.

Complicating matters, many owed their wealth and positions of power to one regime or another. Regime change could mean opportunity, but it could just as easily mean dispossession or execution for treason. The majority might have thought it the safest course not to be identified with any one faction.

Clarence found his new alignment did him little good. He was acknowledged third in line for the succession after Henry VI and Edward of Lancaster but gained little in wealth or influence. His new Lancastrian allies were at best polite and cool towards him. Through his sister the Countess of Oxford, he was soon in secret correspondence with his brother Edward and thinking about changing sides again.

Edward IV had spent the winter in Bruges as guest of the Burgundian noble Louis de Gruthuuse. He hoped that the new Duke of Burgundy, Charles the Bold, having married his sister Margaret the previous year, would support a campaign to regain his kingdom. Charles was sceptical, although not dismissive of the idea, but still he doubted that Edward could succeed and preferred to await further developments. But by the closing weeks of 1470 Burgundy was in open conflict with Louis of France. Warwick would doubtlessly support the French against him, and if only to keep Warwick occupied he warmed to Edward's planned campaign. He gave Edward financial aid and allowed him to raise whatever troops he could. Edward knew that he still had much support in England, but the longer Henry VI continued to sit on the throne the more securely the renascent Lancastrians could consolidate their hold.

Despite Warwick's urging Margaret to return to England, the queen was in no hurry. She knew how volatile the situation could become and may have decided to wait until it was safer. In the spring of 1471 her party did journey to Normandy, but storms in the Channel kept her from setting out for England for so long that she suspected witchcraft. Several times Warwick rode to the south coast hoping to hear of her only to return to London disappointed. He was anxious that she cross to England as soon as possible, certain that Edward IV was planning his own return.

On landing at Ravenser near Hull in March 1471, Edward proceeded first to York and then southwards towards London, joined by supporters as he went. There was little cooperation between the Lancastrian nobles and they were ill equipped to resist. Not only were Somerset and his associates distrustful of Warwick, his brothers and Clarence, but even the Nevilles had cause to suspect the loyalties of John Neville, Marquis Montague, who apparently held back his army when Edward was consolidating his position in Yorkshire. Montague's behaviour in the coming weeks would cast doubt on his allegiances.

Somerset was in London with Warwick and the other Lancastrian leaders when news arrived of Edward's return. But as Warwick prepared to ride north to intercept the Yorkist advance, Somerset, with his kinsman the Earl of Devon, suddenly left for the south coast to meet Margaret; the weather was improving.

The Yorkists besieged Warwick and his confederates at Coventry, but when the latter declined to come out and fight Edward marched for London without any impediment. Clarence, meanwhile, had gone back to the Yorkist camp. The Londoners opened their gates for King Edward in defiance of Archbishop Neville and the Lancastrian defenders. Warwick, together with Oxford and

Exeter, and eventually joined by Montague and his northern men, followed the Yorkist army to London.

Somerset was not present when the two armies fought a pitched battle at Barnet, then some miles to the north of London, on Good Friday, 14 April 1471. Despite initial Lancastrian successes it ended with Edward triumphant, Warwick, Montague and Exeter dead and Oxford in flight to Scotland. If Somerset had been there he might have brought enough troops to turn the course of the battle. If he had planned all along to leave Edward and Warwick to fight it out, it is certain that Oxford and Exeter did not agree with this course of action. Yet he and Devon prioritised joining Margaret, exposing London the risk of a Yorkist takeover.

Margaret landed at Weymouth with her son and a modest force on the day of the battle, and was welcomed by Somerset and Devon. With her were John, Lord Wenlok, formerly Warwick's lieutenant in Calais, and Sir John Langstrother, Prior of the Knights of St John in England, both of whom had been sent from London to escort Margaret's party. Once again a Duke of Somerset headed the Lancastrian army. The seventeen-year-old Prince Edward of Lancaster was too young to be more than a nominal commander and the best Lancastrian generals had been wiped out at Barnet, making Somerset the most senior noble. It is unlikely that he had any experience of leading armies in campaigns; he had conducted an unsuccessful defence at Carisbrooke in 1460, but his time in the Duke of Burgundy's service might have involved some combat and many still believed him one of the better commanders. It is likely that his name and title, exactly the same as his father's, gave him this credence. He would nonetheless acquit himself well enough that the Yorkist *Arrivall of King Edward the Fourth*, a partisan chronicle, describes him as 'knightly and manly'.[5]

Margaret was dismayed when she heard of the outcome at Barnet, but ordered a new army to be raised as she progressed northwards to Bristol and then into Gloucestershire. These were areas where the Beauforts had some influence and could call on plenty of support. The Courtenays were also calling up a following in the Exeter region. Edward was of course aware of this, and was assembling his own force in London. By the time they met in battle, the Lancastrian force was estimated at 6,000 men and the Yorkist host was only a little smaller.

On 4 May the Lancastrians passed through Gloucester. By late afternoon they had reached the town of Tewkesbury, in the shadow of St Mary's Abbey and part of the earldom of Warwick. By this time Margaret's soldiers were tired, having marched for 50 miles with little respite. Edward spent the night at nearby Cheltenham after a shorter march, breaking camp the following morning to bear down on the enemy.

It was unclear just who was in command of the Lancastrian forces on the day. In a foolhardy move Edward of Lancaster was tasked with heading the centre; such a position required an experienced soldier. John, Lord Wenlok and Prior Langstrother were assigned to support him in this, but the Lancastrian cause suffered for the lack of clear leadership in such an important strategic position. While Devon commanded the left flank, Somerset finally gained his important role commanding the right, which would be the vanguard, opposite Richard, Duke of Gloucester. Margaret, who could not participate, watched the battle from a church tower.

Somerset and Gloucester began with the usual exchange of arrows and musket fire, but Gloucester had more of both and Somerset was obliged to advance early. However, his charge abruptly wheeled left. It might have been better if he had fought it out as planned, striking at Gloucester's force, but either on the spur of the moment or because he was uneasy over the prince's leadership, or possibly through simple error, Somerset was soon to the left of the main Yorkist battle, facing King Edward himself.

The *Arrivall* chronicler talks of uncertain ground between the two armies, of 'evell lanes and depe dykes' that the Lancastrian right flank was forced to negotiate before reaching their enemy.

The chronicler believed that they knew the route, and they ended up in a close where Edward, Clarence and the bulk of their army was assembled.[6] Somerset fought bravely, but the Yorkists again outnumbered his men. During the melee that followed Somerset was well placed to do damage but neither Wenlok nor Devon gave him assistance. The latter had Lord Hastings' troops to contend with, and Wenlok might have been so occupied too. Gloucester himself attacked Somerset by the flank, and although the Yorkists were at first hard pressed to gain ground the Lancastrians were put to flight, many up a hillock nearby. At this point a company of Yorkist spearmen emerged from hiding and the former vanguard was engaged from both sides. Some escaped westward to ground bounded by the Coln Brook and the River Severn, where they were cut down by pursuers at a place still known as Blood Meadow. Many others went on running, to the town and beyond. Somerset returned to the fight, furious at the lack of support from the main battle.

Now the Lancastrian centre was under attack. According to legend, Somerset sought out Wenlok and, sure of his treason, buried his own axe in Wenlok's skull. Wenlok had a reputation for turning traitor, but if this act really occurred it hardly aided the Lancastrians as Edward's men set upon them. The Earl of Devon and Sir John Beaufort, Marquis of Dorset were also killed in this onslaught. Another legend has Clarence killing Edward of Lancaster by posing as a helpful relative and stabbing him once he reached close quarters. Margaret was captured the following day. After seeing the Lancastrian army disintegrate, Somerset and Langstrother ran for sanctuary in the nearby Tewkesbury Abbey.

The old tradition of sanctuary was at times broken, and the Yorkists were sure it did not apply to traitors. King Edward was preparing to fight his way into the abbey grounds but was halted by a priest bearing the Host before him. He offered a free pardon to all those inside, but within days he changed his mind. As the abbey and other religious buildings were declared 'polluted' by the fighting and the monks were busy reconsecrating them, it was not difficult for Edward's men to walk in and drag out Somerset and the others before anyone could protest.

The captured fugitives were speedily despatched. A scaffold was already built on the field. A court headed by the Duke of Norfolk as Constable of England and the Duke of Gloucester as Marshal heard the charges. Somerset and the others had taken arms and fought against the king's person, which was treason and punishable by death. Somerset, Langstrother and a handful of Lancastrian knights were condemned; a few, including Fortescue, were pardoned. The sentences were promptly carried out.

On 6 May 1471, when Edmund Beaufort, de facto Duke of Somerset, knelt before the executioner on the Tewkesbury field, the male line of John of Gaunt through Katherine Swynford came to a brutal end. There was no claimant to the dukedom; Edward wanted to eradicate this line of Lancastrian supporters and possible pretenders, and this time there would be no attempt at reconciliation. The Beaufort line survived in several female lines, but few took any account of them at this point. The Beaufort brothers were interred in Tewkesbury Abbey Church in front of the altar in the north part.[7]

The following week, Edward contented himself on hearing that another revolt against him, led by Thomas Neville, Bastard of Fauconberg, had been driven back from London. As soon as he returned to London himself on 21 May he is alleged to have ordered the murder of Henry VI in the Tower, although this has never been verified. Thus he closed the book on the Readeption, the House of Lancaster and the Beaufort dukedom of Somerset all at once. For a time, the triumphant House of York believed that the dynastic civil wars were over. For all his faults, Edward IV was able to rule as a king should, even renewing war against France and then Scotland. He produced ten children, two sons and three daughters surviving him, and his remaining siblings all had issue. The Yorkist succession seemed assured.

Edmund Beaufort (II) did little to secure his faction's victory in 1470, and failed to prevent the Yorkists coming back to retake the kingdom, but there was little that he could do in the circumstances. His brief field command nonetheless showed a young man whose valour partially compensated for his inexperience, even gaining him positive commentary from a hostile chronicler. The most experienced of the Lancastrian fighters had fallen at Barnet, and Margaret was obliged to rely on less experienced commanders on the Tewkesbury campaign. From Somerset's viewpoint, the Lancastrian failure to seize the chance when he was engaging the enemy cost them the battle, but poor communication given his unplanned action could have been to blame. To make the supreme effort and afterwards die a traitor's death was his tragedy; his lifelong devotion to Lancaster as commendable as all of his line.

Surprisingly, the story of the Beauforts has one more chapter, as dramatic and even more unexpected than the rest.

12

MARGARET BEAUFORT

In a memorable case in 1625, Chief Justice Crew passed judgment on a matter of succession to the peerage, and in his summation he was moved to ask, 'Where is Mowbray? Where is Mortimer? Nay, which is more and most of all, where is Plantagenet? They are entombed in the urns and sepulchres of mortality.' He could just as well have asked, 'Where is Beaufort?' It is a phenomenon of later medieval peerages that most did not last more than a few generations from their creation, and the three mentioned were much older. This includes within the Plantagenet dynasty both the houses of Lancaster and York, while the cadet branch we know as the Beauforts itself lasted three generations, leaving the dukedom of Somerset extinct in 1471.

Despite what first comes to mind, the Wars of the Roses did not kill off the noble families. The process had begun long before, and in fact the largest number of extinctions had occurred in the first quarter of the fifteenth century. The reasons are unclear, but in most cases it was the result of failure in the male line. The fifteenth was a century of heiresses.

The Beauforts were typical of the fifteenth-century nobility, although in their case the last generation of males actually died in the civil wars, all unmarried. When Henry Beaufort, third Duke of Somerset was executed in 1464 and his brothers John and Edmund, de facto fourth duke were killed in 1471, there was no man left even to lay claim to the suppressed dukedom. However, the story of the Beauforts did not end at Tewkesbury, for there was still a bastard son of one duke and the heiress of another. With heiresses more important than ever in that century, one in particular succeeded in transmitting the Beaufort claim with resounding effects. Henry Tudor, later Henry VII, was a Beaufort on his mother's side.

Charles, called Charles Somerset, illegitimate son of Henry, third Duke of Somerset, did in fact continue the Beaufort line. In 1514, almost certainly for his connection to the royal house, he would be created Earl of Worcester and grow prominent in Henry VIII's court. The line flourished, first raised to the rank of marquis in 1642, and in 1682 Charles II awarded his descendant with the dukedom of Beaufort. In the present day, David Somerset is eleventh Duke of Beaufort, a descendant of the third Duke of Somerset beheaded on the field at Hexham. The House of Beaufort therefore continues, still bearing the Plantagenet arms distinguished with a bordure gobony of argent and azure exactly as the Beauforts had it in the fifteenth century.

John Beaufort (II), first Duke of Somerset had a daughter born to him and his wife; an only child, Margaret Beaufort (II) was born at Bletsoe Castle in Bedfordshire in 1442. Her birthday was certainly 31 May, as she later required Westminster Abbey to celebrate it. The duke secured agreements with King Henry VI that his child's interests would be maintained and that should he not survive the campaign his duchess would have the keeping of his daughter. But in 1444, after the disappointing French campaign and questions over the duke's death, the king decided otherwise. Soon after John Beaufort's alleged suicide the king changed his mind, or was persuaded to, and gave the wardship to the Duke of Suffolk. A rising star, Suffolk soon married the little girl to his own heir John de la Pole. Suffolk was aware of the advantages that such a marriage could bring his son. Although many of the estates her father held passed on an entail to Edmund Beaufort (I), Margaret was still heiress to lands and incomes that could support a lavish lifestyle. Her wardship, and accordingly the final word on her marriage, was an acquisition that Suffolk must have valued.

The vague claim the Beauforts held to the royal succession saw a brief appearance after the death of Duke Humphrey in 1447, with no heir yet born to Henry VI. When Suffolk was impeached in 1450 he was accused of preparing to make his son king through the boy's marriage to Margaret. For all the assumption it makes on Suffolk's intentions, this accusation does show how seriously the Beaufort claim was then taken.

Margaret Beaufort herself grew up conscious of her status as heiress, for like many girls of aristocratic houses she was all too aware of her value in her family's ambitions and political machinations. Their husbands, the fathers of their children, would be selected for them according to such agendas, and the most they could hope for was to be paired with a likeable young man. Margaret was studious in her nature, a lover of books and learning who spent much time reading and translating pious works from French. She was also deeply religious and known from an early age for her charitable works. She was not as keen on marriage and motherhood as expected of her and would have gladly become a nun, although her family would never countenance that.

Margaret was granted the unusual concession of being allowed to live with her mother while she grew up, and so hardly saw her first husband. But after Suffolk's fall in 1450 her wardship reverted to the crown and new plans were made. In 1455, the twelve-year-old Margaret was informed of a decision to annul her first marriage and to marry her instead to Edmund Tudor, then Earl of Richmond and the king's half-brother. In her old age Margaret told of how she was offered a choice between remaining married to

John de la Pole or marrying Edmund Tudor, and how she prayed incessantly for guidance until a divine messenger in the form of a bishop pointed her way to the latter. In reality she had no choice in the matter.

In a single generation the Tudors had gone from a relatively obscure Welsh gentry family to a brace of earls linked to the royal house by a forbidden romance. Katherine de Valois, who had married King Henry V in 1420 and given birth to the future Henry VI in 1421, was widowed in August 1422. Still living as a royal widow some years later, she took an interest in Owen Tudor, a gentleman groom assigned to her household. Legends abound as to how they met and fell in love, and how some felt that the king's mother should have remained in a dignified widowhood. For all such legends concerning this liaison and eventual marriage, there are few established facts. Owen Tudor was of a Welsh gentry family whose members served in the household of Richard II but later sided with Owain Glyndwr and were finally rehabilitated in the time of Henry V. He was appointed Clerk of the Wardrobe to Katherine, and when they began their affair is unknown. As previously shown, there was some speculation in the 1420s over a proposed marriage with Edmund Beaufort (I).

Nothing was said about Owen and Katherine until 1437, when their four children were already born and Katherine had died after a long illness on 3 January. According to Polydore Vergil's account Owen was then placed in Newgate for his forbidden marriage, escaping early the following year before being recaptured. King Henry VI later had him transferred to Windsor Castle, from which he was conditionally released. He was later killed fighting on the Lancastrian side at Mortimer's Cross in 1461 when the Earl of March, later Edward IV, ordered his execution in reprisal for his own father's death.

There is some question over the ages of the elder sons. Edmund Tudor was said to have been born in 1431 and his brother Jasper the following year. This would mean that they were knighted at a later age than usual for young aristocrats. The children lived at Bermondsey Abbey for three years after their mother's death, but were then brought up at Barking Abbey. Besides Edmund and Jasper there was Owen, who became a monk at Westminster, and an unnamed daughter who is believed to have taken the veil. For some time the two elder sons lived quietly, but after the death of Duke Humphrey there was new concern over the succession and King Henry had his half-brothers brought to the court. Edmund was knighted in 1449 and on 23 November 1452 created Earl of Richmond. Jasper gained the earldom of Pembroke around the same time, possibly on the same occasion.

Plantagenet blood did not run in the veins of Edmund and Jasper, but they were Henry's family. It would defy any understanding of the rules of succession to consider either of them as eligible to inherit the throne at that time, but Henry apparently saw them as possible heirs. The marriage of Edmund with the Beaufort heiress was engineered to facilitate this, it seems. Their presence bolstered the thinned royal family, but it would have been difficult to have them recognised as successors to Henry, even when so many were uneasy over the prospect of Richard of York becoming king.

On 1 November 1455 Margaret Beaufort was married to Edmund Tudor, Earl of Richmond, himself about fourteen years her senior. Besides his immediate access to her estates and their revenues Margaret's new husband had more physical concerns over her. It was often the practice that once a wife could physically bear children she was set to doing so, and at twelve years old Margaret was a wife in every sense in this marriage. She was small in stature and perhaps not ready for childbearing but such concerns did not appear at this phase. Time was never on her dynasty's side and she was expected to produce a son as soon as possible. Early in 1456, Richmond was sent to Wales as the king's representative and brought his pregnant wife with him. They stayed at Caldicot

Castle in the Marches but he left her there when he ventured into Wales.

Division between the nobles had already escalated to the first instance of civil war, and politics were polarizing. Following an altercation with Sir William Herbert, an ally of Richard of York, on 10 August 1456 Richmond was arrested and imprisoned at Carmarthen. He was soon released, but during his stay in the dungeon or the town he contracted the plague. Without leaving Carmarthen, Edmund Tudor died on 1 November.

Margaret, now in her third trimester, immediately fled to Pembroke Castle and sought the protection of her brother-in-law Jasper, Earl of Pembroke. It was there that on 28 January 1457 she gave birth to her son Henry Tudor, future king of England. It was a dire and dangerous labour; at one point it was almost certain that neither mother nor child would survive, and at another the attendants were fighting to save the boy only. Almost by a miracle, both Margaret and her son were still alive after the birth. Both would thrive. Margaret would marry twice more, but never produced any more children; this difficult childbirth had probably damaged her.

According to legend the boy was first baptised as Owen. If true, this was obviously Jasper's idea after his own father and the child's grandfather. But Margaret, on hearing of this, is said to have instructed the bishop to baptise him a second time as Henry. She was determined to ensure his safety and wished the king to stand godfather. This is not a verified story, but serves to link Henry with a Welsh prophecy that an Owen would conquer England.

It remained far from certain whether or not the House of Beaufort had a place in the succession to the throne. When Parliament and Pope had agreed to the transformation back in 1398 from four royal bastards to a legitimate cadet branch of the reigning family it was widely considered that they had at least a vague claim behind others. The pronouncement of 1407 had far from ended the matter, for that could be legally challenged. Still, it was never officially stated that the Beauforts *could* inherit the crown. Did the validity of a retrospective dispensation of legitimacy extend to the royal succession? Henry IV apparently believed it could not, but others were not so sure.

This narrative has been mostly concerned with the men of the Beaufort family. In each generation there were daughters, most of whom married into the nobility and provided a rich network of family connections for which the Beauforts were famous. In the majority of cases the Beaufort women had little opportunity to participate in public affairs, doing little more than dutifully marry whoever was chosen for them and produce their quota of children. Whereas the two Joan Beauforts made the best use of their marriages, little can be seen of the other Beaufort women. One could only imagine the conversations with their husbands and sons across the tables in the halls of their castles, especially when the nobility was riven by faction from the 1450s. Given the shortage of relevant records we are denied insight into whatever influence they might have had.

After the battles of 1471, the House of York believed the conflict over the throne finally resolved. What little hope remained for Lancaster now centred on the person of Margaret Beaufort. Edward IV may have rejoiced in the destruction of the entire Beaufort male line, but the Beaufort heiress remained. By virtue of her status this woman would pick up the Beaufort standard, and eventually her son would bring down the Yorkists and become king, although not as a Beaufort but a Tudor. Margaret had done her duty by giving birth to a son, transmitting the Beaufort claim to the Tudors, and her part in public affairs was believed to have concluded.

But Margaret by her mid-teens had gained some knowledge of the ways of the world. While the Tudors would certainly give her son all he required, she would herself be in need of sustenance, and once she was again able she sought a third husband. From all that is known of her she displayed no interest in romance or married love; her experience of the practicalities of marriage and motherhood left her with no illusions. But she was a widow who still held large estates, and therefore an eligible candidate within the marriage market.

In 1457, when the brief ascendancy of Richard of York was showing signs of slipping, Margaret needed a stable protector. Without too much negotiation she married again, to her cousin Sir Henry Stafford, second son of the Duke of Buckingham, whose mother, Anne Neville, was a daughter of Joan Beaufort (I), Countess of Westmorland. It appears that this new match was mostly Margaret's own choice; they needed papal dispensation to marry as they were first cousins, and this was granted on 6 April. Buckingham himself gave them an annuity of 400 marks, although they lived mostly on the estates Margaret inherited from her father.

Over the next few years, as Margaret reached her late teens, she could only have heard at second hand of the events as they unfolded, the resumption of civil war at Blore Heath and the dismay in 1460 over the Yorkist victory at Northampton. At the end of that year there was cause for optimism on hearing news from Wakefield, and she might have rejoiced soon after on hearing of her cousin Somerset's achievement at St Albans in routing the Yorkists and recovering the king's person. But in March 1461 the family were concerned to hear that the Yorkists were back on the offensive with a king of their own. The outcome could not have been much worse when Margaret's husband returned unharmed with the tidings from Towton. Lionel, Lord Welles, who had married Margaret's mother, had been killed in the battle. The Yorkists had succeeded in winning the country, and both Stafford and Tudor had cause to consider their safety at risk.

In the following months the civil war came close to both, as Sir William Herbert led a campaign to pacify Wales on behalf of

Edward IV. It is believed that Margaret's four-year-old son was in Pembroke Castle during the siege when Jasper Tudor surrendered it at the end of September. While Jasper sailed to join the remains of the Lancastrians in Scotland the whereabouts of both little Henry Tudor and his mother are not recorded, but no harm came to either. In 1462 King Edward gave the wardship of the boy to Lord Herbert, who eventually gained the earldom of Pembroke when Jasper was attainted in his absence. While his estates went to the Duke of Clarence, there was no attempt to divest young Henry of the Richmond title, for the new king had drawn a line under such action against Lancastrians.

As the years passed Margaret played the part of a Stafford wife. She was still a young woman in 1470 with a son in his teens, although she saw almost nothing of him. The new Duke of Buckingham, grandson of her father-in-law and her own nephew, was five years old in 1460, and the Staffords were later received into Edward's grace. Young Buckingham married a sister of Queen Elizabeth Woodville. It is not known what Margaret thought privately of the situation but most of the former pro-Lancastrian families had settled for living under the Yorkist monarchy while little else could be done. She and her husband were given the manor of Woking, formerly of the Duke of Somerset's estates. Richard, Lord Welles, Margaret's stepbrother, fought with Lord Montague's force in the north and contributed to the defeat of the Lancastrians at Hexham.[1]

But whatever pretenses the nobles were obliged to maintain were no longer needed in September 1470 when Warwick and the Lancastrians undertook their invasion and restored Henry VI to the throne. Jasper Tudor wrested both Pembroke Castle and young Henry from the Herberts and they stayed a while with Margaret and her husband at Woking. This short reunion of mother and son was truly a blessing, but soon after this they would be parted for another thirteen years.

According to legend it was when Jasper took his nephew to London that Henry Tudor received a ringing endorsement. It was customary to introduce the boy to the nobles of the court, and Jasper did so meticulously. When he presented young Henry to the king, it was said that the monarch commented on the boy that he would be king one day. This, as reported later by the chronicler Polydore Vergil, was much quoted.[2]

Of course this story is suspect. King Henry's state of mind at the time is uncertain, as is whether or not he was capable of stringing together a sentence. Perhaps he simply remembered that Henry Tudor was a contingency heir and was no longer certain of his own son's survival; after all, he had not seen his immediate family for seven years and was not known for a sound grip on reality in the intervening time. It could even have been Margaret's much exaggerated version of the meeting. Vergil was writing in the next century when the cult of Henry of Windsor was rising to prominence and his canonisation was expected. Naturally, the endorsement of this sainted king would have done Henry Tudor no harm if it was so much as alleged to have happened.

But from March 1471 the tide turned again, to Margaret's sorrow, on the return of Edward IV. Her husband Sir Henry rode off to fight on the Yorkist side and returned from Barnet sorely wounded. He died on 4 October that year. The news of Tewkesbury was also serious, and the deaths of her two Beaufort cousins could only have made things worse. That her son had escaped with Jasper probably brought mixed feelings, but at least he was safe enough in Brittany with his uncle.

Margaret was once again a widow, but she had little time to mourn. She was still a comely young woman and heiress to vast estates, and was now in need of a husband acceptable to the restored Yorkist monarchy. She chose well, for Thomas, Lord Stanley was not only in an undeserved high regard but had shown no axe to grind either way.

Margaret's fourth and final husband was nine years her senior. He held substantial estates and influence in Lancashire and Cheshire, was ruler over the Isle of Man – he was in fact the last to use the title of King of Man – and was Lord High Constable of England. A nominal Lancastrian, in 1459 he had famously kept his men out of the fighting at Blore Heath but had afterwards shown support for the Yorkists. His first wife was Eleanor Neville, a sister of Warwick. He had served Edward IV in keeping the north-west on side, but had then given support to the returning Lancastrians. Now he sat once again on Edward IV's council and was soon Steward of the King's Household. For all his shifting loyalties he had never led any troops into battle on either side. In June 1472, after a noticeably short period of mourning, Margaret married Lord Stanley. Once again a suitor had sought her estates and their incomes, but he was acceptable in the eyes of the returned king and this meant Margaret could live under the Yorkists in safety.

It is far from certain what Margaret herself thought of whoever was on the throne; some say she changed alignment with each marriage. She had thought highly of Henry VI, believing him a saint, but like her third and fourth husbands she was a realist and had to survive despite her convictions.

The second reign of Edward IV saw almost no dynastic quarrelling. With the principal Lancastrians either dead or imprisoned there was no powerful leadership for the discontented, and the few incidences of opposition were swiftly quelled. Edward was forced to have his brother Clarence executed in 1478 when he discovered him plotting again, but otherwise he felt secure enough to restart the Hundred Years War, which would have kept his nobles occupied had they succeeded in regaining lost French lands; alas his invasion of France in 1474 had no lasting results.

If Henry Tudor was still considered as an alternative king, little was said of it. He was still a youth in exile for most of this time, and most of England had stabilised under the Yorkists. Edward had two sons, three daughters and other children who did not survive infancy, and his brothers Clarence and Gloucester both had issue, to say nothing of the daughters of Richard of York and their own children, which gave the overall impression that the Yorkist succession was assured. 'Lancaster' and 'Beaufort' were things of the past, and the claim of Henry Tudor was questionable in any case but now irrelevant.

But over these twelve years Edward's IV's love for rich food and fine wines was doing harm to his constitution, and on 9 April 1483 he died. A further ten years of his rule would have enabled his heir Edward V to succeed as an adult, but at twelve this new king was mostly helpless as Gloucester and the Woodvilles clashed for control over him. Within weeks Richard, Duke of Gloucester, in alliance with Henry, Duke of Buckingham, had gained the reins of government and destroyed the power of the Woodvilles.

The subsequent events are well known. Gloucester's faction presented a case in canon law that rendered Edward IV's marriage to Elizabeth Woodville invalid and its children illegitimate, and by 9 July he had removed all opposition to having himself proclaimed King Richard III. The fate of Edward V and his brother Richard, Duke of York is still uncertain, although the widely accepted accusation that they were murdered while imprisoned in the Tower is still debated.

It was during the first months of the reign of Richard III that Margaret Beaufort, Lady Stanley emerged as a political figure in her own right. Myths abound from that time, alternately suggesting that Margaret was involved in a plan to rescue the princes from the Tower or was responsible for their murders. Stanley was appointed Constable of England when Buckingham later rebelled against Richard III, and Stanley and his wife thereafter had free run of the Tower, but there is no firm evidence of either allegation.

In September the events often known as 'Buckingham's Rebellion' were in motion, although this is a simplistic and inadequate title.

While it was Buckingham who became the figurehead and active leader of this revolt, it was far more than his own bid for the throne. His grandfather Humphrey had been killed at Northampton while his father, another Humphrey, had died at the First Battle of St Albans; he was therefore from a line of committed Lancastrians. His mother was also named Margaret Beaufort, and was daughter of Edmund (I), second Duke of Somerset. This gave him the same claim as Henry Tudor, but the latter would have been able to claim precedence if it ever came to debate between the two. While the claim of Henry Tudor was raised in this revolt, some believe that Buckingham was championing that claim while in fact preparing to advance his own.

Most of the rebels themselves were substantial gentry, largely from the counties of the southern coast of England. To look at those attainted indicates this regional basis, and intriguingly shows links with the Yorkist royal house. While some had been associated with Clarence and others with the Woodvilles, many of the leaders in the counties had been members of the household of Edward IV. There were others, including former Lancastrians such as Sir Nicholas Latimer and three of the Courtenays, so the impression is one of an amorphous revolt with varying agendas united by a rejection of Richard III as king.[3]

But it is certain that the principal conspirators included Margaret Beaufort. Elizabeth Woodville was also involved; it is believed that Bishop John Morton of Ely was the mastermind of the operation and that the two women put up funding. Margaret was obviously seeking to have her son elevated, and there was correspondence with Henry and his uncle in Brittany. It is likely that the two ladies agreed to a marriage between Henry and Elizabeth Woodville's daughter Elizabeth of York, or at least discussed it. It then appears that they met with Morton who linked their cause with that of other elements. One could wonder at how many other agendas were being pursued.

The revolt itself showed its poor planning when it turned out a pitiful failure. Buckingham tried to bring his small army from Wales but was prevented from crossing the Severn when the bridges were destroyed. Forced into Shropshire, where his following melted away, Buckingham was betrayed and captured on the first day of November. The rebels in the southern counties gained some ground – one group seized and held Bodiam Castle for a time – but lack of leadership and direction eventually wore them down and the revolt had petered out before the end of November. In that month Henry Tudor landed in the West Country. He had come too late, the revolt having already fallen apart, and he himself barely escaped seizure by troops loyal to Richard before returning to Brittany.

Richard was far from magnanimous to the rebels. Once Buckingham and several other ringleaders were executed he turned his attention to others who had been involved and to the problem of Henry Tudor as a focus for discontent. It was certain that Margaret had played a part, sending money and intelligence to her son, and this would normally be adequate grounds for ordering her execution too. But Richard had a pragmatic consideration. She was married to Lord Stanley, and Richard could ill afford to lose his support; Margaret's estates gave Stanley a fair income that would be forfeit on attainder. Richard knew how fragile the loyalties of the nobles were and although he might have suspected that Stanley himself was in correspondence with his stepson Henry Tudor, the king was already ruling with the hand of coercion and had added this to widespread suspicion over his nephews' fate. To have a woman executed would have made him more unpopular. He had noticed how so many of the nobles had neither supported the rebellion nor had rallied to him, and although he was personally popular in the north he had not won over many in the greater part of England. It was this pragmatic decision that saved Margaret's life.

At the end of 1483 Margaret was summoned to hear that her death sentence had been commuted to life imprisonment. In addition her husband still had the incomes of her lands while he lived, and this would make no difference to her unless he died during her lifetime. Rather than true captivity, Lord Stanley was instructed to keep his wife in a form of house arrest and unable to intrigue further, which was restricting for Margaret but could have been far worse. She lacked for little in the next two years and Stanley did not prevent her writing to Henry.

Those who have sought to rehabilitate Richard III make him a victim of adverse circumstances that he addressed as best he could. The poor harvest of 1483 was hardly his fault, nor the personal tragedy of the deaths of his only son Edward and then his Queen Anne by early 1485. He was not at all popular but might have made a better mark had he been allowed to reign longer. No matter how spurious Henry Tudor's claim, Richard knew how easily he could be used as a focus for discontent and when the king wrote to the Count of Brittany in 1485 seeking to have Henry and Jasper Tudor brought to him the two fled to the court of Charles VIII of France, who gave financial aid for a new coup. In August that year Henry landed at Milford Haven and surged eastwards with a growing army, while Richard took his troops westward to meet him. On 22 August 1485 the two armies met at Bosworth.

Within two hours, after seeing Margaret's husband Lord Stanley defect and Northumberland refuse to fight, and with his army mostly killed or scattered, Richard III and his remaining retinue fought to the last, with nothing left but to make a good end. The reign of Henry VII, and that of the Tudor dynasty, began that day too. Lord Stanley supposedly found the crown of England in a thorn bush and placed it on Henry's head, although it is unlikely that Richard would have brought it with him.

Now that her son was finally king, Margaret finally came into her own. Her release from house arrest was only the beginning to a long and active public life. Once she met her son at Leicester she assumed her role as 'My Lady the King's Mother' and enjoyed much greater legal and social independence than other married women. Her son's first parliament recognised her right to hold property independently from her husband as if she were unmarried.

Now the Beaufort claim to the throne was fulfilled. Ever since the legitimation of John of Gaunt's four children by Katherine Swynford in 1398 the vague possibility of the Beaufort line succeeding to the throne of England had been a faint but persistent theme in English political affairs. The Beaufort dynasty had failed in the male line, but at least through Margaret their claim was transmitted to create the Tudor monarchy.

Henry Tudor was king after Bosworth simply because he led the victorious army. He was not even a descendant in the male line of any King of England, and although the order of succession was still far from established by 1485 there was cause for dispute in this case. If the succession had been determined by constitutional lawyers, Henry's claim would have at best made the shortlist of the ten strongest.

He was aided by the deaths of Edward IV, his two sons, Richard III and his son Edward, Clarence, Henry VI, Edward of Lancaster and the men of the Beaufort line. Clarence's son Edward, Earl of Warwick was a possible contender but his father's treason had apparently disinherited him in 1478, although there were some prepared to reconsider his position and Henry had quickly placed him in custody for that reason. There were fewer Plantagenet men, but some of Richard of York's grandsons through his daughters might be considered. As Henry became king by force he could still be overthrown by force unless he convinced enough people that he was rightful king. While Henry's claim that his mother was a Beaufort had counted for little over the past century, it had a new significance now that the Plantagenets were all but extinct.

Of his threefold claim, his descent from Katherine de Valois and his father's status as half-brother to Henry VI were the weakest; he was not even a Plantagenet. Through his mother there was some basis for his candidacy; we have seen how the Beaufort claim had persisted, not recognised and still not repudiated altogether. There is enough evidence that this descent from Edward III through John of Gaunt and through the eldest Beaufort and his son was considered a claim, even though it involved a bastard line retrospectively legitimated and also a parliamentary veto by Henry IV. Its link with the Lancastrian kings was also to its advantage. Yet it would be a major mistake to cite Henry's Beaufort parentage on the distaff side as the basis for his accession, leaving as it did scope for anyone with an army and an alternative pretender to challenge.

In fact, his marriage to Elizabeth of York was the strongest element of his justification. She was after all daughter of a king and her two brothers were then believed dead. The new regime made much of the alleged union of the two claims, producing the Tudor Rose and rewriting history to suit. It was the best the Tudors could say of their legitimacy, while they kept an eye open for possible rebellions. One of Elizabeth's great-grandmothers was Joan Beaufort (I), and thus the Tudor monarchy was of the Beaufort connection twice over, but Henry as husband of Elizabeth of York was his best claim. The Tudor propagandists then proclaimed the joining of the two houses under the Tudor Rose, both red and white. In reality little had been seen of either rose during the civil wars, but it was not hard to create a legend in those days.

Margaret now had honours heaped upon her. As Lord Stanley was raised to the earldom of Derby for his judicious defection, Margaret was now styled Countess of Richmond and Derby and usually signed herself as 'Margaret R', conscious of her new royal status. She insisted on a rule whereby she walked half a step behind the queen consort, upstaging Elizabeth Woodville who remained at court. As the king's mother Margaret in fact asserted her status in every area she could. The birth of her first grandchild in 1486 had her organising the child's household with a multitude of ordinances. For the queen, Margaret was an interfering mother-in-law.

There was apparently some tension between Margaret and Elizabeth Woodville. As dowager queen, Elizabeth held a certain claim to precedence. At the baptism of Prince Arthur, first child of Henry and Queen Elizabeth, it was Elizabeth Woodville who was named godmother. While Margaret's husband Lord Stanley stood godfather, it could appear a slight to her even though she was godmother to her namesake Princess Margaret, another child of Henry and Elizabeth. It is often believed that Margaret urged action against Elizabeth Woodville for her complicity in the rebellion, and for her alleged complicity in a later revolt behind the pretender Lambert Simnel. She was eventually banished from court and obliged to live in Bermondsey Abbey until her death in 1492.

Margaret was well known for her large household and sumptuous lifestyle. Her son gave her a large house by the river in London called Coldharbour, although she spent most of the time at the manor of Collyweston in Bedfordshire, which she acquired herself. She was also known for her intense piety. She heard six masses a day. The portrait by which she is best known shows her at prayer, almost certainly as she wished to be seen. Her private apartments in the background are noted for their lavish designs, which contrast with a severe image of Margaret in her widow's black. The royal arms and the Beaufort portcullis are both in sight. The *prie-dieu* at which she is seen kneeling was said to give her back much trouble.

Margaret's piety extended to charitable actions, for which she is best remembered. She was of course one of the richest women in England, but she did much with her incomes. Apart from some awards to almshouses on her estates, her charity had the most effect in the sphere of education. Her association with John Fisher was decisive in this direction. The future Bishop of Rochester and eventual saint following his martyrdom in 1535 for his opposition to the English Reformation so impressed Margaret that he made him her confessor, and he advised her often. Margaret agreed with her chaplain that a well-educated clergy was needed for the good of the Church.

In 1497 she made provision for a free school in Wimborne, Dorset which is still open as Queen Elizabeth's School. She made her first endowment to Oxford University but for the rest of her life showered largesse on Cambridge; Fisher had been a Cambridge scholar. In 1505 she produced the funding and a royal charter that refounded God's House in Cambridge, renaming it Christ's College. Appointing Fisher as its first master, she set up funding from some of her estates and obtained the Abbey of St Mary de Pratis at Creyke, Norfolk so that its estates would also fund the college. Margaret was often in residence at Christ's, her rooms always ready for her. The legend that she called from her window to modify the admonition of a student by a teacher with the cry 'Lente, lente' persists to this day. Her arms still adorn the main gate, flanked by the Yale of Beaufort as supporters and then by the Beaufort portcullis and the red rose. Margaret also set about the founding of St John's College in 1507. This was a more ambitious project which envisaged providing for a Master and fifty students. As she realised that she would not live to see it completed, she bequeathed some of her estates at Great Bradley in Suffolk for its upkeep.

She was also patron of the poet John Skelton and the blind poet laureate Bernard André. She gave support to Caxton in the second half of his career as a printer in Westminster, and made a personal contribution to learning by translating Thomas à Kempis' *Imitation of Christ* into English.

It appears that, however close she was to her husband, Margaret was never fully accepted by her Stanley in-laws. Partially for this reason she took to living apart from Stanley. She lived alone with her servants at Collyweston, although her husband visited her regularly while he lived. In 1499, with Stanley's permission, she took a vow of chastity which she renewed in 1504 when widowed a final time.

The reign of Henry VII did not pass without incident, but civil war was truly a thing of the past after 1487. Margaret saw the tragedies of the death of her grandson Prince Arthur in 1502 and of Queen

Elizabeth the following year. Now in her sixties, a great age in those days, she continued at her devotions and charity. Even then she was struck again with loss when on 23 April 1509 her much-loved son King Henry VII himself died after a long period of intermittent illness. The dying king made his mother executrix of his will, and she prepared to guide her seventeen-year-old grandson Henry in his remaining time of minority. She took a lead arranging the funeral of her son and the coronation of her grandson as Henry VIII, and then acted as his regent for two months. But Margaret herself was in decline, her health deteriorating after losing her only child. On 29 June 1509, the day after her grandson reached his eighteenth birthday, Margaret died in the precinct of Westminster Abbey, where she was interred in the Lady Chapel in a black marble tomb surmounted by a gilded effigy.

The dukedom of Somerset was granted to the king's infant son Edmund Tudor in 1499, but he died the following year. Henry VIII regranted it to his bastard son Henry Fitzroy, who died without issue in 1536. The Somerset title was then recycled as an earldom to Edward Seymour, brother of Henry's third queen Jane Seymour, but again ended in the first generation.[4]

It follows that the Tudors ruled England first through Margaret's grandson Henry VIII and then his three children in turn. The Stuarts inherited their claim through another of Margaret's grandchildren, Princess Margaret, who married James IV of Scotland, himself great-grandson of Joan Beaufort (II). The line of Margaret Beaufort continues to reign over the United Kingdom to this day.

The Beauforts were of the Blood Royal, despite their initial illegitimacy. While at no time was their place in the royal succession fully recognised, their vague claim was never forgotten, and was finally brought to fruition when the houses of Lancaster and York were destroyed. Rather than as kings in waiting, the Beauforts served the Lancastrian kings without any such assurances.

CONCLUSION

In our modern age we are less governed by our parentage and degree in society and it is not easy to appreciate the world of the fifteenth century wherein both opportunities and obligations were largely determined by such factors. To understand this concept of society is to understand the progress of the Beauforts.

The stigma of illegitimacy was the first hurdle that they surprisingly overcame, even if it was never fully eradicated. The four Beauforts showed their mettle before their legitimation, and by the time of the Lancastrian coup they had risen further than many in royal service and prestige.

The overall contribution of the Beauforts to the affairs and progress of the Lancastrian monarchy was positive and they were all loyal servants of their kings. They performed important services in both peace and war in an effective and trustworthy manner and in a time where loyalty and trust were in short supply. The first Beauforts provided two important military commanders for the French wars and an administrator and royal financier who aided the cause of Lancaster where its needs were greatest. Those of the second and third generations varied considerably in their abilities but their loyalties were indisputable.

It is still reasonable to say that the Beauforts were obliged to render such service by virtue of who they were, and their fortunes depended on their standing with the kings. The estates of the first Earl of Somerset were meagre and his various offices brought much-needed incomes. That the Beaufort men were half-brothers to Henry IV was much to their advantage and they gained incomes and power by making their services available to him. They played important roles in keeping Henry on the throne given the controversies over his accession. In the reign of Henry V the two surviving brothers gave effective support to his endeavour to become King of France, and two generations of Beauforts laboured in the cause of conquest until it was finally lost. Whether required to serve or otherwise, the Beauforts could not be said to scant their duties.

Apart from the Beauforts who served in arms up to 1453, the part of Henry Beaufort (I), bishop and cardinal, was exemplary. His service as chancellor three times in separate reigns and his participation in the king's council in the interim proved much to the benefit of his kings, although his activities in the area of royal finance were essential in each reign. Not only were his carefully written sermons effective in mollifying parliaments when money for the wars was needed, but his role as the king's banker using the resources of the Winchester bishopric was indispensable in making ends meet. It is hard to see how the Lancastrian monarchy could have proceeded in peace and war without his ministrations.

The accession of Henry VI brought upheaval and uncertainty, with decisive leadership from the monarch unobtainable throughout. The Beauforts, particularly Bishop Henry, struggled to keep the Lancastrian monarchy and its endeavour in France on track despite the serious prospect of the whole affair falling apart. After the early deaths of his brothers, Henry Beaufort worked in conjunction with John, Duke of Bedford to maintain the status quo and averted the initial crisis. His quarrel with Humphrey,

Duke of Gloucester was the result of his conviction that the duke could not be trusted to govern England over a long period, and some of Humphrey's actions show good reason to believe so. Cardinal Beaufort was unpopular with the people as a whole; not only was Humphrey well thought of but the prelate was associated with unpopular measures which he believed were for the best. Beaufort was stubborn, bombastic and high-handed but always a loyal servant of his king.

The Beaufort women were mostly excluded from the affairs of the realm and mainly functioned as promoters of claims and alliances like most medieval women. The two Joan Beauforts were remarkable, despite their restrictions. The story of Joan Beaufort (I) concerns the creation of the Middleham Nevilles, a separate dynasty and an alternative monarchy, against which the Beauforts would campaign later in the century. Joan Beaufort (II) was Queen of Scotland, and on her husband's murder she laboured to establish her son as king independent of the insurgents.

Both Cardinal Beaufort and his nephew Edmund Beaufort (I) had the same problem as Richard III: a bad press in the Tudor era. Shakespeare not only presented the cardinal as a cold, odious character, which was accurate but only part of the picture, but depicted Edmund as the cause of the ills that brought down Henry VI. While there are reservations over the career of this second Duke of Somerset there was much about him that was commendable. Despite the advantages of being born first cousin of Henry V, Edmund was penalised as the youngest son of the first earl, and mostly rose through his personal efforts as a soldier in the French wars under Bedford's patronage. His services defending Paris and his rescue of Calais were much commended, and he rose as peer in his own right before finally inheriting the dukedom of Somerset from his unstable brother.

Edmund's behaviour in 1449 that lost Normandy to the English was a stain on his exemplary career to this point. The truce with

France was not strong, and encouraging its violation was not the action of a responsible commander. He was probably acting on Suffolk's orders, but there is no way of knowing. If he intended to lose Normandy it went against all he had sought to accomplish his entire adult life, but nonetheless he took the blame for it.

Rather than the devious manipulator of the sainted Henry VI and alleged secret lover of his queen, Edmund Beaufort was in an unenviable position. He was trying to make sense of a kingdom that suffered when its king was inept and unable to address its ills, and in the tradition of his family he was seeking good government. Despite popular opinion he had reason to see Richard of York as a dangerous adventurer and sought to defend the Lancastrian monarchy against him. That York's good work maintaining Normandy was undone when Somerset replaced him was a myth, and neither could have succeeded when the council declined to fund its defence. The troubled kingdom had little direction in the early 1450s. Somerset certainly tried to dispense good government together with others on the council, and in his view Richard of York was the cause of the trouble. While justice and peacekeeping had become partisan and uncertain in the provinces, Somerset's quarrel with Warwick over the Glamorgan inheritance was typical of the disputes that decisive kings would otherwise resolve. Somerset was no more to blame than any noble uncertain of material needs, although his actions, coupled with instability in the north, virtually forced the Nevilles to the camp of Richard of York. Edmund Beaufort's death at St Albans was an uncharacteristic end to a long and distinguished military career.

A third generation of Beaufort men then maintained their family's tradition of service to the Lancastrian monarchy, although hampered by less military experience. They were loyal, even when their side suffered defeat. While Henry Beaufort (III), the third duke, walked out on his place in the court of Edward IV to give his all to the cause of Lancaster he might have been spurred by the opposition of the court to his rehabilitation, but what is taken as loyalty to Henry VI was consistent with the commitment of the entire Beaufort line to the Lancastrian kings. While Edmund (II) and his brother John (III) showed themselves a poor imitation of the previous Beauforts, their loyalty to Lancaster also cannot be disputed. After 1461 it was altogether possible for even the most prominent Lancastrians to reconcile with the Yorkist monarchy, but they and their elder brother still supported their cause in defeat and remained when most had gone, the brief restoration notwithstanding.

The question of a Beaufort succeeding as King of England appeared again and again after the legitimation of the first Beauforts, but not once did a Beaufort male openly seek recognition for a place in the royal succession even though both supporters and enemies alluded to it. It would have been dangerous ground, but given the uncertain order of succession it is reasonable to say that the Beauforts would have had a case had it ever been raised. They were of the Y-chromosome of John of Gaunt, whose senior line produced the Lancastrian kings, and he himself was a son of King Edward III and descendant of all the Plantagenet rulers. The first Beauforts were born out of wedlock, which would have excluded them, but would the act of legitimation have enabled them? Not according to the 1407 statute, but this may have been challenged at a later date and their eligibility was not out of the question. Still, the Beauforts were not said to have shown any interest in being king, and either out of loyalty or prudence, or both, they always declared their support for the House of Lancaster.

The marriage of Margaret Beaufort to Edmund Tudor transmitted the tenuous claim to their son Henry, adding a vital component to the case for the Tudor kings. In doing so she fulfilled the logical progression in the fourth generation when Henry Tudor, a Beaufort on his mother's side, became king.

In a century that saw intermittent foreign warfare give way to continual civil war, kings displacing each other by force, and the long and disastrous reign of an inept monarch, it was precarious for any aristocrat to survive. The Beauforts were bound to the same state of affairs as so many of their social station, and their loyalty was for the most part commendable.

Appendix I

THE BEAUFORT ESTATES

After G. L. Harriss, *Cardinal Beaufort,* Appendix II and additions from *Inquisitions Post Mortem* Vol. XX and other documents.

I The estates of John Beaufort (I)
II The estates of Thomas (I) Duke of Exeter
III The estates of Margaret, Duchess of Clarence
IV The estates of Edmund Beaufort (I) second Duke of Somerset
V The estates of Lady Margaret Beaufort

Estate	I	II	III	IV	V
CAMBRIDGESHIRE					
Babraham and Bassingbourne					*
Orwell	*				*
DEVON					
Aller Peverell	*		*		*
Halberton Hundred	*		*		
Sampford Peverell	*		*		
Samford Hundred	*		*		*

DORSET					
Corfe	*			*	
Ryme				*	
GLOUCESTERSHIRE					
Cirencester Abbey (rent)			*	*	*
HAMPSHIRE					
Andover Fee Farm					*
Basingstoke Fee Farm				*	*
Bedhampton					*
Carisbrook Isle of Wight				*	
Romsey Fee Farm					*
HEREFORDSHIRE					
Newland			*		
Walsh Newton			*		
Wigmore Castle			*		
HERTFORDSHIRE					
Maidcroft			*		
Tydbolt			*		
LEICESTERSHIRE					
Enderby		*		*	
LINCOLNSHIRE					
Bolton messuage					
Billingborough					
Bourne					
Deeping		*			
Appilby					

MIDDLESEX				
Edgware		*	*	
Stanmore Parva		*		*
NORTHAMPTONSHIRE				
Brampton Parva	*			
Buckley	*	^		*
Eydon	*		*	
Maxey	*			
Overstone	*			
Torpell	*	*	*	*
SOMERSET				
Beth priory fee farm	*	*	*	*
Burton	*		*	*
Hovethrorne	*	*		
Kingsbury Regis	*	*	*	
Milburn Port fee farm		*	*	
Queen Camel	*	*		
Matthew Gournay lands				*
SURREY				
Woking	*		*	*
Sutton		*	*	
SUSSEX				
Iden (rent)		*		
WORCESTERSHIRE				
Droitwich (fee farm)	*			

YORKSHIRE		
Cottingham	*	
Scotton		*
Farnley Magna		*
Farnley Parva		*
Okenshawe		*
Clakheton		*
WESTMORLAND		
Grasmere		*E
Loughrigg		*E
Langdale		*E
Casterton		*E
Amblesside		*E
Kendal		*E
Troutbeck		*E
WALES		
Glyndwrdy lands	*	

An attempt to list and estimate the estates of the Beaufort dynasty is problematic and would entail a study more detailed than this volume could produce. The above information combines the findings of G. L. Harriss's listings with later records of the second and third dukes' possessions.[1]

It appears that the inquisitions post mortem are incomplete, and it is likely that in some areas the tribunals did not sit. It also shows that some estates, including those of Thomas, Duke of Exeter, apart from one, are not accounted for in the later assessments.

There is also the division of estates on the death of John (II), first duke from 1444. A large part went to Margaret Beaufort, but some were inherited by Edmund (I), second duke, as on an entail. This duke appears to have had fewer estates than his elder brother, those on an entail that Margaret could not inherit. He did gain some grants of lands in this time; the Matthew Gournay lands in Somerset included Farrington, Gournay, Deoform, Ingolstad, Widdecombe, Lanerton, Shepton Mallet, Westhampton, Worymale and Westchapter and were listed as Edmund's but returned to the crown after his death.[2] The Lordship of Carisbrooke on the Isle of Wight was also in Edmund's hands, but although said to have been returned was still in practice a possession of his son Henry (III), third duke with his two brothers as his deputies when taken by the Yorkists in 1460.

Some of the estates listed (marked with E) were held in dower by Eleanor, dowager duchess from 1444. John Beaufort (II) received the Barony of Kendal; it was reported as returned to the crown on his death, but Eleanor held it in dower.

Given the anomalies in the documentation it is difficult to reach an estimate of the incomes of the Beauforts. There was serious economic upheaval in the previous century and in many cases revenues from the estates were reduced. A detailed study of the Patent and Fine Rolls would reveal a number of grants of incomes rather than landed estates, and this is probably the source of the wealth that the dukes acquired to sustain their affairs.

There are many references to grants of fee farm to John (II) which Edmund (I) was deemed to have inherited, such as that of £500 paid annually from the Port of London and £20 from Burton, Somerset, both of which passed to Edmund in tail male after 1443.[3]

The payments made to Edmund first from the Exchequer from 1442 and then from specified Welsh lordships were designated while the king could not grant him estates, and it is not certain when these disbursements in fact ceased, if not when he received his brother's entailed lands.[4] There were other arranged cash payments. This shows how the Beauforts could not easily rely on incomes from their lands to sustain them but were heavily dependent on payments attached to the offices they held and payments from the revenues of counties and other sources of royal revenue.

The Surrey lands, in Sutton and Woking, were listed as passing to Edmund but it is certain that Margaret was in occupation of the latter in 1471.

When Henry (III), third duke was attainted in 1464 there are only two entries in the *Calendar of Inquisitions Post Mortem*, of which the first deals with Monketon and Berchington in Thanet, neither of which appear in an earlier inquests. The second reference deals with Corfe Castle, which was granted to Clarence soon after.[5]

There is no record of any estates in the possession of Edmund (II), fourth duke, or his brother John, later created Marquis of Dorset. They probably subsisted as Margaret of Anjou's pensioners during the Readeption but no grants of estates or royal incomes to them were known.

The landed estates of Cardinal Beaufort were those of the Bishopric of Winchester, and were said to have exceeded £4,000 per annum.

Appendix II

GENEALOGICAL TABLES

Table I. Plantagenet, Lancaster and Beaufort.

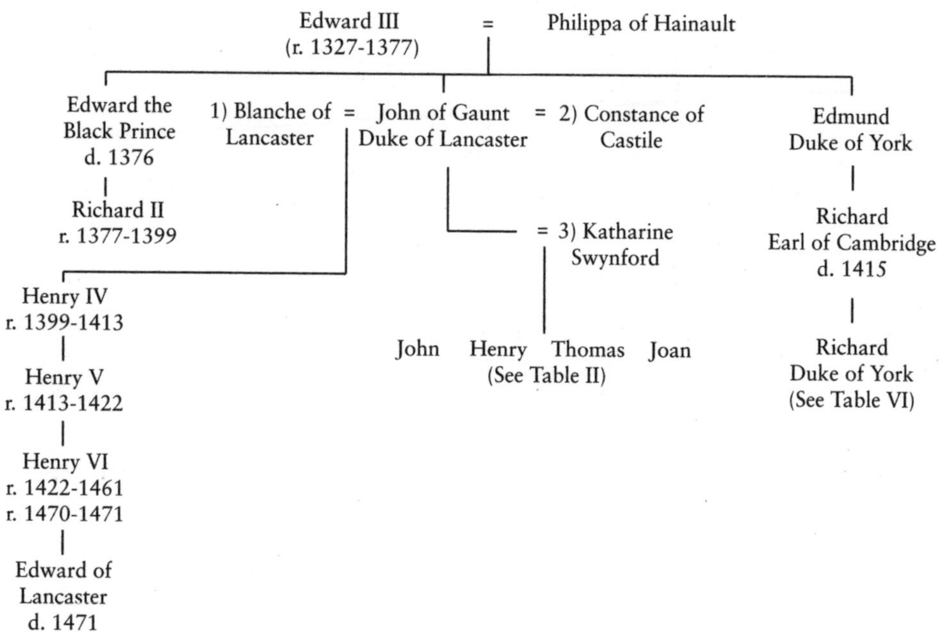

Table II. The Beauforts: the first generation.

John of Gaunt
Duke of Lancaster
=
Katharine
Swynford

John Beaufort (I) Earl of Somerset 1373-1409	Henry Beaufort (I) Bishop of Lincoln & Winchester Cardinal Beaufort 1375-1447	Thomas Beaufort (I) Earl of Dorset Duke of Exeter 1377-1426	Joan Beaufort (I) 1379-1440
See Table III	Joan (illegitimate)	Henry (predeceased)	See Table V

Table III. The Beauforts: the second and third generations.

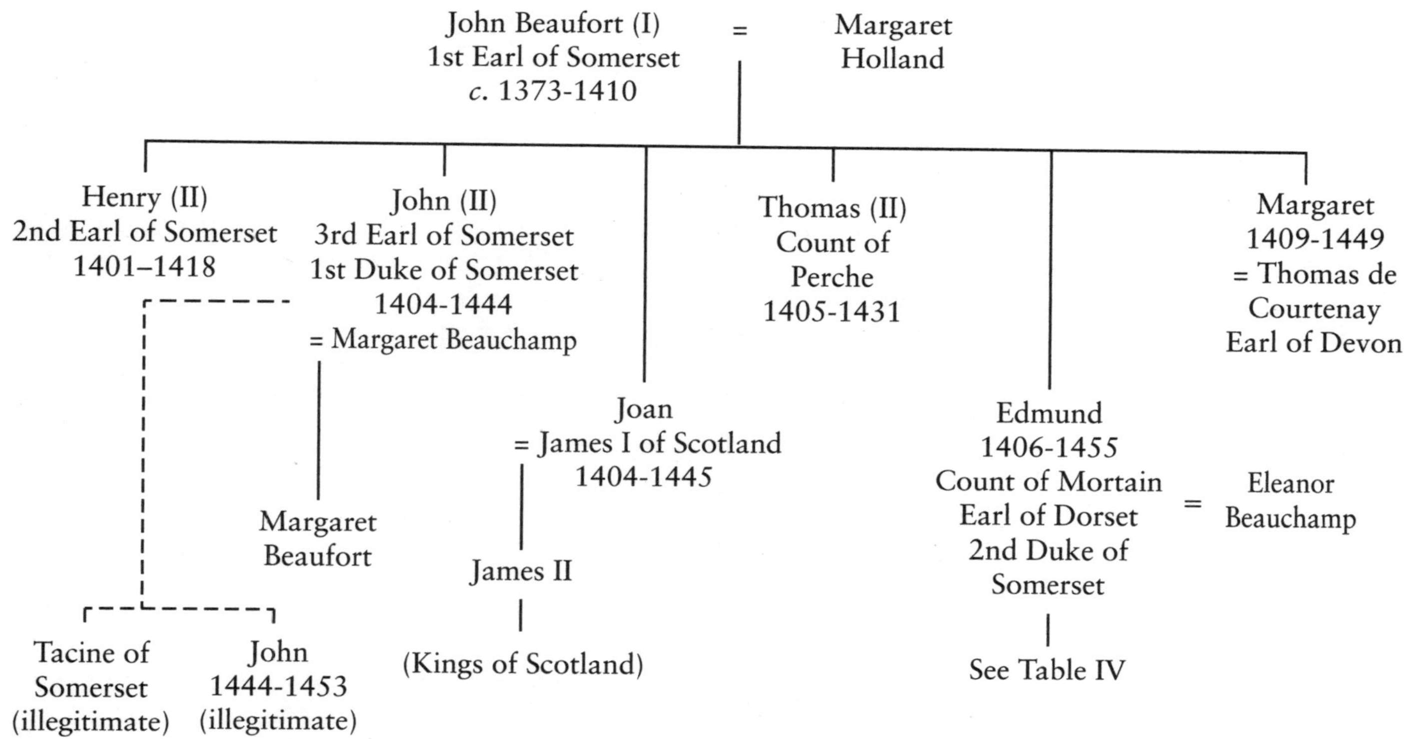

Table IIIb. The Family of Edmund Beaufort (I).

Edmund Beaufort (II)
2nd Duke of Somerset
1406-1455
=
Eleanor
Beauchamp

Eleanor
= 1) James Butler
Earl of Ormond
= 2) Sir Robert
Spencer

Elizabeth
= Sir Henry
FitzLewis

Henry (III)
1436-1464
3rd Duke of
Somerset

Charles Somerset
(illegitimate)

Margaret
= 1) Humphrey
Earl of Stafford
= 2) Sir Richard
Dayrell

Edmund (II)
'4th Duke of
Somerset'
1439-1471

Anne
= Sir William
Paston

John, Earl of
Dorset
1465-1471

Robert St Lawrence, = 1)
Baron Howth
Sir Richard Fry = 2)

Joan
d. 1518

Thomas (II)
d. 1463

Mary

Table IV. Roelt, Swynford, Beaufort and Chaucer.

- Sir Gilles 'Paon' de Roelt
  - Walter
  - Elizabeth
  - Philippa = Geoffrey Chaucer
    - Thomas Chaucer
      - Alice Chaucer
        - = 1) Sir John Phelip
        - = 2) Thomas Montague Earl of Salisbury
        - = 3) William de la Pole Earl & Duke of Suffolk
  - Katherine
    - = 1) Sir Hugh Swynford
      - Margaret
      - Sir Thomas Swynford
      - Blanche
      - Dorothy?
    - = 2) John of Gaunt Duke of Lancaster
      - The Beauforts (See Table II)

Table V. Neville and Beaufort, the Middleham Nevilles.

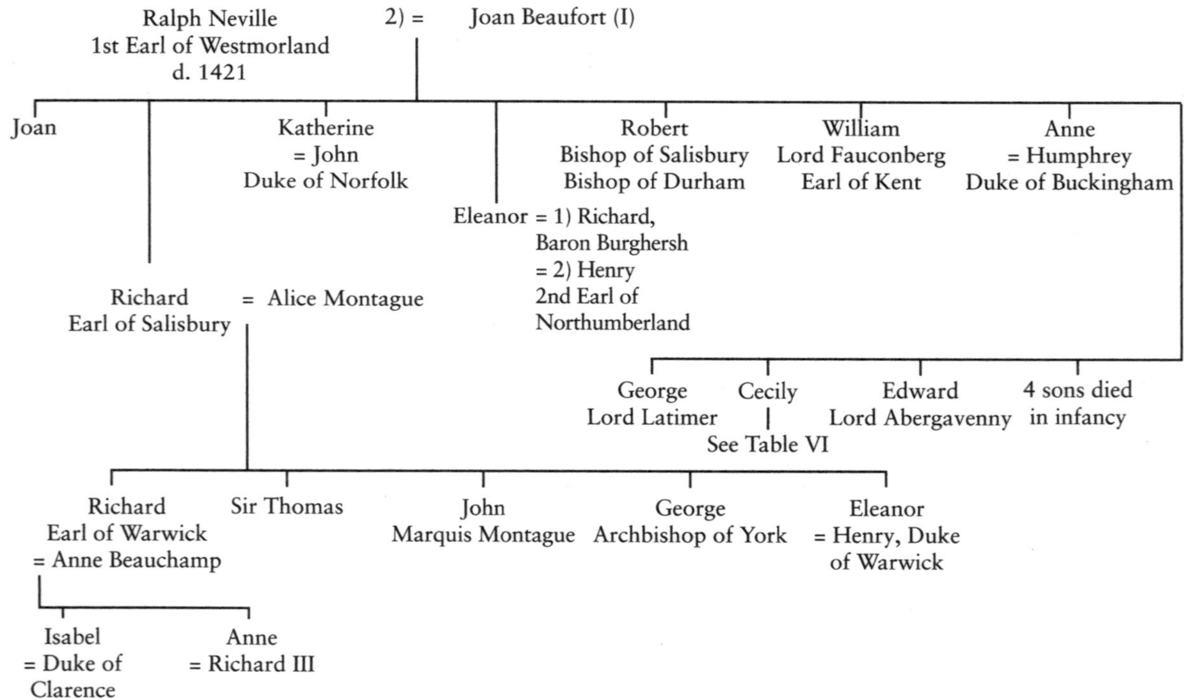

* Ralph Neville first married Margaret Stafford in 1370, and his senior line produced the earls of Westmorland

** Joan Beaufort (I) was previously married to Robert Ferrers, Baron Boteler of Wem c 1392 and had issue.

*** Katherine Neville later remarried in turn to Sir Thomas Strangways, John Viscount Beaumont and then Sir John Woodville

Table VI. Beaufort and the Stewart Kings.

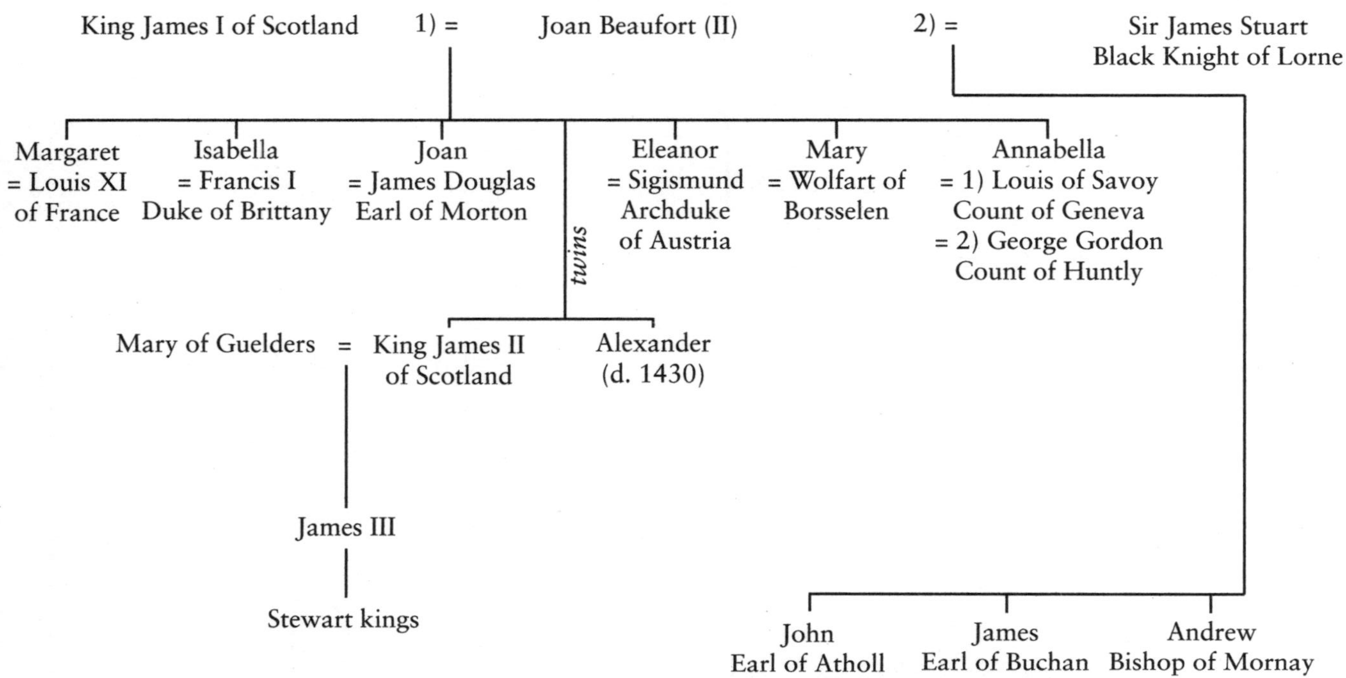

Appendix III

MAPS

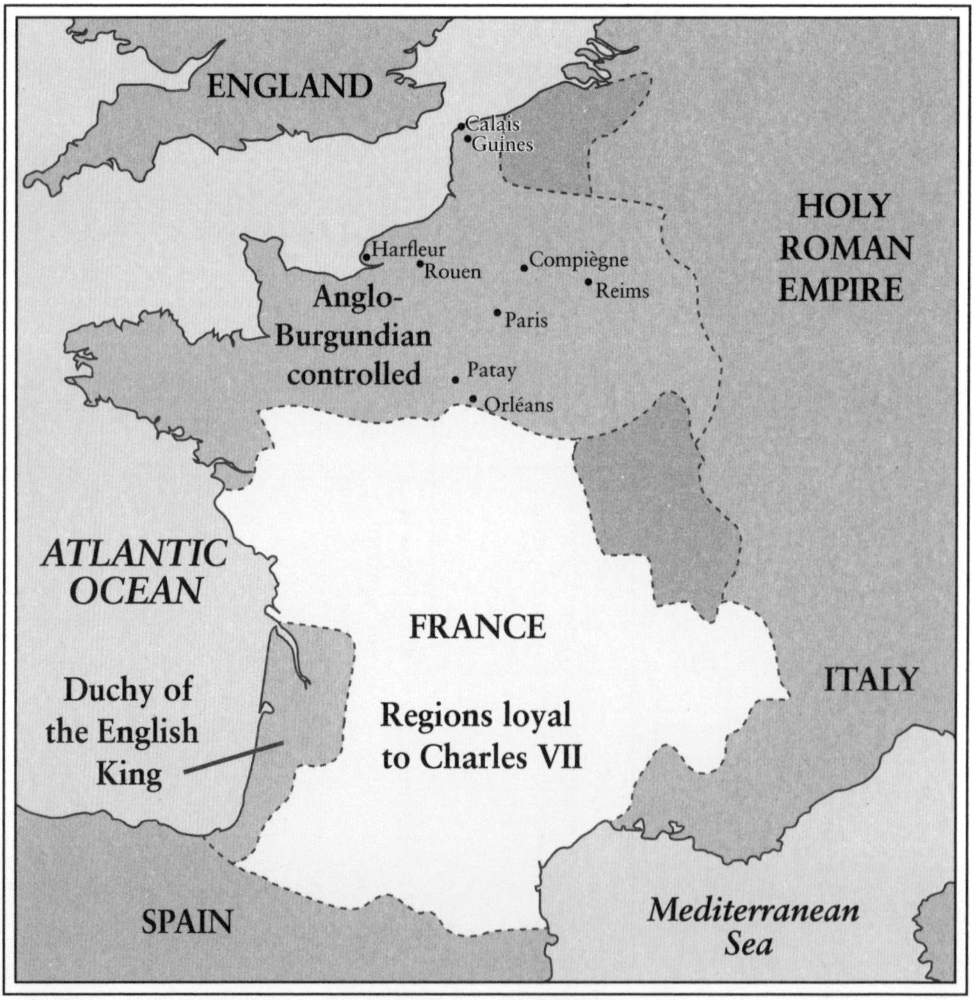

French territories at the time of the Treaty of Arras, 1435.

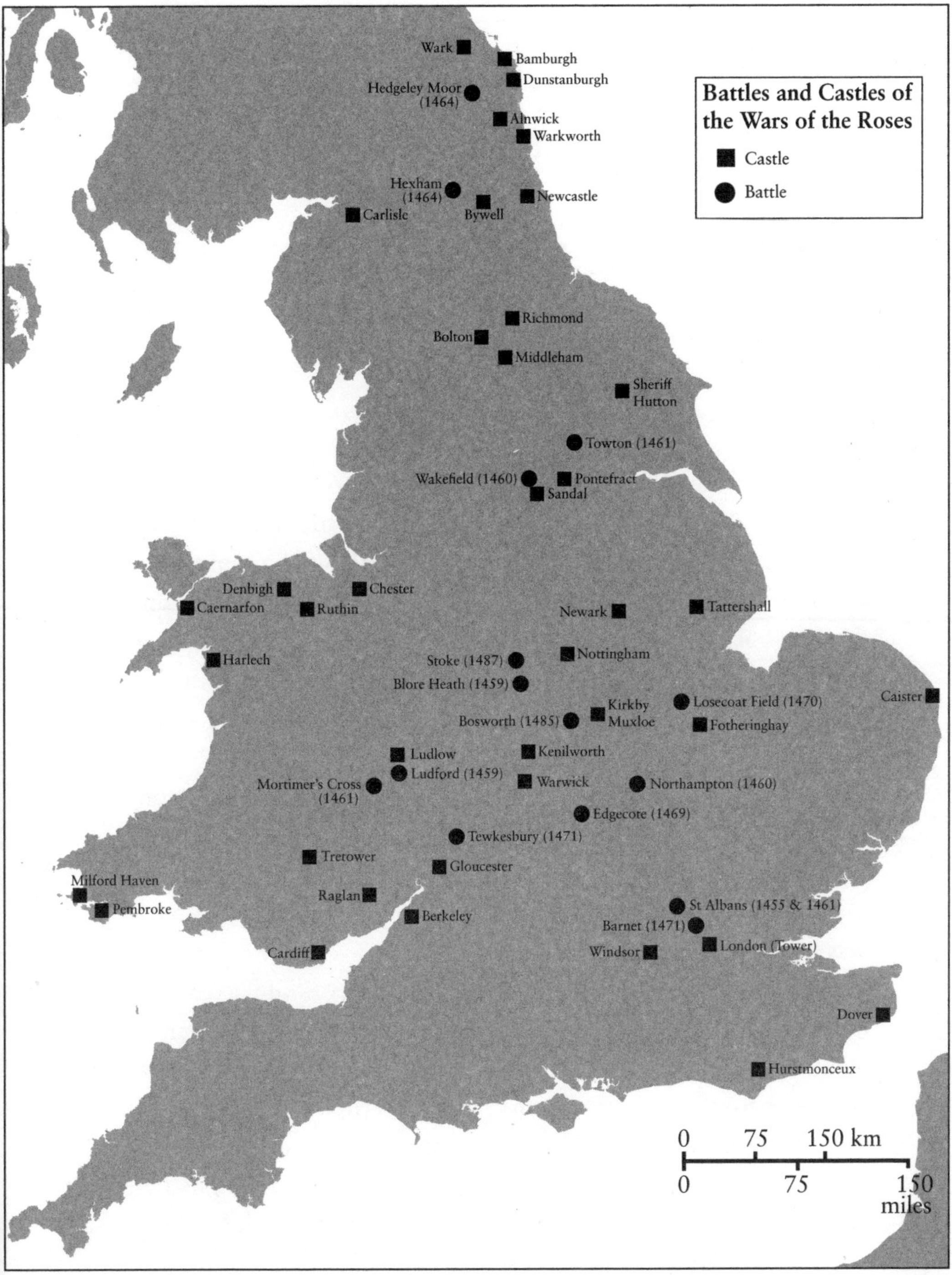
Battles and Castles of the Wars of the Roses
Castle
Battle
Wark
Bamburgh
Dunstanburgh
Hedgeley Moor (1464)
Alnwick
Warkworth
Hexham (1464)
Bywell
Newcastle
Carlisle
Richmond
Bolton
Middleham
Sheriff Hutton
Towton (1461)
Wakefield (1460)
Pontefract
Sandal
Denbigh
Chester
Caernarfon
Ruthin
Newark
Tattershall
Harlech
Stoke (1487)
Nottingham
Blore Heath (1459)
Kirkby Muxloe
Losecoat Field (1470)
Caister
Bosworth (1485)
Fotheringhay
Ludlow
Kenilworth
Ludford (1459)
Mortimer's Cross (1461)
Warwick
Northampton (1460)
Edgecote (1469)
Tewkesbury (1471)
Trerower
Gloucester
Milford Haven
Raglan
Pembroke
Berkeley
St Albans (1455 & 1461)
Barnet (1471)
London (Tower)
Windsor
Cardiff
Dover
Hurstmonceux
0 75 150 km
0 75 150 miles

Appendix IV

ON REGALIA AND LIVERIES

The popular legend of the plucking of the two roses, which still holds a place in school textbooks, is now understood to have been a myth, almost certainly engendered by the supporters of Henry VII, who claimed to have reunited England with the symbol of the red and white roses together. The title of the 'Wars of the Roses' as emerged in the Romantic era of historical literature has since persisted, for want of a better name.

In reality comparatively few roses of any kind were seen among the regalia of either side. While Richard of York was known to use the white rose as his personal badge no sign of the red rose can be found at the time. The real picture may have been colourful, but it was highly complex.

The entire question of regalia and heraldry is an exact and fascinating study. Each aristocrat had a unique design which he wore on his surcoat and shield in order to identify himself. Such designs, known as 'coats of arms', were inherited and worn by the head of the family, other members wearing 'differenced' versions. This was only a part of the culture of symbols and designs that played such an important part in the everyday lives and military activities of that day and continues to do so.

The Beaufort Arms

As a knight in Henry Bolingbroke's crusade John Beaufort bore the first coat of arms, which was obviously based on his father's. John of Gaunt bore the royal arms with a difference (quarterly France and England, on a label ermine.)

John (I) first bore the following: Per pale azure and argent, on a bend dexter gules, in bend three lions passant guardant or clawed azure and a label argent with fleur-de-lys or. He does not make use of the bend sinister, which denotes bastardy, and which would have linked him, somewhat dubiously, with his royal father.

The Plantagenet family all used differenced versions of the royal arms, effectively the three Plantagenet lions of England and the lilies of France (quarterly, first and fourth, azure, on three fleur-de-lys, second and third, gules, on three lions passant guardant or.)

After 1397, when the Beauforts were legitimated, John adopted a version of the royal arms which effectively stated the Beauforts' place as Princes of the Blood. Their arms thenceforth were quarterly France and England within a bordure gobony of azure and argent. This was similar to the differences of the Plantagenets' arms. Humphrey, Duke of Gloucester as one example used the royal arms differenced with a bordure argent.

The younger sons of John (I) and Edmund (I) wore differenced arms, but as three sons of the first and two of the latter inherited the earldom and dukedom these all adopted this blazon in due course.

Badges and Liveries

The followings of nobles may wear liveries, distinctive uniform dress, and often badges to show their affinity. Badges, usually made of cloth sewn to garments, were the usual symbols of political and military affinity. Many other forms of this can be seen, from the SS collar for Lancaster on portraits and tomb effigies to the cartouche of the boar that Richard, Duke of Gloucester placed on Barnard Castle.

Richard of York used the white rose but was more often associated with the falcon and fetterlock, and others on both sides showed their separate contingents with other symbols as their badges. Richard Neville, Earl of Warwick inherited from the Beauchamp earls the bear and ragged staff and these symbols, particularly the latter, were seen about his supporters, who followed his alignment as it changed. On the morning of his victory at the Battle of Ludlow, Edward, Earl of March was so moved by the optical illusion of three suns rising that he adopted the sun in splendour as his personal badge thereafter, and did not inherit his father's white rose.

Much is also said of liveries, garments of a particular colour combination or design that nobles would hand out to their followings. Whereas the Earl of Warwick's men wore red after the uniform of the Calais garrison, those of the Duke of Clarence would wear a design in murrey and blue. Certainly by the civil wars the livery of the Duke of Somerset was a white and blue combination. It was likely that an immediate following drawn from a noble household and other close affinity would wear such garments, and others would content themselves with the badge, for large retinues would be expensive to clothe. Conversely, it would have been an indicator of status to have large followings in their colours and some lords were willing to meet such a bill. Cardinal Beaufort clothed his henchmen in vermillion tunics, each with the word 'Honour' embroidered on the sleeve. At Arras in 1435 over 600 of his party arrived in this livery, again a mark of status.

This haphazard system of regalia caused many problems, as events showed. Somerset's livery used the same colours as Salisbury's brother Lord Fauconberg, and this could have caused confusion when the armies met at Towton. There was one case of serious misidentification among the Lancastrians at the Battle of Barnet, when Montague's musketeers opened fire on the Earl of Oxford's men returning to the battle under the banner of the rayed star, mistaking it for Edward's sun in splendour. Believing this to be treachery, Oxford promptly withdrew his force.

Battles and other gatherings of nobles and followings must have been very colourful events, but clearly fraught with pitfalls. It was difficult for all involved to remember which livery or badge stood for which magnate, and which side they were fighting on at the time, given that many changed sides during the conflict.

For the Beauforts the two badges with which they were identified were the portcullis and the yale, both from the time of John Beaufort (I), first Earl of Somerset. It is possible that John's office of Captain of Calais inspired his adoption of the first symbol. He was the keeper of the gate to England, the nearest foothold the English had in France, and John saw himself as protector of this route. There is no doubt that he took his office in Calais seriously. In typical fashion the Beaufort family retained the use of the portcullis as their badge and a popular ballad of about 1450 identifies the portcullis with them.[1]

Through Margaret Beaufort (II) the Tudors inherited the portcullis and it became a prominent device in the architecture and regalia of the Tudor dynasty after 1485, now surmounted with a crown. The symbol made a reappearance when Charles Barry redecorated the restored Palace of Westminster in the nineteenth century; it was still much in evidence from the Tudor era. Parliament itself has since adopted the portcullis as its own symbol; it appears on its documents and seat covers. John Beaufort's personal token has come a long way.

The yale of Beaufort, as was included among the statues of the queen's beasts as commissioned in 1953, was Margaret's own heraldic device and appears on the gates of the two Cambridge colleges she endowed. It subsequently appeared at Hampton Court and where the queen's beasts are depicted. It is a mythical creature, a kind of goat whose horns can swivel, and is the most puzzling member of the collection. How John Beaufort (II), first Duke of

Somerset acquired it as one of his personal badges is debatable. It was originally used by John, Duke of Bedford, and is shown in the Bedford Hours. Some say that John Beaufort inherited the yale when the Barony of Kendal, previously of Bedford's possessions, was regranted to him. On Somerset's achievement, that is his full coat of arms, the yale is the sinister (i.e. left-hand) supporter. The yale was often embroidered and used as a badge of the supporters of the Beauforts during the civil wars.

The yale of Beaufort. A popular image.

Appendix V

EDMUND BEAUFORT AND KATHERINE DE VALOIS

Some narratives on the Tudor monarchy hint at a tantalising question concerning the true lineage of Henry VII. There has been a suggestion that his father Edmund Tudor was the son not of Owen Tudor as the story goes but of Edmund Beaufort (I), eventually second Duke of Somerset. Our study of the Beauforts therefore requires some investigation into this and although the allegation is short on concrete evidence the facts are given here.

The Tudors themselves had no claim in the male line to the throne; as Welsh gentry they were hardly of the Blood Royal and the marriage of Owen Tudor to Katherine did not change this for all of Henry VI's honouring of his half-brothers. Only Edmund Tudor's marriage to Margaret Beaufort gives Henry Tudor even a vague claim to the succession and his marriage to Elizabeth of York made his accession viable, at least to most. It is certain that had he submitted his claim to arbitration rather than winning the Battle of Bosworth his chances would have been poor indeed by the standards of the day.

Katherine de Valois was widowed at twenty and forced into the role of dowager queen to Henry V and mother to the infant Henry VI, playing little or no part in his upbringing. As a young woman 'unable fully to curb her carnal passions', as one source commented,[1] she would look to eligible young men, and was frustrated in this role that demanded her chastity. It is not known when her affair with Owen Tudor began but it could have been as late as 1434, as will be shown.

It appears that her remarriage was under discussion sometime around 1425. It was also rumoured that Sir Edmund Beaufort was considered for her second union, and that several who did not favour the Beauforts prevented this by Act of Parliament. This would give rise to speculation concerning the real paternity of her children, and as this issue does appear in many narratives on the Tudor monarchy, the facts need examination. One could conclude that while the speculation cannot be refuted, no real evidence can be found. G. L. Harriss admitted to an 'agreeable possibility' that Henry Tudor's parents were first cousins, due to Edmund Beaufort's liaison. However, while Edmund Tudor could easily have been the son of Edmund Beaufort Harriss wrote of the evidence as 'less than conclusive'.[2] One more recent writer on the subject refers to this matter, but also concludes that the allegation is inconclusive.[3]

The tantalising fact that Katherine named her first son Edmund alone prevents this story from dismissal as historical gossip. It was not a common name, and while it was usual to name the eldest son after the father, Katherine called the third son Owen instead. The eldest might alternately have had his godfather's name, but no corroborating record survives. It was also common to name a child after the saint's day, but Edmund's date of birth is unknown. It is certain that someone named Edmund had a major effect on Katherine, and Edmund Beaufort was the only one of that name known in her life at that stage.

Edmund Beaufort had just come to manhood in the mid-1420s. He had little standing at the time; he was only a knight, a younger brother of an earl, and could not expect an inheritance. But his eldest brother, John, the Earl of Somerset, was imprisoned in France with the next brother Thomas, and Edmund, nephew of the

Chancellor Bishop Beaufort, might have brought some influence and protection with him. As a widow Katherine was not obliged to remarry against her will, and while she might have found him an agreeable young man. Edmund could equally have been attracted to her dower lands as much as to her.

If the matter was under discussion its opponents quickly acted. In the parliament of 1427–28 it was stated that no man of any status could marry a Queen of England without special licence of the king, 'when the latter is of the age of discretion, on pain of forfeiture of all lands and tenements'. This does not appear in the parliamentary rolls but a copy of the enrolment in that parliament has been verified.[4]

There had already been in the previous parliament a statute that forbade remarriage of widows without royal assent, although this new pronouncement may not have been related.[5] The specific reference to dowager queens in the later parliament makes it likely that such a remarriage had been discussed.

The petition was delivered in the name of some of the most senior prelates of England; Archbishops Chichele and Kemp, the bishops of London, Rochester and Ely and the abbots of four high-profile religious houses. Chichele and his associates were uneasy over the increase in influence of the Beauforts.[6] It is also tempting to think that Humphrey, Duke of Gloucester was stirring them up as an attack on Bishop Beaufort, but nothing was said of it among his other documented accusations. One may wonder what prompted this concern. Of the two dowager queens then in England, Katherine de Valois and Joan of Navarre, Joan's advanced age made it unlikely that she was seeking a new husband, and she had anyway been in disfavour since the witchcraft allegations of 1419. Nor is there any mention of this matter in relation to Joan. Isabella, Richard II's child queen, had returned to France and remarried when she reached a more appropriate age. Katherine was the only possible candidate.

The marriage with Edmund was therefore prevented, and would need to wait at least ten years before it could come about while the king was a minor. Whether the two had an affair after this judgment is purely a matter of speculation. Bishop Beaufort fell from grace that year and as cardinal then occupied himself with the Bohemian crusade, and there was no way of having the restriction reversed. In February 1427 Edmund was ordered to muster with a contingent of soldiers to fight in France, and there he remained for some time, apart from the expedition to Bohemia later that year.[7] He took part in the defence of Paris in 1429, was briefly in England in 1430 on his way to his embassy to Scotland but was seen at Paris again the same year, defending it from Joan of Arc's attack. It is not shown where he was during the coronation campaign, but more than likely he was again in Paris with the English coronation party. He was on the Louviers campaign in 1431.

But the whereabouts of Katherine cannot be so easily established. After the marriage controversy she was ordered to attend the royal household; perhaps she was not trusted to remain chaste. Although there is no record of her being there it is likely that she accompanied her son and his large household to Paris, and could have met Edmund again there. She was at her manor of Waltham soon after Christmas 1430.[8]

The whereabouts of Edmund Beaufort are uncertain for the three years after Louviers. He might have returned to England with the coronation party in or shortly after 1431. He was chosen in 1434 as a lay ambassador to Basel[9] and in 1435 he married Eleanor Beauchamp, any question of marriage with Katherine definitely at an end by that point. One could conjecture that only when Edmund departed from her life Katherine then took an interest in Owen Tudor. Owen appears to have returned to England in 1427 in the company of Lord Hungerford and was made Keeper of the Queen's Wardrobe when his patron gained the keeping of the Royal Household. His association with Katherine could have dated from this appointment or up to seven years later.[10]

There were many legends concerning the meeting of Katherine with Owen Tudor, mostly appearing in the times of Tudor propaganda. The tale of Katherine peeping on him as he bathed in the river and afterwards accosting him disguised as her maid is one such. Another was how at a ball Owen's unsteady footwork had him fall into Katherine's lap. The details of their affair and marriage are sketchy to say the least and such stories are of little relevance here.

In reality the story of Katherine and Owen Tudor is imprecise as to the dating and order. It was only when Katherine died in January 1437 that it was even revealed that they had married; it was a secret marriage, not even documented. When it took place and whether it really happened are uncertain. How knowledge of it was withheld from King Henry for so long and why nobody acted on what was an illegal union appears strange, as Owen was thrown into prison for this only after her death. Some say that once Katherine had died he no longer had her protection, but this appears to have overestimated how effective her protection was. Katherine was not too powerful, as her previous treatment shows. In 1434 she granted Owen a wardship in her gift, which may or may not show her interest in his affairs.[11]

Four children were acknowledged as their own, which meant that Edmund Tudor the eldest was born no later than 1433. It is generally believed that he was born in or about 1430 and his brother Jasper the following year, but the apparent late age at which both were knighted, unless this was only because the king acknowledged them at all at that time, presents the possibility that they were born later than believed.

It is hard to see how Katherine produced four children without this coming to the attention of the king's council. She was apparently still sustained by the royal household when her first two sons were born, Edmund at Hadham and Jasper at Hatfield – both royal manors. It seems a matter that was never discussed while she lived and while the king was still a minor it was probably kept from him.[12] After the royal party returned to England in 1431 she left the court and went to live in Hertfordshire. It defies belief how her four pregnancies were not noticed or commented on, and it is possible that the last two at least happened after leaving the royal court.

Given such facts it is possible, although no evidence directly supports it, that Katherine may have conducted a long-term affair with Edmund Beaufort, similar to Katherine Swynford in her relationship with John of Gaunt, from about 1425 to possibly as late as 1434, although interrupted when Edmund was on campaign. Although prevented by Parliament from marrying they might have continued in the hope of her son's blessing as soon as his minority ended. Edmund's absence in France notwithstanding, they could have associated again either during the coronation expedition or afterwards. Edmund and Jasper Tudor may have been born of Katherine and Edmund in 1433 and 1434 or thereabouts. This would have meant that in 1434 or the following year Katherine's marriage with Owen Tudor took place, probably after Edmund Beaufort abandoned the relationship and opted for a Beauchamp marriage. Perhaps Owen, son of Katherine *was* Owen Tudor's firstborn son after all.

Needless to say, this is where historical research ends and historical gossip begins. The only evidence we have of any of this is that someone called Edmund had a strong influence on Katherine at the time her eldest son was born, and that Owen Tudor was condemned for illegally marrying her before her death in 1437. It can also be said that if such an affair lasted any length of time word of it would have almost certainly found its way to the sources. Such secrets could not easily be kept for as long.

The presence of the Beauforts in Katherine's life even after the suggested marriage was prohibited is also in evidence. It has been shown that Cardinal Beaufort was in her company at Waltham soon after Christmas 1430 and she granted the stewardship of some of her lands to Thomas Chaucer and then the Earl of Suffolk. This shows that she associated with the de la Poles as much as the Beauforts, the two families close at the time. Her children were placed in the care of Barking Abbey, whose abbess was then Suffolk's sister.[13]

There is always gossip over those in high places. Some twenty years later tongues wagged over the close association of the same Edmund Beaufort and Queen Margaret of Anjou. Any allegations that Edmund was the real father of Edward of Lancaster can only remain allegations, but the Yorkists took them as fact, in order to declare the boy disinherited.

Even if Edmund Beaufort was Henry Tudor's grandfather it would have made little difference. Being the son of Margaret Beaufort, herself daughter of John Beaufort, first Duke of Somerset, was Henry's one claim to the Blood Royal of England. The line of Beaufort had a questionable claim at best, and to name his paternal grandfather as Edmund the second duke would not have strengthened his claim, but would have declared him of a bastard line if it was ever raised. The one change it would have made was to the Welsh dimension of the Tudor legend, and would have cut Owen Tudor out of the pedigree, relegating him to Edmund Tudor's stepfather. This again meant little, for the Tudor monarchy did not really profit from being Welsh. It would have simply invalidated much propaganda and rendered a number of prophecies redundant.

To this incomplete puzzle one more piece is added, which itself yields no firm evidence either. A Paston letter reported Richard III's condemnation of Henry Tudor's *double* bastard ancestry in 1485 and this could be relevant.[14] While one 'bastard' line was that through Margaret Beaufort to John of Gaunt's Beaufort children, which was the other? He does state that this was Owen Tudor's line, but one may wonder: was Owen's legitimacy ever called into question? His lowly status was derided, but none called him a bastard. Nor was the secret marriage with Katherine ever disputed. Paston might have referred to allusions on Katherine's lack of chastity and the possible paternity of her children. It does not lay a trail to Edmund Beaufort but at least hints at such concerns.

But the final analysis cannot give credence to this matter. There is no evidence that Katherine to Edmund ever saw each other again once the marriage was prohibited. While her elder sons might have been born some years later than believed, and her marriage to Owen, if it ever took place, could have occurred later, no documentation supports any of this. It is just as likely that Edmund gave up on marrying her either in 1427 or later, and that possibly as early as 1429 Katherine married Owen. Any allegation that she and Edmund's affair lasted long enough to beget Edmund Tudor, certainly in or after 1430, remains speculation, the stuff of historical fiction.

All we know for sure was that Katherine and Edmund Beaufort abandoned their plans of marriage in or after 1427 but by 1434 at the latest, and also that her association with Owen Tudor began in or before 1435, and in addition Edmund Tudor was born between 1428 and 1433. While this makes it possible that Edmund Beaufort was the father of Edmund Tudor, it does not at all make it certain.

Some would have been concerned that the king would have fallen under Beaufort's influence as he grew up. While the Beauforts were at their most powerful at that time there was growing concern among some council members, Archbishop Chichele and of course Gloucester in particular, that Edmund would as the king's stepfather exert undue influence. Although no sign of Humphrey's direct involvement is in evidence he would have been concerned about this match, and perhaps he encouraged the prelates in this – not that they needed much encouragement.

But one might like to think that Katherine did not forget Edmund Beaufort, for she almost certainly named her son after him.

Appendix VI

EDMUND BEAUFORT AND THE SIEGE OF CALAIS, 1436

Popular ballad, as quoted in *Brut* Vol. 2 pp. 582-584

Whene the Flemmyng wer fresh, florisshed in your flouris,
And had welth at your will, ye wolde be conquerouris
Of Caleis, that litill toune, : as it come in yhour mynde;
But ye, to conuere Caleis, it cometh you not of kynde.
Remembers on that wurship ye wann the first day,
When the Erle of Mortein come passing with his pray
Before youre toune of Grauenyng, ehere ye, as men bold,
Come rennying on hem fersli, as lyone of Cotteswold,
With habirgeons & hounsculles, & rusti ketill hates,
With long pykes, golden daghes for to stikke the rates,
With messis & meskins, & eke with side takes,
Doune unto mydde the leg, of kanuas lyke to sakes;
Stoppid al with hempen tawe, and that in straunge wyse,
Stiched like a matrace, al of newe gyse,
Ye laid upon englisshmen so mightily with your handes
Til of you iij hundred lay stretchid on the sandes.
Ye fled the into Gravenyng, and wolde no longer bide,
And gave the Erle leve to passé over that same tyde

In saafte with his prisoners, & lost never a man :
This was the first wurship, of Caleys that ye wan.
Remembres how ye laide seege, with gret pryde & bost,
To Caleis, that littil toune: the number of youre host
Was a hundred thousand & fifty, to reken by the pollis,
As it was that same time founden by youre rollis ;
And yette, for a your egret host, erly nothir late,
Caleis was so ferd of you, they shitte never a gate.
Remembres how ye drowned att full see for the nones,
With shippes, Caleis haven, massoned with stones,
And how that the Calisers hem brake the next day,
And when it was lawe water, and bare lxiii clene away,
Every stikke and stone, and lafte not ther one log.
Remembres eke on Goby, the water-baliffes dog,
How he scarmysshed with you twyes upon the day,
And among you, on the sandes, made many a fray.
Remembers ye of Brugges; how ye ferst wan youre shone,
How ye come forth to scarmyssh upon an aftirnone
With pavyses & crossbows, on Saynt Petirs playne,
And how sone the Calisers made you to turne agayne,
And overthrew you sodeynly, or ever that ye wist,
And brought you in-to Caleis, tyed fast by the fist.
Remembres ye of Gaunt eke: for al youre pride and bost,
Wonnen was youre bulwark, beside youre gret host,
And slayne al that was therin: & ye, that same night,
Fled ovir Gravenyng water; but go that go might,
And youre lord with you, for dreed and for fere
Of the Duyk of Gloucester; & yette was he not ther
Wel was hym might go before with pisone and with paunce,
And laft behind you, for hast al youre ordynanuce
Remembers, ye Picardes, at seege eke as ye lay
Of Guysnes, that strong Castel, how ye fled away
For ryngyng of the larume bell, shamfulli in a morowe,

As ferd as the Flemmynges,with hertes full of sorowe.
Ye lost there your ordinaunce, of gunnes that was cheff:
To you & to all Pycardis, shame and gret repreff.
Remembres now, ye Flemmynges, upon youre owne shame;
When ye laide seege to Caleis, ye wer right still to blame;
For more of reputacioun, ben Englisshmen then ye'
For Flemmynges come of Flemmed me ye shal wel understand,
For fflemed men & banshid men enhibit first youre land.
Thus prove I that Flemmynges is but a flemed man,
And Flaunders, of Flemmyngs, the name first began.
And therefore, ye Flemmynges, that Flemmynges ben named,
To compare with the Englisshmen, ye aught to be ashamed !
Ye be nothing elles worth, but gret wordes to camp;
Sette ye still, & bith in pees, God gyve you quadenamp!

NOTES

Abbreviations

CCR – Calendar of Close Rolls
CPR – Calendar of Patent Rolls
DNB – Dictionary of National Biography
EHR – English Historical Review
POPC – Proceedings and Ordinances of the Privy Council
Rot Parl – Rotuli Parliamentorum
TRHS – Transactions of the Royal Historical Society

1 A Brood of Royal Bastards

1. *Complete Peerage* Vol 7 pp. 401 – 416
2. Anthony Goodman *Katherine Swynford* (Honywood Press 1994) p. 10
3. Froissart *Chronicles p.* 11
4. *Excerpta Historica pp.* 158-159
5. Goodman *Katherine Swynford p.* 12
6. *ibid*
7. Chris Given-Wilson *The English Nobility in the Late Middle Ages* p. 52
8. Froissart *Chronicles pp.* 418-420
9. *ibid* p. 428
10. *Complete Peerage* Vol 12 Part 2 pp. 41
11. *Parliament Rolls* Vol VII p. 322
12. *ibid*
13. *Paston Letters* Vol 3 p. 320
14. Harriss, G L *Cardinal Beaufort A Study of Lancastrian Ascendancy and Decline* Clarendon 1988) p. 8
15. DNB Vol 4 p. 643

2 The King's Half-Brothers

1. Complete Peerage Vol 5 p. 201

2. Harriss *Cardinal Beaufort p.* 9
3. Parliament Rolls Vol VIII pp. 164-165
4. CPR 1399-1401 pp. 79, 173, 281,386, 387, 434, 263 *et al*
5. *English Chronicle p.* 34
6. Stephen Hyde Cassan, *The Lives of the Bishops of Winchester* Vol I London 1827, p. 256
7. Parliament Rolls Vol VIII p. 227; Harriss *Cardinal Beaufort p.* 30
8. After Harriss *Cardinal Beaufort p.* 401 from E 101/43/38
9. Harriss *Cardinal Beaufort p.* 8
10. Complete Peerage Vol 5 p. 203
11. CPR 1399-1401 pp. 160, 176, 243,393 *et al*
12. BL Cotton Caligula E, I.f. 152; BL Cotton Faustina E, VII, f. 17, as reproduced in *The Chronicles of Calais* Camden Society 34 (1846) pp. xxxv-vi
13. E 101/68/182
14. Complete Peerage Vol 5 p. 203; Harriss *Cardinal Beaufort pp.* 25-26
15. J L Kirby The Council of 1407 and the Problems of Calais. (English Society and Government in the Fifteenth Century Olivier & Boyd London 1967) pp. 71-86
16. *English Chronicle* p. 41
17. Clifford Brewer *The Death of Kings pp.* 79-81
18. *Rot Parl* Vol iii p. 343; CPR 1405 p. 384
19. Parliament Rolls Vol VIII p. 358
20. *Brut* ii p. 369
21. Harriss *Cardinal Beaufort p.* 46
22. Calendar of Inquisitions Post Mortem, Vol XIX 7-14 Henry IV 1405-1413. ed J L Kirby (London HMSO 1992)
23. Harriss *Cardinal Beaufort p.* 47
24. *ibid*
25. *Rot Parl* iii p. 622; Harriss *Cardinal Beaufort p.* 54
26. Parliament Rolls Vol IX p. 290
27. Registry of Henry Chichele vol ii (Canterbury and York Society) p. 295
28. Charles Lethbridge Kingsford, *The first English Life of King Henry the Fifth*, p. xxii

3 *The King's Uncles*

1. Parliament Rolls IX p. 5; J H W Wylie *The Reign of Henry the Fifth* Vol I p. 24
2. Harriss *Cardinal Beaufort p.* 69
3. E 101/ 69/3/355
4. *Complete Peerage* Vol 2 p. 71; Vol 5 p. 730
5. Brut ii p. 554
6. English Chronicle p. 45
7. *Ibid p.* 49
8. F R H Du Boulay *An Age of Ambition* Thomas Nelson 1970
9. Harris *Cardinal Beaufort p.* 80
10. K B MacFarlane 'Bishop Beaufort and the Red Hat 1417-21' *EHR Vol LX 1945 pp. 316-348*

11. Harris *Cardinal Beaufort p.* 87
12. *Complete Peerage* Vol 5 p. 202
13. *Complete Peerage* Vol 5, p. 202; *Ibid p.* 203
14. *Brut* Vol 2 pp. 387-389, 419-421
15. *Complete Peerage* Vol 5 p. 45
16. *Complete Peerage* Vol 5 p. 203; Waurin Vol 39 p. 364
17. *Complete Peerage* Vol 12 Part 2 pp. 45
18. *The Kingis Quair*, as reproduced in TEAMS Middle English Texts https://d.lib.rochester.edu/teams/text/mooney-and-arn-kingis-quair-and-other-prison-poems-james-i-scotland-kingis-quair Accessed 16 June 2020. ll. 274-280
19. *Complete Peerage* Vol 4 p. 327

4 *The Bishop and the Good Duke*

1. Rymer *Foedera* iv iii 146
2. E Carleton Williams *My Lord of Bedford 1389-1435* Longmans 1963 p. 116. The London Chronicle p. 58
3. *A Short London Chronicle p.* 59
4. Harriss *Cardinal Beaufort p.* 47
5. *ibid p.* 155
6. Harriss *Cardinal Beaufort* p. 207
7. Parliament Rolls Vol X p. 213
8. Harriss *Cardinal Beaufort – Patriot or Usurer?* (TRHS 20, 1970 pp. 129-148)
9. Harriss *Cardinal Beaufort (1988)* Appendix III pp. 412-413
10. E401/743, E 28/56, E401/748 *et al*
11. After Harriss *Cardinal Beaufort (1988) See* Appendix I
12. *ibid*
13. Letters of Queen Margaret of Anjou Bishop Becklington and others written in the reigns of Henry and Henry VI (Camden Soc 1863) p. 49
14. William Worcester *Itineraries pp.* 356-9
15. *Complete Peerage* Vol 5 p. 203
16. P A Johnson *Duke Richard of York p.* 1
17. SC 8/136/998
18. Harriss *Cardinal Beaufort p.* 121
19. *Chronicle of London p.* 78
20. *ibid p.* 84
21. Harriss *Cardinal Beaufort p.* 277
22. Parliament Rolls Vol X p. 290
23. *ibid p.* 288
24. *ibid p.* 290

5 *The Cardinal's Crusade and the Coronation Campaign*

1. CCR 1422-1429 p. 472
2. Thomas A Fudge – The Crusade against heretics in Bohemia 1418-1437. Crusade Texts in Translation. Ashgate, Aldershot 2002 p. 225
3. *ibid* p. 230
4. Michael Brown *James I p.* 110
5. *ibid*

6. Harriss *Cardinal Beaufort p.* 183
7. Papal letters vii 38.39; Lewis Bostock Radford *Henry Beaufort Bishop, Chancellor, Cardinal* London 1908 p. 167
8. Harriss *Cardinal Beaufort p.* 208
9. Radford *Henry Beaufort p.* 205
10. Daniel Hobbins (trans) *The Trial of Joan of Arc* (Harvard University Press 2005) p. 190
11. Radford *Henry Beaufort* p. 208; Harriss *Cardinal Beaufort p.* 209
12. Vickers *Humphrey Duke of Gloucester p.* 224
13. *ibid p.* 233

6 *War and Peace*

1. Harriss *Cardinal Beaufort p.* 144 et al
2. CPR 1422-1429 p. 404
3. CPR 1429-1436 p. 331
4. Harriss *Cardinal Beaufort p.* 206
5. CPR 1429-1436 pp. 340,342
6. *ibid pp.* 340, 498
7. *ibid pp.* 331, 510
8. E 30/1517
9. Stephen Hyde Cassan, *The Lives of the Bishops of Winchester* Vol I London 1827, p. 256
10. Brut ii p. 575
11. ibid pp. 578-581
12. ibid p. 577
13. CPR 1429-1438 p. 160
14. *ibid pp.* 188, 318
15. *Complete Peerage* Vol 12 part 1 p. 47
16. Ingulph's Chronicle of the Abbey of Croyland trans Henry Riley London 1854 pp. 398-399
17. Harriss *Cardinal Beaufort p.* 278
18. Wolffe *Henry VI p.* 92
19. E 30/448
20. Griffiths, Ralph A *The Reign of Henry VI: The Exercise Of Royal Authority 1422-1461* (Ernest Benn 1981) p. 449

7 *The False Peace, and the Loss of France*

1. *Complete Peerage* Vol 12 part 1 p. 51
2. CPR 1441-1446 pp. 54, 231
3. *Complete Peerage* Vol 12 part 1 pp. 46, 47
4. *ibid*
5. *Testamenta Vetusa p.* 254; POPC V p. 288; *Complete Peerage* Vol 4, p. 19n
6. POPC V 225-226
7. *ibid p.* 377
8. Harriss *Cardinal Beaufort p.* 336
9. Harriss Cardinal Beaufort p. 335

10. Croyland Chronicle p. 399
11. *Select Cases before the King's Council* (Seldon Society 1918) p. 102
12. E 328/109; DURH 3/43 mm 2
13. Entry No 1112 Register of Thomas Langley (Surtees Society, Vol 4 1958), p 132; Dobson *Durham Priory p.* 190
14. After Watts, John, *Henry VI and the Politics of Kingship* (CUP 1996)
15. *Excerpta Historica* pp. 43-46
16. Vickers, Humphrey Duke of Gloucester, pp. 288-289
17. Polydore Vergil, p. 15
18. Harriss *Cardinal Beaufort pp.* 377-78
19. English Chronicle p. 70
20. Stevenson Letters and Papers II i p. 313
21. Stevenson Letters and Papers I pp. 207-220, 223-232
22. *ibid pp.* 308-309, 313
23. Stephen Cooper The Real Falstaff: Sir John Fastolf and the Hundred Years War (Pen & Sword Books 2010) p. 113
24. Stevenson Letters and Papers II ii pp. 718-722
25. Stevenson II Part ii p. 723; Cooper *The Real Falstaff pp.* 115-116

8 Faction and Fighting

1. *English Chronicle* p. 72
2. P A Johnson Duke Richard of York 1411-1460 p. 83
3. *Parliament Rolls Vol V pp.* 184-5
4. C 1/1/66
5. *Parliament Rolls Vol V p.* 166
6. CPR 1441-1446 pp. 419,435,443,446,449 *et al*
7. K B McFarlane 'The Beauchamps and the Staffords' *The Nobility of Later Medieval England* (OUP 1973) p. 199
8. KB 9/15. KB 9/109, KB 9/94/1 *et al*
9. Paston Letters Vol I pp. 78-77
10. *English Chronicle* p. 73

9 Civil War

1. *Complete Peerage* 12 part 1 p. 54
2. C 49/30/15; Parliament Rolls XII p. 326
3. CPR 1452–1461 pp. 53,404
4. *ibid* pp. 211,212,213
5. *ibid pp.* 458,477,549
6. *ibid p.* 93
7. *ibid pp.* 392,61,365, 346
8. *Complete Peerage* 12 part 1 p. 54
9. Waurin 39, p. 327
10. Helen Cox *The Battle of Wakefield revisited* (Herstory New York 2010)
11. English Chronicle pp. 106-107
12. Waurin 39 p. 325
13. *English Chronicle* p. 106

14. Waurin 39 p. 324
15. Waurin 39, pp. 339-340

10 *Somerset and Edward IV*

1. Paston Letters Vol 1 p. 151
2. Parliament Rolls Vol XIII pp. 42-47
3. *ibid pp.* 43-46
4. Charles Ross *Edward IV pp.* 51-52
5. William Worcester *Annales,* Stevenson II Part ii p. 779; William Worcester *Annales,* Stevenson II Part ii p. 779; Ross *Edward IV p.* 85; Annie L Dunlop The Life and Times of James Kennedy Bishop of St Andrews p. 277
6. CPR 1467-1477 pp. 31,36
7. *ibid* p. 121
8. *ibid pp.* 86, 94, 100, 343
9. *Complete Peerage* Vol 8 p. 604
10. Paston Letters no. 273 Vol 2 p. 46

11 *The Last Beaufort Duke of Somerset*

1. Complete Peerage 12 part 1 p. 57n
2. Paston Letters Vol II p. 50
3. Philippe de Commynes *Memoires of the Reign of Louis XI 1461-83* (Penguin Books 1972) *p.* 190
4. *Arrivall p.* 14
5. *Arrivall p.* 29
6. *ibid*
7. Complete Peerage Vol 12 part i p. 58

12 *Margaret Beaufort*

1. *Complete Peerage* Vol 12 part 2 p. 444
2. Polydore Vergil p. 135
3. Charles Ross *Richard III* (Methuen 1988) *pp.* 105-125
4. *Complete Peerage* Vol 12 part 1 pp. 58-59

Conclusion

1. Harriss *Cardinal Beaufort. Appendix II*
2. C 139/160/38
3. *Calendar of Inquisitions Post Mortem* Vol XXVI numbers 188,192 *et al.*
4. CPR 1441-1446 pp. 54, 231
5. *Calendar of Inquisitions Post Mortem.* (HMSO. London 1898); CPR 1467-1477 pp. 31,36

Appendix III

1. Excerpta p. 161

Appendix IV

1. Giles *Incerti Scriptoris p.* 17
2. G L Harriss *Cardinal Beaufort p.* 144
3. Terry Breverton *Owen Tudor: Founding Father of the Tudor Dynasty*. (Amberley Publishing, Stroud 2017) *pp.* 134-37
4. *Parliament Rolls* Vol X p. 365; C 49/16/11; R A Griffiths 'Queen Katherine of Valois and a missing statute of the realm' *Law Quarterly Review* No 93 (1977) p. 253
5. *Parliament Rolls* Vol X p. 308
6. C 49/16/11
7. CPR 1422-1429 p. 404
8. Griffiths *Henry VI p.* 61
9. CPR 1429-1436 pp. 340,342
10. Ralph A Griffiths and Roger S Thomas *The Making of the Tudor Dynasty* (Alan Sutton Stroud 1985) p. 30
11. *ibid p.* 31
12. H T Evans *Wales During the Wars of the Roses p.* 43
13. Griffiths *Henry VI p.* 61
14. Paston Letters Vol 3 p. 320

BIBLIOGRAPHY

Documents

National Archives
E 101/68/182
E 101/ 69/3/355
E 328/109
E 401/743
E 28/56
E 30/1517
E 401/748
DURH 3/43
SC 8/136/998
C 49/30/15
C 49/16/11
C 139/160

Books

Calendar of Close Rolls Vols 1422-1429 (HMSO 1933)

Calendar of Patent Rolls Vols 1422-1429,1429-1436,1436-1441,1441-1446,1446-1452,1452-1461,1461-1477, 1467-1477 (HMSO 1897-1910)

Rymer *Foedera* Vol IV (London, 1739-1745)

BL Cotton Caligula E, If. 152; BL Cotton Faustina E, VII,f. 17, as reproduced in *The Chronicles of Calais* Camden Society 34 (1846)

Calendar of Inquisitions Post Mortem, Vol XIX 1-6 Henry IV 1399-1404 ed J L Kirby, Vol XX 7-14 Henry IV 1405-1413, Vol XXVI (London HMSO 1992), also Vol XXVI 21-25 Henry VI 1442-1447 (Boydell (2009)

Dictionary of National Biography (Vol 4 London: Offices of the Royal Historical Society, 1935)

Proceedings and Ordinances of the Privy Council Vols 4-6, ed Sir Harris Nicolas (HMSO 1835-1837)

The Brut, or The Chronicle of England 2 Vols (Early English Texts Society London 1908)

Parliament Rolls Vols 8-13 (Boydell 2005)

Rotuli Parliamentorum Vols III, V and VI (London: Parliament) 1767-1777

An English Chronicle 1377-1461 ed William Marx (Boydell 2003 edition)

Ingulph's Chronicle of the Abbey of Croyland (trans Henry Riley London 1854

'A Short English Chronicle' from *Three Fifteenth Century Chronicles with Historical Memoranda by John Stowe*, ed James Gairdner (Camden Society 1880), pp 58-78.

Chronique de la trahison et mort de Richard Deux, Roy Dengleterre, (ed B Williams London 1846)

The Crowland Chronicle Continuations 1459-1486) ed Michael Pronary and John Cox (Richard III and Yorkist History Trust 1986)

The Arrivall of Edward IV (Camden Society 1838)

Polydore Vergil English History in Henry VI, Edward IV and Richard III ed Rev Henry Eltham (Camden Society 1854)

Philippe de Commynes *Memoires of the Reign of Louis XI 1461-83* (Penguin Books 1972)

Jean Froissart *Chronicles* (Penguin Classics 1978)

Jehan de Waurin *Chronique de Anchiennes Istoire de la Grant Bretagne a present nomme England* Vol V 1447-1471 (HMSO 1891)

Itineraries of William Worcester: edited from the unique MS Corpus Christi College, ed John Harvey, (Cambridge,: Clarendon Press. 1969).

Select Cases before the King's Council (Seldon Society 1918)

Letters and papers Illustrative of the War of the English in France During the Reign of Henry VI King of England ed Rev Joseph Stevenson 2 Vols (London 1804)

Receuil des Chroniques et Anchiennes Istoires de la Grant Bretaigne a present nomme Engleterre par Jehan de Waurin. Ed Sir William Hardy Vol 39 1447-1471 (HMSO 1891)

The Paston Letters in three Volumes ed John Warrington (Letchworth Everyman 1924,1956)

The Paston Letters, ed James Gairdner (Gloucester, Sutton 1983)

Letters of Queen Margaret of Anjou Bishop Becklington and others written in the reigns of Henry V and Henry VI (Camden Soc 1863)

Register of Thomas Langley (Surtees Society, Vol 4 1958)

Registry of Henry Chichele vol ii (Canterbury and York Society)

Excerpta Historica or Illustrations of English History ed Richard Bentley, (London 1833)

Testamenta Vetusta being Illustrations from Wills ed Nicholas Harris Nicholas (Nicholls London 1826)

The first English Life of King Henry the Fifth, Called The Translator of Livius (ed Kingsford, Charles Lethbridge. Oxford, Clarendon Press 1911)

The Trial of Joan of Arc edited and translated by Daniel Hobbins (Harvard University Press 2005)

Giles J A (ed) *Incerti Scriptoris Chronicon Angliae de regnis Henrici IV, Henrici V et Henrici VI* (1848)

Secondary Sources

Amin, Nathen *The House of Beaufort: The Bastard Line That Captured the Crown* (Amberley, 2017)

Breverton, Terry *Owen Tudor. Founding Father of the Tudor Dynasty* (Amberley, 2017)

Brewer, Clifford *The Death of Kings* (Abson Books London 2001)

Brown, Michael *James I* (Canongate Press. Edinburgh 1994)

Cassan, Stephen Hyde *The Lives of the Bishops of Winchester* Vol I (London 1827)

Complete Peerage of England, Scotland and of the United Kingsom ed GEC St (Catherine Press (1910-1929)) 12 Vols

Chrimes, S.B *Henry VII* (Methuen 1972)

Cooper, Stephen *The Real Falstaff: Sir John Fastolf and the Hundred Years War* (Pen & Sword Books 2010)

Cox, Helen *The Battle of Wakefield Revisited.* (Herstory New York 2010)

Dobson, R B *Durham Priory 1400-50.* (CUP 1973)

Downie, Fiona *She Is But A Woman. Queenship In Scotland* 1424-1463. (John Donald Edinburgh 2006)

Du Boulay, F R H *An Age of Ambition* (Thomas Nelson 1970)

Dunlop, Annie L *The Life and Times of James Kennedy Bishop of St Andrews* (Oliver and Boyd Edinburgh 1950}

Evans, H T *Wales and the Wars of the Roses* (Alan Sutton 1995)

Fudge, Thomas A *The Crusade against heretics in Bohemia 1418-1437.* (Crusade Texts in Translation. Ashgate, Aldershot 2002)

Given-Wilson. Chris *The English Nobility in the Late Middle Ages* (Routledge & Keegan Paul 1987)

Goodman, Anthony *The Wars of the Roses* (Routledge & Kegan Paul 1981)

Goodman, Anthony *Katherine Swynford* (Honywood Press 1994)

Gregory, Philippa *The Lady of the Rivers (*Simon and Shuster 2012)

Griffiths, Ralph A *The Reign of Henry VI: The Exercise Of Royal Authority 1422-1461* (Ernest Benn 1981)

Griffiths, Ralph A 'Queen Katherine of Valois and a missing statute of the realm' *Law Quarterly Review* Vol 93 (1977)

Ralph A Griffiths and Roger S Thomas, *The Making of the Tudor Dynasty* (Alan Sutton Stroud 1985)

Griffiths, Ralph A and Thomas, Roger S *The Making of the Tudor Dynasty* (Alan Sutton 1985)

Harriss, G L *Cardinal Beaufort A Study of Lancastrian Ascendancy and Decline* Clarendon 1988)

Harriss, G L *Cardinal Beaufort – Patriot or Usurer?* (TRHS 20, 1970 pp 129-148)

Jacob, E F *The Fifteenth Century 1399-1485* (Oxford History of England. Clarendon Press Oxford 1960)

Johnson, P A *Duke Richard of York 1411-1460* (Clarendon Press Oxford 1988)

Jones, M K *Edward IV and the Beaufort family: Conciliation in Early Yorkist politics.* (Ricardian Vol VI no 83 Dec 1983)

Kirby J L 'The Council of 1407 and the Problems of Calais.' *English Society and Government in the Fifteenth Century* (Olivier & Boyd London 1967)

Kingsford, Charles Lethbridge *The first English Life of King Henry the Fifth* (Clarendon Press, Oxford 1911)

MacFarlane, K B 'Bishop Beaufort and the Red Hat 1417-21'(*EHR Vol LX 1945 pp 316-348)*
MacFarlane, K B 'The Beauchamps and the Staffords' *The Nobility of Later Medieval England* (OUP 1973)
Radford, Lewis Bostock *Henry Beaufort, Bishop, Chancellor, Cardinal* (London 1908)
Ross, Charles *Edward IV* (Methuen 1975)
Ross, Charles *Richard III* (Methuen 1988)
Vaughan, Richard *Philip the Good, The Apogee of Burgundy* (Longmans 1970)
Vickers, George *Humphrey Duke of Gloucester* (Archibald, Constable & Co 1907)
Warner, Marina *Joan of Arc* (Weidenfeld & Nicolson 1982)
Watts, John *Henry VI and the Politics of Kingship* (CUP 1996)
Williams, E Carleton *My Lord of Bedford 1389-1435* (Longmans 1963)
Wolffe, Bertram *Henry VI* (Methuen 1981)
Wylie, James Hamilton *The Reign of Henry the Fifth* 3 Vols (Cambridge 1914-1929)

Online Sources

James I of Scotland: *The Kingis Quair*, as reproduced in TEAMS Middle English Texts: https://d.lib.rochester.edu/teams/text/mooney-and-arn-kingis-quair-and-other-prison-poems-james-i-scotland-kingis-quair [Accessed 16 June 2020]

INDEX

Abergavenny 101, 193-4
Aberystwyth Castle, Constable of 132, 142
Aberystwyth 132, 142
Admiral of England 55, 61, 240
Admiral of the North 28, 42
Agincourt. Battle 46, 67, 68, 72, 78, 88, 91, 102, 143, 148, 156, 159
Albergati, Cardinal 140
Albret, Charles d' 67
Alençon, Duke of 67
Alexander V, Pope 70
Alnwick 234, 236, 296
André, Bernard 275
Angoulême, Edward of 18
Count of 130
Aquitaine, Duchy of 12, 14, 16, 18, 29, 56, 65, 177, 188, 240
Arundel, Thomas, Archbishop of Canterbury 26, 29, 33, 43, 45, 48, 50, 52, 54, 56, 57, 61, 63, 71, 72
Arundel, Earl of 55, 61, 107
Arques 228
Ashton, Sir Richard 141
Athol, Earl of 295
Armagnac (faction) 47, 52, 55, 56, 58, 64, 65, 66, 67, 69, 78, 79, 80, 83, 84, 90, 91, 94, 96, 135, 137, 138, 151
Armagnac, Count of 47, 69, 78, 91
Arras, Congress of 134, 135, 136, 137, 138, 139, 140, 142, 147, 150, 177, 296, 300
Audley, lords 212, 214, 230
'Auld Alliance,' 95, 209
Auxerre 137
Avignon Papacy 24, 69
Aysgoth, William, Bishop of Salisbury 180, 182
Avranches 175
Bamburgh 232, 237, 248, 297
Barbary Crusade 20
Barking Abbey 14, 261, 309
Barnet, Battle 252, 256, 266, 297, 300
Bar, Duchy of 67
Barnard Castle 299
Barnard's Heath 221
Baron Howth 239, 292
Basel, Council at 132, 140, 306
Bath and Wells, Bishop of 96
Baugé, Battle of 83, 84, 103, 118, 129
Bayeux 76, 175
Baynard's Castle 104, 222
Bayonne 157, 187
Beauchamp
family 192, 193, 308
Anne (senior) 193, 294
Anne (child heiress) 193
Eleanor 142, 239, 291, 306
Henry earl of Warwick, Duke of Warwick. 162, 192, 193, 300
Margaret 291, 292
Richard, Earl of Warwick 53, 62, 190, 192, 193. 194. 196, 192, 217
Beauchamp of Bletsoe, John 158
BEAUFORT
family 7, 8, 9, 17, 20, 21, 22, 23, 24, 25, 27, 28, 29, 30, 33, 34, 35, 36, 38, 40, 41, 42, 46, 47, 48, 49, 50, 52, 54, 55,

56, 57, 58, 59, 61, 62, 70, 80, 81, 82, 83, 84, 85, 86, 95, 101, 102, 110, 124, 139, 147, 158, 159, 160, 162, 180, 181, 190, 191, 193, 194, 199, 203, 204, 206, 212, 213, 227, 229, 233, 234, 237, 242, 243, 244, 252, 255, 258, 259, 262, 263, 266, 271, 273, 275, 276, 277, 278, 279, 281, 282, 283, 286, 287, 289, 290, 291, 292, 293, 294, 295, 299, 301, 308, 309
Edmund (I) second Duke of Somerset 116, 120, 124, 130, 131, 141, 142, 143, 157, 162, 167, 171, 178, 179, 189, 202, 203, 205, 217, 225, 237, 259, 279, 280, 283, 303, 304, 305, 306, 308, 310, 311
Daughters of Edmund (I) 237
Edmund (II) 242, 244, 247, 249, 255, 256, 257
Henry (I) Cardinal Beaufort 8, 9, 17, 21, 26, 29, 30, 37, 38, 39, 40, 41, 48, 50, 56, 57, 58, 61, 64, 65, 66, 67, 71, 72, 73, 74, 75, 76, 81, 85, 87, 89, 94, 95, 96, 97, 98, 99, 101, 102, 103, 104, 105, 106, 107, 108, 109, 110, 111, 112, 113, 114, 115, 116, 117, 118, 119, 120, 121, 123, 124, 125, 126, 127, 128, 129, 130, 132, 133, 135, 136, 137, 138, 139, 140, 141, 143, 144, 145, 146, 147, 148, 149, 150, 151, 152, 153, 154, 155, 157, 159, 160, 163, 164, 165, 169, 170, 171, 186, 278, 279, 300, 305, 306, 309
Henry (II) Second Earl of Somerset 62, 81, 129, 206
Henry (III) Third Duke of Somerset 168, 202, 205, 217, 225, 227, 237, 257, 280
Joan (I), Countess of Westmorland 17, 22, 23, 27, 40, 100, 162, 193, 229, 258, 264, 279, 283, 301
Joan (II), Queen of Scotland 81, 82, 94, 95, 129, 145, 276, 279
John (I), First Earl of Somerset 14, 17, 20, 21, 25, 29, 30, 34, 35, 36, 42, 44, 45, 46, 50, 51, 53, 54, 55, 57, 80, 81, 129, 143, 159, 160, 210, 299
John (II), Third Earl and first Duke of Somerset 82, 83, 84, 99, 103, 129, 287, 302
John (III), Marquis of Dorset 206, 249, 254
Thomas (I), Earl of Dorset, Duke of Exeter 17, 20, 21, 27, 34, 36, 39, 42, 54, 58, 59, 61, 66, 67, 69, 70, 76, 80, 81, 82, 86, 100
Thomas (II) 82, 124, 129, 130, 194
Thomas (III) 206
Margaret (I) 82, 210, 281, 309
Margaret (II) 9, 181, 210, 258, 259, 260, 261, 263, 268, 269, 286, 288, 301, 303, 309
Beaufort, Duke of, *see* Charles Somerset
Beaufort, Roger 17
Beaufort Castle 17
Beaufort Portcullis 274, 301
Beaumond-le-Vicomte 160
Beaumont, Viscount 168, 296
Bedford, John, Duke of 62, 69, 77, 87, 88, 89, 90, 91, 92, 92, 93, 96, 97, 103, 104, 105, 106, 107, 108, 109, 110, 118, 119, 121, 123, 125, 126, 127, 131, 132, 133, 134, 135, 138, 139, 140, 144, 153, 157, 163, 172, 231, 240, 258, 279, 279, 302
Bedfordshire 258, 274
Bellingham, Henry 296
Benedict XIII Pope 74
Benedict III, Pope 93, 135
Berri, Duke de 35, 61
Bermondsey Abbey 261, 274
Berwick 36, 120, 209, 228, 229
Bishop Beaufort, *see* Henry Beaufort (I)
Blount, John 68
Bodiam Castle 270
Boniface IX, Pope 24, 69
Booth, Laurence, Bishop of Durham 110, 227, 231
Booth, William Archbishop of York 183
Bourchier, Thomas, Archbishop of Canterbury 198, 206, 207, 210
Bourchier, Viscount Henry 206, 207, 210, 249
Bishopsgate 222
Blackfriars 183

Blanche, Duchess of Lancaster 11, 12, 13, 16, 17, 289
Blanche, daughter of Henry IV 37
Bledlow, Thomas 239
Bletsoe Castle 158, 258
Blois 58
Blood Meadow 254
Blood Royal 276, 303, 309
Blore Heath, Battle 264, 267, 297
Bohemia, Bohemian 70, 114, 115, 116, 118, 120, 121, 122, 123, 132, 140, 201, 306
  Anne of 19
  King of, *see* Sigismund
Bolingbroke, Henry, *see* Henry IV
Bolingbroke, Roger 152, 153
Bonville, Lord 188, 221, 242
Bordeaux 46, 47, 58. 187, 188
Bosworth, Battle 272, 298, 303
Boulogne 137, 141
Bourbon, Duke of 20, 67, 136
Bourges 91, 118, 151
Bowet, Henry Archbishop of York 75, 96, 103
Brabant 67, 92, 93, 109
Brétigny, Treaty 27, 64
Bretons 118, 172, 173, 174, 176, 188
Brezé, Pierre de 243
Bristol 252
Brittany 92, 149, 160, 161, 173, 266, 269, 270, 271, 295
Bruges 41, 229, 244, 250
Bubwith, Nicholas Bishop of Bath and Wells 52, 96, 103, 163
Buckingham
  Earls and Dukes of, *see* Stafford
Buckingham, John, Bishop of Lincoln 26
Burgundy, Duchy of 242
Burgundy, faction 78, 79, 93, 149, 165, 240
Burgundy, Dukes of
  Charles the Bold 243, 245, 248, 250, 152
    as Count of Charolais
  John the Fearless 46, 47, 52, 55, 56, 64, 65, 77
  Philip the Good 79, 91, 92, 103, 109, 117, 122, 125, 132, 134, 138, 141
  Yolande (duchess) 150
Bury St Edmunds 168
Butler, James
  the elder 184, 255
  the younger, as Earl of Wiltshire 185, 292
Byzantine Empire 115
Cade, Jack 181, 182
Caen 91, 175, 205
Calais 13, 18, 28, 41, 42, 43, 44, 46, 47, 53, 55, 56, 58, 61, 62, 66, 67, 90, 92, 93, 94, 109, 111, 114, 123, 134, 135, 136, 139, 140, 141, 142 143, 149, 175, 176, 177, 179, 187, 188, 205, 207, 208, 210, 211, 212, 213, 214, 215, 217, 239, 240, 242, 243, 244, 245, 252, 279, 296, 300, 301, 311
  Captain of 33, 36, 37, 40, 41, 43, 61, 139, 141, 196, 210, 213, 214, 217, 301
Caldicot Castle 261
Cambridge
  town and university 21, 156, 168, 275, 289, 301
  Richard, Earl of 62, 66, 102
Camoys, Lord 141
Canterbury, Archbishops, *see* Arundel, Chichele, Bourchier, Pole
Cardiff 194, 195
Cardigan 40, 158
Carisbrooke Castle 195, 242, 252
Carlisle 228, 229, 230, 297
Carmarthen 40, 44, 158, 262
Castile 13, 16, 17, 19, 22, 289
  Constance of 16, 17, 22
Castle Inn 202
Castle Rising 27
Cathars 115
Cauchon, Pierre, Bishop of Beauvais 125
Caterik, John 39, 72
Caxton, William 275
Chamberlain of England 36, 157, 240
Chancellor of England 37, 223, 240
Channel 42, 55, 56, 64, 66, 88, 134, 139, 210, 214, 213, 214, 215, 246, 251
Charles IV of France 10
Charles VI 47, 64, 79, 137, 139, 171
Charles VII 91, 124, 125, 133, 135, 136, 137, 151, 157, 228, 296
  as Dauphin 77, 78, 79, 91, 93, 118, 119, 119, 121, 123, 124, 151

Charles VIII 271
Chaucer, Alice, Dowager Duchess of Suffolk 101, 157, 190, 293, 309
Chaucer, Elizabeth 14
Chaucer, Geoffrey 13, 82, 84
Chaucer, Thomas 51, 55, 89, 101, 163
Cheltenham 253
Cherbourg 144, 158, 159, 160, 175
Cheshire 29, 104, 211, 267
Chichele, Henry, Archbishop of Canterbury 53, 56, 71, 72, 74, 75, 76, 87, 89, 98, 105, 110, 113, 123, 131, 145, 164, 305, 319
Chilton, John 37
Chief Justice of South Wales 150
Chinon 171
Christ's College, Cambridge 275
Church of St Mary, Warwick 192
Cinque Ports 68, 215
  Warden of 28, 88, 92, 139, 210, 240
Clarence, George, Duke of 229, 239, 245, 246, 247, 249, 250, 251, 254, 265, 267, 268, 269, 274, 283, 288, 294, 300
Clarence, Lionel Duke of 28
Clarence, Thomas, Duke of 56, 57, 58, 61, 62, 80, 82, 83, 84, 95, 130
Clarendon 195
Clerk of the Wardrobe 260
Clifford family 197, 198, 202
Clifford, Thomas, Eighth Baron 200, 202
Clifford, John, Ninth Baron 208, 209, 216, 219, 220, 224, 230, 240
Clovis 124
Cobham, Lord 185
Cobham, Eleanor 94, 109, 146, 151
Cock Beck 223
College of Cardinals 112
Collyweston 274, 275
Coln Brook 254
Colonna family 73
Colonna, Odo, Pope Martin V 73, 112
Colonna, Prospero 96
Constance, Council of 70, 71, 73, 74, 75, 95, 112, 115, 132
Constance of Castile 16, 17, 22, 23
Commons, House of 35, 37, 38, 42, 46, 50, 51, 52, 55, 66, 75, 85, 97, 98, 106, 170, 180, 181, 183
Compéigne 124
Commynes, Philippe de 248
Richemont 67
  Constable de 139
Constable of England 182, 255, 267, 268
Constable of the Army 132
'Cousins' War' 191
Conwy 29
Corfe 183, 215, 239, 284
Council for the Regency 100
Countess of Richmond and Derby 273
Courtenay family 72, 82, 244, 253 269
Coventry 28, 211, 251
Cravant, Battle 91
Crécy 13, 27
Crew, Chief Justice 257
Creyke, Norfolk 275
Crichton, Sir William 146
Cromwell, Ralph Lord 127, 144, 189
Crowland Abbey 144, 161
Crowland Chronicler 161
Dacre. Lord 224, 230
Dartford 185
Dauphin, *see* Charles VII
Dauphin Louis 65
  Louis XI as 243
Dauphinists 118, 122, 125, 133, 135, 137
Deeping, Lincs 144, 284
Deputy Warden of the Welsh Marches 43
Despenser, Lady Constance 45
Devon
  earls of, *see* Courteney
Dorset
  earls and marquis of, *see* Beaufort
Douglas, Earl of 146, 295
Dover, Kent 136
  Constable of Dover Castle 28, 126, 210
Dublin 184, 196, 239
Dublin Castle 176, 214
Duchesne 173
Dudley, Lord 183
'Duke of Buckingham's Rebellion' 268, 269, 270
Duke of Exeter *see* Beaufort, Holland
Dunstanburgh Castle 232, 297
Durham
  bishop of, *see* Langley, Neville, Booth

Bishopric 39, 48, 190, 210, 231, 294
City 227, 232
County 40, 101, 102, 145, 163, 163, 210, 228
Priory 163
Edward, Duke of York 45, 62
Edward of Lancaster 187, 196, 197, 208, 209, 210, 222, 243, 245, 246, 247, 250, 252, 253, 254, 272, 289, 301
Edward of Middleham 193
Edward I 10, 44
Edward II 10, 33
Edward III 10, 11, 12, 13, 15, 18, 27, 32, 33, 38, 41, 46, 49, 64, 67, 113, 133, 136, 137. 148, 180, 273, 281, 289
Edward IV 223, 224, 225, 227, 228, 229, 230, 231, 232, 233, 234, 236, 237, 238, 239, 241, 243, 244, 245, 246, 247, 250, 251, 252, 253, 254, 255, 260, 263, 265, 266, 267, 268, 280, 300, 301
as Earl of March 205, 221, 227, 272, 300
Edward V 268, 269
Edward, son of Richard III 269, 272
Edward the Black Prince 289
Eighth Crusade 115
Elizabeth, daughter of John of Gaunt 12
Elizabeth, daughter of Paon de Roelt 13
Elizabeth Berkeley 192
Elizabeth of York 273, 303
Elizabeth Woodville, Queen 240, 248, 265, 268, 269, 273, 274, 275, 276
Eltham 105
Epiphany 63, 219
Eton College 156, 165
Eugenius IV, Pope 132
Exchequer 42, 43, 158, 160, 172, 197, 207, 239, 387
Exeter
dukes of, *see* Holland, Beaufort
bishop of, *see* George Neville and Stafford
Falaise 76, 175
Farnham 163
Fastolf, Sir John 68, 91, 121, 131, 148, 157, 159, 166, 173, 177, 212
Fauconberg, *see* William Neville
Ferrara, Council 132
Ferrers of Wem, Lord 22
Ferrybridge 224
Fisher, John 274, 275
FitzAlan, Alice 37
Fitzhugh, Lord 225, 247
FitzLewis, Sir Richard 239, 292
Fitzwalter, Lord 106, 225
Fitzroy, Henry 276
First Protectorate 208, 209
Fleming, Richard. Bishop of Lincoln 96
Flemings 93, 97, 135, 140
Formigny 175
Fortescue, Sir John 244, 255
Fougères 173, 174
Foul Raid 77
Four Members 135, 140
Fourth Crusade 115, 116, 121
France 7, 8, 10, 11, 14, 17, 18, 19, 21, 22, 29, 41, 46, 47, 52, 53, 55, 58, 62, 64, 65, 66, 68, 69, 77, 78, 79, 80, 81, 82, 83, 84, 85, 86, 87, 88, 90, 91, 93, 95, 96, 98, 99, 100, 103, 105, 108, 110, 111, 116, 118, 119, 121, 122, 123, 124, 125, 126, 129, 130, 131, 132, 133, 135, 136, 137, 138, 140, 143, 144, 147, 149, 150, 151, 153, 154, 155, 157, 159, 163, 165, 166, 168, 169, 171, 173, 175, 177, 179, 181, 187, 201, 206, 209, 228, 230, 235, 240, 241, 243, 250, 255, 267, 271, 278, 280, 293, 294, 295, 299, 301, 304, 305, 306, 308
French 8, 10, 16, 17, 19, 27, 36, 41, 42, 46, 47, 53, 58, 61, 62, 64, 65, 67, 68, 69, 70, 71, 73, 77, 78, 79, 81, 84, 86, 90, 91, 95, 97, 103, 106, 110, 115, 117, 119, 120, 121, 123, 124, 125, 126, 131, 134, 135, 136, 137, 139, 142, 144, 147, 148, 149, 150, 151, 156, 157, 158, 159, 160, 161, 165, 166, 167, 170, 171, 173, 174, 176, 177, 178, 179, 188, 203, 212, 215, 217, 221, 229, 232, 235, 237, 242, 243, 250, 258, 259, 267, 277, 279, 296
Frederick II, Emperor 115
Fresnoy 175

Friar Randolph 105, 107
Froissart, Jean 13, 14, 23
Garter, Order of 25, 34, 94, 120, 123, 158, 173, 175
Gate, Sir Geoffrey 242
Gaunt, John of, Duke of Lancaster 7, 11, 12, 13, 14, 15, 16, 17, 18, 19, 20, 21, 22, 23, 24, 26, 27, 28, 29, 33, 34, 38, 49, 54, 135, 147, 153, 169, 229, 255, 272, 273, 281, 289, 290, 293, 298, 209, 312
Ghent 11
Gisors 132
Glamorgan 194, 197, 198, 280
Gloucester
  Humphrey, Duke of 8, 48, 62, 87, 88, 89, 92, 93, 94, 97, 98, 99, 104, 106, 107, 108, 110, 117, 121, 128, 129, 140, 147, 148, 153, 167, 200, 202, 205, 231, 239, 261, 269, 278, 292, 294, 299, 310
    Arthur, bastard son 88
    Antigone, bastard daughter 88
  Richard, Duke of, *see* Richard III
  Bishop of 127
Gloucestershire 252, 284
Glyndwr, Owain 34, 35, 36, 44, 46, 47, 55, 62, 64, 260
Golden Fleece, Order of the 135
Good Parliament 15
Gournay 132
Gravelines 149, 150
Great Bradley 275
Great Council 211
Great Schism 24, 61, 64, 69, 74, 75, 96, 132
Great Seal 39, 54, 76, 97, 245
Greenwich Park 88
Gregory XI 17
Gregory XII 69
Grey, Sir Ralph 234, 235, 236, 237
Grey, Sir Thomas 66
Grey, Lord Reginald 159
Greystoke, Ralph, Lord 216, 230
Grosmont, Henry, Duke of Lancaster 12
Gruthuuse, Louis de 250
'Guardian and Lieutenant of England' 88
Guyenne 28, 30, 61, 62, 118, 139, 148, 157, 159, 165, 177, 187, 188, 196, 207
Guyenne King of Arms 13
Hadham 308
Hafsid Caliphate 20
Hainault 11, 13, 14, 42, 53, 92, 93, 97, 104, 109, 110, 133, 289
Hallam, Robert, Bishop of Salisbury 71, 73, 74, 113
Harfleur 66, 67, 68, 69, 72, 76, 77, 85, 88, 118, 139, 144, 147, 158, 172, 175, 296
Harlech 237, 297
Harrington, Lady 36
  Sir Thomas 220
Hastings, William, Lord, Earl 246, 248, 254
Hatfield 308
Hedgeley Moor 236, 297
Henry of Monmouth, *see* Henry V
Henry of Trastamara 16, 17
Henry IV 8, 29, 31, 32, 33, 34, 35, 36, 45, 47, 48, 49, 51, 52, 56, 57, 58, 59, 62, 70, 77, 99, 105, 107, 114, 118, 122, 136, 137, 146, 148, 149, 250, 263, 273, 278, 299
  as Henry Bolingbroke 21, 22, 27, 28, 57, 63, 64
Henry V 8, 22, 25, 35, 60, 61, 62, 64, 65, 67, 68, 69, 70, 73, 77, 79, 81, 83, 84, 85, 86, 87, 88, 91, 97, 99, 107, 110, 134, 139, 151, 170, 260, 278, 279, 303
  as Prince of Wales 49, 56, 57
Henry VI 8, 87, 91, 97, 99. 101, 105, 119, 120, 1234, 124, 129, 135, 136, 137, 139, 140, 143, 144, 146, 148, 149, 152, 153, 154, 155, 156, 165, 166, 173, 180, 181, 185, 186, 190, 192, 195, 197, 199, 200, 202, 206, 209, 215, 216, 221, 223, 225, 226, 229, 231, 234, 235, 236, 237, 238, 241, 247, 248, 250, 258, 259, 260, 261, 265, 266, 267, 272, 279, 281, 303, 307
Henry VIII 75, 113, 258, 276
Henry the Navigator, Prince 12

Henry VII 273, 274, 275, 276
as Henry Tudor 9, 248, 258, 261, 265, 266, 267, 268, 269, 270, 271, 272, 281, 303, 309
Herbert, William 262. 264, 265
Hereford 44
Heron Sir John 224
Hertfordshire 199, 308
Hexham, Battle of 237, 240, 241, 258, 268, 297
High Constable 168, 267
Hill, Joan 206
Holland, John, Earl of Huntingdon 25, 77, 147
Holland, Henry 157
Holland, County 93
Holy Roman Empire, *see* Sigismund
Honfleur 175
Hôtel de Ville 125
Hotspur, *see* Henry Percy
Hospital of St Cross, Order of the 164
House of Valois 10
Hume, John 152, 153
Hundred Years War 8, 23, 27, 83, 138, 154, 188, 267
Hungerford, Sir Walter 109, 286
Huntingdon, Earl of, *see* Holland
Hussites 71, 73, 115, 117, 123
Ile-de-France 79, 157
Ireland 29, 37, 48, 51, 56, 61, 167, 176, 182, 184, 185, 213, 216, 240
Isabeau, Queen of France 52, 79
Isabel of Portugal 135
Isabella, Queen 10, 11
Capet 147, 305
of Valois 20, 23
Isle of Man 267
Isle of Wight192, 195, 242, 264, 287
'Jack Sharpe' 127
João, King of Portugal 12, 17
Jacqueline of Hainault 92, 93, 94, 109, 110, 117, 133, 138
Jacquetta of Luxemburg 134, 340
James I 81, 82, 91, 93, 105, 111, 119, 120, 145, 146, 190
James II 190, 209, 228, 276, 295
James III 228
James IV 276
Jargeau 121, 157
Jerusalem 74, 115, 165
Joan (II), Queen of Scotland 81, 94, 95, 120, 129, 130, 145, 146, 153, 263, 276, 291
Joan of Arc 119, 121, 123, 124, 125, 133, 151, 157, 171, 306
Joan of Navarre 107, 151
Joan of Kent 18
John of Thoresby 113
John II of France 83
John, Duke of Brabant 92
Joseph, William 206
Jourdain, Margery 152
Katherine of Lancaster 17
Katherine Swynford 14, 17, 54, 153, 229, 255, 272, 308
Keeper of the Royal Wardrobe 207
Kemp, John, Archbishop of York and Canterbury 72, 87, 89, 96, 109, 127, 135, 144, 145, 149, 163, 183, 184, 186, 196, 205, 305
Kenilworth 209, 297
Kennedy, James. Bishop of St Andrews 228
Kentish rebels 181
Kettlethorpe, Lincolnshire 17
King John 18
Kingis Quair 81
King of Bohemia 116
'King of Bourges' 91
King of Castile and Leon 17
King of Man 267
King of the Romans 70, 116
King's College Cambridge 156
Kingston 185
Knights of St John 252
Kyriell, Sir Thomas 175, 221, 242
La Trémouille 134
Lancashire 104, 219, 227, 237, 243
Lancastrian faction 8, 9, 31, 35, 43, 44, 47, 85, 86, 88, 97, 98. 110, 129, 131, 133, 134, 135, 145, 147, 153, 156, 169, 170, 172, 176, 177, 189, 190, 199, 200, 201, 202, 203, 204, 206, 210, 211, 212, 213, 214, 215, 216, 217, 218, 219, 220, 221, 222, 223, 224, 225, 227, 228, 229, 229, 230, 231, 232, 233, 234, 235, 236, 237, 238, 240, 241, 242, 243, 247, 248, 249, 250, 251, 252, 253, 254, 255, 256, 260, 265, 270, 273, 276, 278, 280, 281, 300

Langham, Simon, Archbishop of Canterbury 113
Langstrother, Sir John, prior of the Knights of St John 253, 254, 255
Duke of Lancaster 12, 289
Latimer
Sir Nicholas 269
Baron 209, 290, 216, 269, 294
Le Guerche 160, 161
Le Mans 166
Leicester Castle 28
Leulinghem, Truce of 19
Levant 114
Lieutenant of Rouen 78
Lincoln
Bishopric 26, 33, 38, 39, 94, 124
Cathedral 26, 28, 96
Lincolnshire 14, 17, 28, 144
Lisle Barony 194
Lithuania 21, 35, 115
Lisieux, Thomas 210
Lollard, Lollardy 43, 61, 63, 64, 70, 71, 118, 119, 147, 170
Loire 83, 91, 118, 136
London, Londoners 37, 39, 54, 63, 66, 93, 97, 98, 104, 105. 121, 140, 152, 163, 181, 182, 183, 184, 189, 199, 207, 209, 211, 215, 217, 218, 222, 223, 228, 232, 237, 239, 241, 258, 251, 252, 253, 255, 266, 274, 287, 297, 305
London Bridge 183
Loos 141
Lorraine 119
Louis XI 228, 235, 242, 243, 295
Louis Duke of Bourbon 20
Louviers, siege 130, 132, 306
Love Day 211
Low Countries 41, 42, 92, 94, 103, 104, 106, 117, 122, 140
Ludford Bridge 212, 213
Ludlow 39, 185, 217, 297, 300
Ludlow Castle 211
Lumley, Lord 36
Luxembourg 125, 134, 137, 240
Mâconnais 137
Mahdia 21
Maine 69, 118, 158, 160, 165, 166, 174, 177, 210
March, Earl of, *see* Edward IV
Marck 141
Margaret, Holland, Countess of Somerset and later Duchess of Clarence 57, 58, 83, 130, 158
Margaret of Anjou 165, 166, 180, 196, 208, 241, 243, 288, 309
Marie of Maine 210
Marshal of France 151
Martin V, Pope, *see* Colonna, Odo
Mary of Guelders, Queen of Scotland 238, 235, 295
Mary Bohun 22
Master Porter 212
Market Drayton 211
Maud Countess of Leicester 12
Meaux 144, 150
Melun 81, 82, 100
Middleham 82, 297, *see also* Middleham Nevilles
Midlands 161, 199, 209, 211, 215, 216
Milford Haven 29, 271, 297
Moleyns, Adam, Bishop of Chichester 172, 177, 179
Mons 13, 93
Mont St-Michel 99
Montague, *see* Neville, Montague
Montague family 120
Thomas Montague 101, 188, 120, 157
More, Thomas 52
Mortain, Count of, *see* Edmund Beaufort
Morton, Earl of 145, 295
Morton, Doctor John 244
Morteon, John Bishop of Ely 269
Mortimer, Roger 43, 44, 184
Mortimer, Anne 62
Mortimer, Sir Edward 90
Mortimer, 'Lord', *see* Cade, Jack
Mortimer's Cross, Battle 220, 221, 260, 297
Mowbray, Thomas, Earl of Buckingham 44
Mundeford, Osbert 212
Najera, Battle 16
Nancy 165
Naples 165
Neufchâtel 132
Nellport, John 183

NEVILLES
Senior branch:
Ralph, First Earl of Westmorland 27, 29, 30, 34, 40, 54, 80, 84, 89, 100, 101, 102, 103, 162
Ralph, second earl 100, 162, 163, 219
John, Westmorland's heir 80
Lord John 100, 219, 224
Middleham Branch:
Richard, Earl of Salisbury 40, 90, 101, 118, 124, 145, 157, 159, 160, 162, 168, 180, 185, 189, 190, 192, 193, 196, 197, 198, 199, 203, 207, 211, 212, 213, 215, 217, 220, 239, 293, 294, 300
William, Lord, Fauconberg 101, 190, 191, 200, 213, 215, 221, 255, 294, 300
Edward, Lord Abergavenny 101, 190, 193, 294
George, Lord Latimer 190, 194, 216, 294
Robert, Bishop of Salisbury and Durham 96, 101, 102, 145, 163, 210, 254
Cecily 102, 229
Cecily, daughter of Salisbury 193
Richard, Earl of Warwick 'the Kingmaker' 40, 185, 190, 193, 194, 195, 196, 197, 198, 199, 201, 202, 203, 208, 210, 211, 212, 213, 214, 215, 216, 217, 219, 220, 221, 222, 223, 228, 233, 235, 236, 239, 240, 242, 243, 245, 246, 247, 248, 249, 250, 251, 252, 253, 265, 267. 272, 280, 294, 300
Sir Thomas Neville 189, 220
John, Lord Montague, Earl of Northumberland 221, 226, 237, 228, 245, 246, 246, 248, 249, 251, 252, 265, 243, 300
George, Archbishop of York 216, 223, 240, 245, 249
Isabel, duchess of Clarence 245, 293, 294
Anne, Queen to Richard III 246, 264, 271, 294
Thomas, Bastard of Fauconberg 255
Sir Thomas Neville of Hornby 27
Newcastle 207, 227, 233, 297
Newcastle Emlyn 40
Newham Bridge 214, 215
Norfolk, Duke of 27, 28, 102, 190, 196, 197, 198, 206, 224, 239, 255, 275, 294
Norham Castle 236
Normandy 55, 65, 66, 67, 69, 74, 76, 77, 78, 86, 91, 118, 131, 132, 136, 139, 149, 157, 159, 160, 165, 166, 167, 171, 172, 174, 175, 176, 177, 178, 179, 181, 183, 184, 188, 196, 203, 205, 207, 212, 251, 279, 280
Northampton 213, 215, 216, 231, 233, 246, 264, 269, 297
Northumberland 227, 228, 232, 233, 235, 236, 243, 248
earl of, *see* Percy and Montague
Nuremburg 117
Ogle, Sir Robert 217
Oldcastle, Sir John 63
Oldhall, Sir William 182, 184
Orleans 101, 118, 119, 120, 138, 157, 296
Dukes of 46, 47, 67, 101, 103, 118, 119, 120, 138, 148, 149, 150
Oxford University 19, 21, 26, 35, 39, 64, 70, 88, 96, 127, 132
Oxford, earls, *see* de Vere
Oye 141, 152
Palm Sunday 53, 74, 226
Papacy70, 71, 73, 94, 121, 126
Papal Curia 74, 75, 96, 140, 170
papal provision 96, 109, 111
Paris 47, 62, 64, 76, 78, 79, 80, 83, 84, 91, 121, 123, 124, 125, 130, 133, 135, 137, 138, 139, 140, 141, 142, 148, 165, 246, 279, 296, 306
Archbishop of Paris 124
Parliament 15, 24, 31, 37, 38, 42, 45, 47, 49, 52, 55, 57, 61, 66, 68, 72, 76, 88, 89, 95, 97, 98, 106, 107, 108, 109, 113, 127, 131, 147, 167, 168, 172, 177, 180, 182, 186, 199, 200, 206, 209, 229, 237, 262, 272, 273, 278, 301, 304, 305
Parliament of Bats 107
Parr, Sir Thomas 225
Paston, Sir John 239, 244

Peasants' Revolt 19
Pedro, Duke of Coimbra 105
Pedro the Cruel King of Castile 16
Earl of, *see* Tudor, Jasper
Pembroke Castle 262, 265
Perche, Count of 130, 131, 291
Percy, Henry, First Earl of
  Northumberland 29, 30, 34, 36, 45
Percy, Henry, Second Earl 80, 89. 90.
  101, 189, 190, 145, 200, 201, 202
Percy, Henry, Third Earl 208, 209, 216,
  217, 219, 223, 224, 225, 227, 230
Percy, Henry, Fourth Earl 246, 248, 271,
  294
Percy, Henry ('Hotspur') 30, 34, 43, 80
Percy, Thomas, Lord Egremont 189, 215
Percy, Sir Ralph 232, 234, 236
Perrers, Alice 15
Peterhouse College Cambridge 21
Philip VI 10
Philippa of Hainault 11, 13, 289
Picardy 41, 53
Pickering, Sir James 220
Pisa, Council of 70, 71
Plantagenet family 10, 35, 46, 49, 62,
  139, 146, 257, 258m 261, 272, 281,
  299
Poitiers 27
Pole, John de la 259, 260
Pole, William de la 156, 293 *see also*
  Duke of Suffolk
Polydore Vergil 169, 260, 266
Pont de l'Arche 174
Pont l'Evêque 174
Pontefract 29, 45, 197, 218, 220, 297
Ponthieu 65, 137
Pontoise 157
Praemunire 73, 115, 120, 128, 133, 150,
  164, 170
Privy Council 167
Prokop the Great 116
Queen's Beasts 301
Queen's College Oxford 21
Raby 163
Rais, Gilles de 151
Readeption 248, 249, 255, 288
Regent of England 88
Regent of France 87
Reims 120, 124, 133
René, Count of Anjou 165
Republic of Genoa 21
Resumption, Act of 186, 194
Bishop of Rochester 42, 274
Rolin, Nicholas 134, 136
Rouen 77, 78, 123, 125, 135, 138, 148,
  160, 173, 175, 205, 296
Roxburgh 77, 120, 128
St Albans 88, 118, 200, 202, 205, 206,
  207, 208, 211, 217, 221, 222, 225,
  229, 231, 229, 231, 242, 264, 269,
  280, 296, 297
St Cloud 55
St Cross 164
St David's 53, 71, 72, 135
St George's Day 120
St John, Sir Oliver 158
St Mary de Pratis, Abbey of 275
St Mary Overy 95
St Mary of the Tower 99
St Nicholas of the Tower 177
St Paul's 72, 104, 211
St Remegius 124
Saint-Mihiel 243, 249
Sangatte 141
Saye and Sele, Lord 182
Scrope, Lord 41
Scrope, Richard, Archbishop of York 44,
  45, 48, 55, 69
Scrope of Masham, Lord 66
Second Protectorate 209
Seine, River 66, 67, 76, 83
Severn, River 254, 270
Seymour, Edward 276
Shrewsbury, Battle of 43
Shrewsbury, Earl of, *see* Talbot
Sigismund, Holy Roman Emperor 68, 70,
  71, 73, 92, 115, 116, 122
Simnel, Lambert 274
Skelton, John 275
Smithfield 223
Southwark 95, 104, 163
Southwell, Thomas 152
Somerset 21
  earl and dukes, *see* Beaufort
Stafford
  Family 264, 265, 294
  Margaret
  Earl of Stafford 190

John, Bishop Stafford of Exeter, Archbishop of Canterbury 37, 87, 89, 96, 103, 109, 163, 190
Dukes of Buckingham 168, 201, 203, 208, 209, 210, 211, 212, 264, 265, 268, 269, 270, 294
Duchess of Buckingham 102
Sir Henry 264
Staindrop 163
Stanley, Thomas, Lord 61, 190, 207, 249, 270
earldom of Derby 273
Steward of the King's Household 267
Stewart, Sir James, Black Knight of Lorne 146, 295
Stradling, Sir Edmund 37
Strangways, Sir Thomas 294
Suffolk, earl and Dukes, *see* Pole
Swynford, Katherine, also Roet, Roelt 7, 14, 17, 22, 54, 153, 229, 255, 272, 308
Swynford, Thomas 14
Sydenham, Simon 95, 109
Tachov 117, 122
Tacine, also Thasnya, Thomasina 159, 291
Tailboys. Sir Robert 224
Talbot, John, First Earl of Shrewsbury 99, 121, 131, 148, 157, 175, 187, 188, 190, 194, 210
Talbot, John, Second Earl of Shrewsbury 210, 231, 247
Teutonic Knights 21, 115
Tewkesbury, Battle 253, 254, 256, 258, 266, 297
Tewkesbury Abbey 255
Thames, River 42, 107, 177, 185
Tutbury, Thomas 52
Thorp, John 207
Thorp, Thomas 206, 207
Tiptoft, Lord 127
Tombelaine 212
Tours 165, 170
Tower of London 237
Towton, Battle 223, 224, 225, 226, 227, 229, 231, 243, 264, 297, 300
Treaty of Troyes 79, 90, 91, 135, 136
Archbishop of Trier 117
Trollope, Andrew 212, 213, 214, 218, 219, 220, 221, 222, 223, 224, 226, 230, 239
Trollope, David 212
Tudor, Edmund 180, 190, 210, 259, 260, 261, 262, 279, 281, 303, 304, 307, 309, 310
Tudor, Henry, later Henry VII 9, 25, 248, 258, 262, 266, 267, 268, 269, 270, 271, 272, 281, 303, 304, 309
Tudor, Jasper, Earl of Pembroke 180, 244, 247, 260, 262, 265, 266, 271, 307, 308
Tudor, Mary 113
Tudor, Owen 260, 261, 262, 203, 303, 304, 306, 307, 308, 309, 310
Tudor Rose 273
Tunstall, Sir Richard 237
Tunis 20, 21, 114
Tyburn 90
Tyne Valley 236
Umfraville, Sir Gilbert 83
Valois, House of 10, 20, 84, 140, 172
Valois, Katherine de 87, 131, 137, 138, 260
Valognes 175
Venice 74
Venables, Richard 91
Verneuil 91, 95, 118, 119, 134, 137, 159
De Vere, Aubrey de 231
De Vere, John, Twelfth earl 238
De Vere, John, Thirteenth earl 238, 248, 249, 250, 251, 252, 300, 301
Vincennes 84
Wallingford, Constable of 28
Wagenburg 117
Wakefield, Battle of 218, 220, 221, 225, 229, 264, 297
Wakering 103
Walere 173
Wales 34, 36, 37, 40, 43, 44, 45, 47, 48, 50, 51, 52, 55, 56, 60, 62, 63, 100, 107, 132, 150, 167, 168, 195, 227, 233, 267, 261, 261, 264, 270, 195
Waltham 306
Warden of the Welsh Marches 43
Warden of the West March 34, 80, 100, 145, 162

Wars of the Roses 8, 25, 195, 199, 203, 257, 297, 298
Warwick, earldom, *see* Beauchamp, Neville
Waterton, Sir Robert 102
Waynflete,William, Bishop of Winchester 169, 210
Wedmore prebendary 26
Welles, Lionel. Lord 224, 230, 264, 265
Welsh raids 39
Wenlok, John Lord 239, 252, 253, 254
West Country 184, 213, 218, 247, 270
Westminster 86, 106, 107, 124, 152, 160, 163, 202, 160, 210, 216, 229, 248, 275, 301
Westminster Abbey 258, 261, 276
Westmorland, *see* Neville
William of Bulleyn 142
William of Wykeham 38
William Perkins, *see* Jack Sharpe
Willoughby, Lord 90, 139
Wimborne 161, 275
Winchelsea 141
Winchester bishopric 38, 39, 72, 87, 98, 113, 122, 137, 164, 210, 278, 288
Winchester Palace 164, 169
Winchester Cathedral 95, 169
Windsor 53, 297
  Castle 143, 197, 202, 260
Wine Crane's Wharf 104
Witch of Eye, *see* Jourdain, Margery
Woking 265, 285, 288
Wolvesley 163
Wolsey. Thomas, Cardinal Archbishop of York 75, 113
Woodville, Elizabeth 240, 248, 265, 268, 269, 273, 274, 294, 336
Woodville, Richard, First Earl Rivers 104, 105, 109, 139, 187, 213, 225, 231, 240, 245
Woodville, Anthony, Second Earl Rivers 225, 246
Woodville, John
Wool Staple 188
Wool trade 56, 68
Worcester, William 235
Wycliffe, John 19, 70
Yolande of Aragon, *see* Burgundy
York, City 198, 223, 224, 236, 249, 251
Yorkist faction 8, 40, 102, 171, 177, 187, 199, 200, 202, 207, 208, 210, 211, 212, 213, 214, 215, 216, 218, 219, 220, 221, 222, 223, 224, 225, 228, 230, 231, 232, 233, 234, 236, 237, 238, 239, 240, 242, 244, 246, 247, 248. 249, 251, 252, 253, 254, 263, 264, 265, 266, 267, 268, 269, 272, 276, 261, 287, 309
York, House of 9, 40, 49, 227, 232, 234, 255, 256, 257, 263, 276
  Edmund, Duke of York 30, 44
  Edward, Duke of York 45, 46, 58, 62, 66, 67
  Richard, Duke of York 102, 144, 146, 157, 160, 166, 167, 172, 176, 178, 179, 180, 181, 182, 183, 184, 185, 186, 190, 191, 196, 197, 198, 199, 200, 201, 202, 203, 206, 207. 208, 209, 210, 211, 212, 213, 214, 216, 217, 218, 219, 223, 229, 260, 261, 264, 268, 280, 289, 298, 300
  Elizabeth of York 269, 303
  Margaret of York 243, 244, 272, 273
York, Archbishop of, *see* Scrope, Bowet, Kemp
  Yorkshire 27, 40, 45, 80, 101, 211, 213, 217, 220, 251
Young, Thomas 180
Zeeland 92, 104, 106
Ziška, Jan 116